PRAISE FOR JULES BROWN

Jules' travel writing is funny, inspiring, quirky, and always engaging

> MARK ELLINGHAM, ROUGH GUIDES FOUNDER AND PUBLISHER OF 'DRIVING OVER LEMONS'

I feel I have been travelling with a new, entertainingly witty friend.

> SUE BAVEY, BOOK-BLOGGER

Informative funny, inspiring – loved this book!

> 5-STAR AMAZON REVIEW

I can't give more than five stars for this travel memoir but I would if I could.

> 5-STAR GOODREADS REVIEW

I laughed so much I scared the cat!

> 5-STAR AMAZON REVIEW

ALSO BY JULES BROWN

Born to Travel series

Don't Eat the Puffin

Never Pack an Ice-Axe

Watch Out for Pirates

The Born to Travel Collection

On the Rails series

Not Cool: Europe by Train in a Heatwave

Far Out: By Train to the Edges of Europe

FAR OUT

BY TRAIN TO THE EDGES OF EUROPE

JULES BROWN

Copyright © 2025 by Jules Brown

All rights reserved.

ISBN: 978-1-916694-11-8

No part of this book may be reproduced in any form or by any electronic or mechanical means, including information storage and retrieval systems, without written permission from the author, except for the use of brief quotations in a book review.

Cover design: Chris Hudson Design, chrishudsondesign.co.uk

To the honourable Elaine,

These pages, which she has been so good as to peruse and approve of, are dedicated, in the hopes that other fair readers may follow her example,

*By her very affectionate
Husband and Servant,*

Jules Brown

[after the dedication in 'The Handbook for Travellers in Spain' by Richard Ford, 1845]

FAR OUT: THE JOURNEY

North, East, South, West – Europe By Train

NARVIK

E
UIMAHARJU

- OSLO
- STOCKHOLM
- HELSINKI
- COPENHAGEN
- NEWCASTLE UPON TYNE
- HAMBURG
- AMSTERDAM
- BERLIN
- **OSNABRÜCK**
- LONDON
- WARSAW
- PARIS
- PRAGUE
- VIENNA
- BUDAPEST
- BUCHAREST
- **PRAIA DAS MAÇAS**
- SOFIA
- BARCELONA
- ROME
- ISTANBUL
- MADRID
- W
- LISBON

S ALGECIRAS

CHAPTER 1

HOME

As is the way with these things, on the downward slope of the wine bottle, it all seems so simple.

North. East. South. West. That will be my route.

Travel to the four cardinal points of the compass in Europe, and do it all by train.

There's even a handy mnemonic to remind me to go the correct way around. Never Eat Shredded Wheat – or Naughty Elephants Squirt Water, depending on where you went to school.

My school stood firmly on the anti-breakfast-cereal side of the matter, but there's nothing wrong with being pro-elephant instead, as long as you go north, then east, then south, then west. Because that's the rule, primary school teachers say so.

And why would I want to travel to the edges of Europe by train? Well, partly, I refer you to the wine bottle, and partly to my well-used Rail Map of Europe (3rd Edition, 2nd Revision), which just begs a man in possession of a large glass of Bordeaux to trace his finger along the arterial rail routes of Europe and dream.

Also, and I can't stress this clearly enough, why not?

I love travelling by train, sitting for hours as different views – hell, different countries – rattle by. Europe's railway network is, for the most part, a thing of interconnected beauty. There's no excuse to fly between major cities; it's often quicker, and always more enjoyable, to let the train take the strain, as the old British Rail ads used to say.

It's not like I've got anything else to do. I used to write travel guidebooks for a living, but I haven't done that for years. I'm now what you call a 'freelance writer,' and 'semi-retired,' which, according to my wife, Elaine, means that I am 'under-employed' and 'always around.'

"Off you go," she says, "You'll enjoy it." She has a spring in her step, I notice, and is ordering something off the internet. Her finger hovers over the projected delivery date. "When did you say you were going?"

"I haven't decided yet. Anyway, I might not go. Don't you remember what happened last time?"

That was when I travelled by train through nine cities in nine countries in nine days, during a record-breaking heatwave. That trip turned into a book called *Not Cool*, which I am told is highly entertaining, though frankly I'm still in recovery. I nearly melted. I looked like Demi Moore at the end of *The Substance* by the time I got back.

"You had a lovely time and wrote a book about it," she says, distractedly, while opening a WhatsApp group on her phone called 'Let's Stitch, Bitches.' "Let me know if you need some help packing."

Well, that's not happening. There's no way I'm letting Elaine do my packing. It'll be all flattering shirts, stylish shackets, and tailored trousers, instead of what a gentleman traveller really requires, namely – elasticated waists, vintage band T-shirts, and the bomber jacket I got in the charity shop that, to certain eyes, makes me look like I'm on day-release from a home for 1980s DJs.

In our house, unsupervised purchases are frowned upon, unless they can be fed through one of the four sewing machines that take up space in our dining room, sorry, design studio. Elaine has never met a piece of fabric that can't be cut down, altered, shaped, transformed, or otherwise beaten into submission. You don't want to sit still too long in a pair of oversized chinos – yes, they *were* in the sale, how did she know? – that's all I'm saying.

Anyway, it's not the packing that's the problem. On further investigation, it's the whole north, east, south, west business.

I might have known it wasn't as straightforward as simply following routes to the far ends of the map. Because we're talking here about trains – and, more specifically, railway stations – which means nothing is quite as clear-cut as it seems.

It all starts with how you define Europe. Did you know, for example, that forty percent of Europe's total landmass is in Russia? Europe, in fact, stretches all the way to the Ural mountains and to the border with Asia – almost two thousand kilometres east of Moscow – which is hunky-dory, I'm sure, for Russia, but no help at all to me.

Technically, it means that the northernmost and easternmost train stations in Europe are both in Russia, and there's a phalanx of little men on Reddit arguing about which is which. None of the candidates – Murmansk, or possibly Zapolyarny, in the north, Vorkuta in the east – set the pulse racing.

Vorkuta, for example, is both the easternmost and the coldest town in Europe, with temperatures plunging to minus fifty Celsius in winter but rising to a balmy plus thirteen in high summer. It's big on coal mining and forced labour camps, while the indigenous Tundra peoples of the area know the town as 'Bear Corner.'

That description is not the result of just one bear wandering into town every now and again, is it? That's a multiple-bear destination. The walk into town from the train station must be fun.

As it happens, the UK Foreign Office currently holds very stern views about visiting Russia, for obvious reasons. And anyone with a scintilla of empathy and humanity is not going to go to the land of the great aggressor on a jaunty train holiday, probably for many years to come.

So, at a swoop, my trip just got easier. If you take

Russia out of the equation, the northern and easternmost points of Europe almost select themselves, just by squinting at a map.

Except, not really. I told you it wasn't simple.

In the current geopolitical climate, the furthest north you can go on the European mainland is Nordkapp, or North Cape, in northern Norway. There are lots of reindeer, and you can see your breath in the air in August. It's bleak, windswept, inhospitable country, and undeniably grand in its way, but what it doesn't have is a railway station.

The nearest one is seven hundred kilometres away to the southwest, at a fjord-side port town called Narvik, and *that* is the northernmost train station in Europe. It's reached in turn on the northernmost passenger railway service in Europe, which starts its run all the way south in Stockholm in Sweden.

There are more little men on Reddit who have opinions on the veracity of even this fact, but let's put those to one side for now and say that this is a route – Stockholm to Narvik – that is entirely do-able. The first guidebook I ever wrote for Rough Guides was to Scandinavia. I've travelled its length and breadth by train and bus, and I've even been to Narvik once before, though admittedly a long time ago.

I know this part of the trip can be done. That's N for Never and North sorted.

E for Eat and East is subject to the same initial caveats, for the same reasons. Ukraine – which, after Russia, has the continent's easternmost train stations –

is understandably off-limits. The whole of eastern Ukraine is the most heavily depredated part of the country, bitterly fought over by the invading Russian forces. Indeed, a horrifying Russian rocket attack on Kramatorsk railway station in 2022, in Ukraine's far east, killed scores of people, children included.

The trains are still running in Ukraine, heroically so, you might think – and there are cross-border services from Poland – but an idiot writer on a made-up mission is the last thing those brave people in that brave country need.

The political situation means that Belarus, the neighbouring country run by Putin's pet puppet dictator, is out, too. That leaves me running a finger down the map, trying to figure out where the safest, most accessible, easternmost train station in Europe might be.

It's probably not where you think.

The Black Sea coast of Bulgaria or Romania would be a decent guess. There's a station, for example, at the Romanian Black Sea resort of Constanta, which you can reach by direct train from Bucharest. That's a long way east, in anyone's book.

Or, if you're clever and map-smart, you might plump for Istanbul in Türkiye. Only five percent of the country is in Europe – the rest lies over the Bosporus Strait in Asia – but international trains from western Europe all stop at Halkali on the European side, in Istanbul's far-flung suburbs. From there, you can jump on a local train to historic Sirkeci station, right in the heart of European Istanbul. Surely, that's the easternmost train station in Europe?

Nope. And the Baltic countries – Estonia, Latvia and Lithuania – don't come into it either.

Much further east than any of them, and stretching even further east than St Petersburg, is the lower bulge of Finland, known as Karelia.

The slow train from Helsinki runs out this way, heading east into a region of boundless lakes and forests. If you chug along in Finland for several hours, parallel to the Russian border, eventually you pass through the small town of Uimaharju, whose station is – by my convoluted reckoning – the easternmost railway station in Europe.

Granted, it's in the absolute middle of nowhere, and the trip is going to take some planning, but Uimaharju and Europe's far east is definitely do-able, too.

"Still looking at your little map?" says Elaine, as she passes by. Skips by, I should say. "When are you leaving, by the way?" She doesn't wait for an answer, and I hear her on the phone saying, "Well, we'll need more fabric, chocolate, and Prosecco than that, he'll be gone for weeks by the looks of it."

There's what can only be described as a cackle from the other end of the phone, and then Elaine snorts, "Sewing club, yeah right," in a way that puts the words 'sewing club' firmly in italics.

The minute I leave, there'll be women of a certain vintage, from all corners of the country, arrowing in on some obscure fabric shop they've seen on Instagram. I once drove Elaine for two hours, deep into the Yorkshire Dales, to a remote barn up a farm track that was filled with satin-backed shantung, Bedford cord, fine muslin, and Harris Tweed. She conducted lengthy negotiations with the proprietor, while I sat in the car and listened to an entire football match. Both Elaine and the barn-fabric specialist thought this was a completely normal way to spend a Saturday.

All of which is to say, I'll be lucky if I can get in the dining room, sorry, design studio, by the time I'm back. It already looks like a bomb exploded in a curtain factory, and that's before Elaine and her friends have bought up the entire contents of a bankrupt worsted mill.

Anyway, back to the planning.

It's something of a relief that S for Shredded and South is more straightforward. There's a train nerd or two – said with love and respect – who argue for the small resort of Pozzallo, on the southern coast of Sicily, as having Europe's southernmost train station. I've been to Pozzallo, too, back when I was researching the *Rough Guide to Sicily*. It's all right, it's got a Lidl, but I wouldn't rush back.

And luckily, I don't have to, because general agreement has it that the southernmost railway station in Europe is instead at Algeciras, in Andalusia, in southern Spain. I've never been there, and it should be a positive breeze to get to, given Spain's excellent train service. It is an exacting five thousand kilometres from eastern Finland, and God knows how many changes of train, but I'll worry about that later.

Finally, here I am, with only W for Wheat and West to go, and this is the easiest of all, since western Europe basically runs out when you get to Portugal.

The westernmost point of mainland Europe is Cabo da Roca, around forty kilometres west of Lisbon. It's wild and windy, as you might expect from a place where the cliffs fall straight into the Atlantic Ocean, and it's most certainly a dramatic place to stand and realise you are on the edge of an entire continent.

There isn't a train station there, that would be far too convenient. But the local train out of Lisbon runs west as far as Sintra, a beautiful hill town full of castles and palaces, and that is where you'll find the westernmost train station in Europe.

Or is it?

Going down a Google-search rabbit hole, I'm intrigued to find that there is a single-track tram service that runs west for thirteen kilometres from Sintra to the coast at Praia das Maçãs, just a little way north of Cabo da Roca.

If we're counting trams as trains – and I think we are, they run on a track – then I'm calling it for the tram terminus at Praia das Maçãs as my ultimate, westernmost destination.

But hold on, you might say, if you have been on the internet as much as I have in pursuit of this madcap route... hold on right there.

It's all well and good discounting the dangerous

parts of the continent that you currently can't go to, or saying 'Europe' this and 'Europe' that in a fashion that brooks no argument. Isn't Cyprus in Europe, you might say? Isn't it, in fact, in the European Union? And isn't the island of Cyprus a long way further south than Algeciras in Spain?

To which I reply, yes, yes and yes. And also, no, because Cyprus hasn't had a railway service since the 1950s. Neither does the Greek island of Gavdos, by the way, which lies south of Crete and is undisputedly the southernmost point in Europe. No trains, no vote.

Mind you, if that's the game you want to play, then Réunion island – between Madagascar and Mauritius in the Indian Ocean – has a claim to be the southernmost point of the European Union.

It's been an official region of France since 1946, and it actually did have a passenger railway line as late as the 1960s, with a more recent light rail system planned but not built. Even if Réunion did have a proper railway line, I don't see me getting a trip there past Elaine. I can just about badge this trip as work. The Indian Ocean, I suspect, would be very much seen as a holiday.

What about the far north then? Iceland, say?

I'm on safe ground here because even though it's technically in Europe, and part of the European Economic Area, Iceland doesn't have any trains. Even if it did, its latitude is such that Icelandic railway stations would all be further south than the northernmost one I've already identified in Narvik, Norway.

There is a short railway line in Svalbard, the Norwegian archipelago which lies about halfway between the north of Norway and the North Pole. That is undeniably very north, and still European, but it's a freight and not a passenger railway, so I'm relieved that doesn't count. Svalbard has one polar bear for every ten inhabitants, which means you have to be able to run faster than at least one other person at any given time, and I'm a bit out of shape.

Tenerife, though, does have passenger trains, or at least it has a tram service, which as we've seen, I'm allowing. And Tenerife is one of the Canary Islands, off the coast of West Africa, so that would win location of the westernmost train station in Europe, hands down, because Tenerife has been part of Spain since 1496. And Spain's definitely in Europe, you can trust me on that, because I'm looking at the map right now.

Ultimately, what all this means is that I'm defining Europe to my own satisfaction for the purposes of this trip, which is to visit by train the furthest-flung, cardinal-point railway stations in continental, mainland Europe.

Incidentally, this also means ignoring the United Kingdom, where I live, which doesn't matter because the UK's westernmost train station – Arisaig, on the Scottish West Highland Line – is still not as far west as Sintra or Praia das Maças in Portugal.

I'll tell you what does lie further west than those two, though, and that's the station at Tralee in County Kerry, in the Republic of Ireland. If there was any justice in the world (there isn't), and if I hadn't just come up with a definition that I was happy with, then I'd probably have to go to Tralee. It is, after all, unarguably, home of the westernmost train station in Europe.

But suck it up, Ireland. You are not part of mainland Europe, and it's my book.

I fold the Rail Map of Europe (3rd Edition, 2nd Revision) away carefully. I'll be needing that. For now, I'm done.

Never. Eat. Shredded. Wheat.

North. East. South. West.

Narvik. Uimaharju. Algeciras. Praia das Maças.

That's the route. Around seven thousand kilometres by train, if I start in the far north and end in the extreme west. But it's going to be a much longer trip than that, because I live in northern England and have to start from my local station, before heading all the way around Europe.

Look, rules are rules.

A rough calculation tells me I'll be travelling more like eleven thousand kilometres in total. And what I also need is an embarkation point in mainland Europe that makes sense of the journey – that fits all the destinations together. I have an idea about that, too.

But I've had enough of looking at the rail map for today, and anyway, there is a banging noise coming from the attic, where Elaine is throwing down various backpacks "to save you some time."

She's certainly being very helpful about it all. When

she drives me to York station the following week for the 11.02 train, she gets us there nice and early to see me off.

Her phone pings, and it's a pin for the designer bar at the old railway hotel, which has an entrance virtually on the platform. "Bye, darling," she says, "have a lovely time," while at the same moment, answering her phone. "11.03," she says in answer to someone, cryptically, and then, "Gin. And put me down for twenty metres of the linen."

The train pulls away, Elaine waves and then sprints down the platform, and I'm on the rails and off around Europe. Again.

CHAPTER 2

NEWCASTLE TO OSNABRÜCK

"Conditions are fine at the moment," says the captain over the intercom, "but during the crossing we anticipate some wind at around four o'clock in the morning."

I mean, come on? This joke is going to write itself. I'd be a fool to pass it up. Something about how a man of my age always expects wind at four am. I'll work on it, see if I can punch it up a bit, but hats off to the captain for the straight-man soft-serve.

And what am I doing in the middle of the North Sea, on the Newcastle-to-Amsterdam ferry, when this is a book about long-distance train travel?

We'll come to that. Right now, all you need to know is that the sea is calm, and I've just ordered scallops and chorizo, a grilled seabass, and what is referred to vaguely but cheerily as a bottle of 'ship's red.'

I haven't been on an overnight ferry since I slept

outside on the deck of an Italy-to-Greece rust-bucket, back in the day. That is not happening tonight, I can tell you. My cabin accommodation is altogether superior to a sleeping bag on a metal gangway next to a row of backpackers with guitars and bongos.

It very nearly wasn't. Originally, I had booked a tiny box of a cabin with bunk beds and a theoretical sea view, if you discounted the lifeboat hanging in plain view outside – reassuring or alarming, depending on your tastes. But then I showed the pictures to my friend and best man, Steve, who knows a lot about cruises. I'm just saying, the man has his own dinner jacket and knows how to mix a Negroni.

"Oh, dear me, no," was his considered response. "And where do you plan to eat, before retiring to that cell?" he asked.

I showed him the website, which had pictures of harassed parents, young children, and hefty truck drivers tucking into a buffet that featured all the major carbohydrates.

"Oh, dear me, no," said Steve again. "What you want to do is go to reception the minute you get on board and ask for an upgrade. Any cabin with the word 'Deluxe' in the title should do the trick."

Which is how I find myself eighty quid lighter but ensconced in the wood-panelled Commodore Deluxe, with a complimentary minibar, a wall-mounted TV, a double bed with a furry bed quilt, and the best view on the ship – straight out to sea over the pointy bit at the front.

I know this is called the bow, but when you're FaceTiming a man who makes much of his knowledge about cruise ships, the temptation is just too great.

"Good call," I say to Steve. "The cabin's great. I'd have been cross if it had been at the back of the ship."

"Stern," he says. I knew he wouldn't be able to resist the correction.

"Stern? I'd have been bloody furious."

Steve might know a lot about cruises, but he has much to learn about retrofitting ship jokes into a train-travel book.

Later, I fall asleep amid the pillowy soft bedding in my Commodore cabin – until woken rudely by a terrible lurch and thump at, oh let's see, yes, four am. It is wild weather outside, if the rain lashing against the cabin window is anything to go by. Well done, Captain, spot on with the forecast.

After that I spend the next few hours with my stomach going one way and the ship the other. Last night's scallops don't know whether to stick or twist and when I eventually struggle out of bed, my legs do a passable imitation of a 1920s flapper dance. Under these choppy conditions, the shower is an entertainment in itself – the water appears to be going sideways, or I am, it's not clear which.

I manage to get out on deck in the early morning as the ferry moves into the more sheltered, calmer waters of the deep-water port of IJmuiden. (Don't worry, I checked – the double capital letter is not an error, it's just the language being all mysterious and Dutch.)

This is as far as the ferries come, docking at the seaward end of the canal that was cut between Amsterdam and the North Sea in the 1860s. Anyone expecting to sail straight through to Amsterdam – ahem, I couldn't possibly say – is in for a bit of a shock, not least because IJmuiden's brutal docksides look like the scene of a terrible accident involving discharged thermo-nukes.

Flaming towers, billowing chimneys, clanking conveyor belts and chutes, filthy barges and monumental tankers. It's very possible Skynet has triggered the machine war while I've been busy holding on to both the shower grab rails and last night's dinner.

There's a bus waiting on the dockside to run us the forty minutes into Amsterdam itself, and there are definitely worse places to start a round-Europe train trip. Fabulous city, nice people, good coffee, great beer – given all of which, you'll be surprised to learn that I'm not stopping. It's not that I don't like the city, or don't want to stop, but I have a mad train adventure to start, and it doesn't begin in Amsterdam.

I mean, it does, obviously, because I'm heading for Amsterdam city centre, but the true start of my trip is elsewhere – a carefully calculated location that fits perfectly with this entirely invented train challenge. I'm not saying that place is better or more interesting than Amsterdam – it probably isn't, though I've never been, so we'll see – but it makes sense.

Also, if I spend a night or more in every fascinating city that I pass through on my way north, east, south and west, this trip will take for ever. I have to go home at some point, if only to try and clear a way through the accumulated bales of cloth.

However, I have a couple of hours before my first train, and it's time for lunch in one of Europe's most handsome stations – Amsterdam Centraal. (I know, they just chuck a double 'a' in words when they feel like it. I've had to pay the proof-reader to *leave in* the spelling mistakes.)

It's a rather fine sight from the outside, a huge, red-brick Gothic/Renaissance Revival palace with slender turrets and ornamental stone reliefs. Admittedly, they've mucked about with it inside, adding modern underground galleries with shops and cafés, but the station hides one of the best secrets in European raildom, whispered about in model-railway club-houses and dark-web chatrooms alike.

Go through the main entrance and look past the soaring brick pillars to the staircase in the righthand corner, just in front of the ticket gates. Up here and tucked away along a rather beautiful, tiled corridor is the former waiting room, designed in the 1890s for the station's first-class passengers.

It's an absolute treasure of polished wood, shining brass, gleaming tiles, and stained glass, with high ceilings and arched windows. And at this point I'd be telling you all about the relaxed lunch I had in the Grand Café 1e Klas, the restaurant that occupies the space, if only it hadn't closed down in the meantime, following a court dispute. It had been there for forty years, so this was rather unexpected – and a shame for the restaurant's white cockatoo, called Elvis, whose daily perch was on the bar, where he could chat to the customers.

The space is still there, and I can only assume another restaurant will eventually open up inside. For now, you'll have to take it from me that it's worth trying to take a peek.

From Amsterdam, my plan is to head two hundred and fifty kilometres due east for the true start-point of my grand adventure, and here's why.

Back at home, I'd traced the routes out on Google maps, just to check the distances. From Narvik in the north to Algeciras in the south, it's a shade over five thousand kilometres, down through Sweden, Denmark, Germany, Belgium, France and into Spain. The direct route would take me through grand cities, such as Stockholm, Copenhagen, Hamburg and Paris.

East to west, from Uimaharju in Finnish Karelia to the Atlantic coast at Praia das Maças in Portugal, it's just under five thousand kilometres, again by the most direct route, which involves crossing by ferry from Helsinki to Stockholm.

Now, the routes as traced on the maps – north-south and east-west – don't follow the train lines, which often steer a different course to the roads. So I wouldn't be following *exactly* those routes, travelling by train, but I would end up passing through stations in all the same towns and cities. In short, although plotted by road on Google maps, it was a good enough representation of the journey I was going to make.

What I couldn't help noticing, when I studied all this, was that the two lines crossed at a city somewhere in northwestern Germany – not exactly halfway along each route, but close enough to think that the universe might be trying to tell me something.

Where the lines crossed – in the notional mid-point of the whole trip – is obviously where I should start from. That city would be my Ground Zero for a trip to the far-flung stations at the cardinal points of the European compass.

So I zoomed in, and it's not Düsseldorf, Dortmund or Hanover, though they are all close by. It's not, in fact, any place you've ever heard of, and at this point you might be thinking, Jules, mate, why do you do this to yourself? You're making the entire trip up anyway. It's not even a thing – it's a confected challenge you've set yourself. No one cares. Why not just fudge the whole thing and start in Amsterdam? Relax, have a couple of those strawberry beers they do, and then head off towards Narvik the next day. We'd never know.

Have you ever met me? Pointless excursions to unknown towns in the middle of nowhere are my speciality. I could indeed stay in Amsterdam and have an agreeable evening, but those crossed lines on the map would be nagging away at me. I'd always regret the missed opportunity to go to a random destination, just for the hell of it.

Before I got too carried away, I did first check that

this fabled place has a train station. Wouldn't that be a kicker?

Not only does it have a train station, it turns out that Ground Zero city is very important in the European train-travel world. The Amsterdam-to-Berlin and Cologne-to-Hamburg lines cross there. You can travel to Munich and Basel and on to Austria and France, or head north towards Denmark and Sweden. It's a rail crossroads, of sorts, which has to be some kind of sign.

It's decided, then, and the train from Amsterdam is almost ready to depart. It ends its run in Berlin, but I'm getting off about halfway along the route.

The fourth-largest city in Lower Saxony, and site of the signing of the 1648 Treaty of Westphalia, here I come.

Three hours later, in the mid-afternoon, I step out of the station at – ta-da! – Osnabrück. To say I'm underwhelmed is a little unfair. After all, they didn't know that I had plucked their fair city at random to sit at the centre of my train-based odyssey. But a stack of bikes, a Burger King, and a Best Western hotel is not putting your best face forward, Osnabrück.

A twenty-minute walk from the station, though, and things improve immeasurably, as I leave the modern streets behind and enter the old town, the Altstadt. It's a tight kernel of landscaped squares and narrow streets, tucked in between the river and the ring road. There are houses with stepped gables, a sprinkling of slender church spires, and a large, twin-towered cathedral.

All right, it's not Amsterdam, where I could have stayed, though there is a pleasant riverside walk, and signs pointing the way to a couple of local museums.

But I know what you're thinking. A stroll around a reasonably attractive German town is all well and good, but when are we going to hear more about the 1648 Treaty of Westphalia?

The place to find out is the city hall, the Rathaus, built in the early sixteenth century and looking very impressive, with its sculpted ornamentation and twin stone staircase rising to a heavy oak door. The so-called Peace of Westphalia, which ended the Thirty Years' War, was declared from these very steps on 25 October, 1648, and I wave at imaginary crowds as I ascend.

If you think you're going to find out substantially more than that, then you have clearly never wrestled with the baffling geopolitical intricacies of the Holy Roman Empire.

I don't understand it, and I've got a history degree, but basically everyone in Europe was at war from 1618 – Catholics versus Protestants, Habsburgs against Bourbons, and France and Sweden against almost everyone else. Battles erupted across central Europe, as imperial armies and their proxies fought to a standstill – some estimates put the deaths of soldiers and civilians over the period at between five and eight million.

All we really need to know is that Osnabrück is where all the carnage ended, and it promotes itself nowadays as a 'City of Peace,' which seems fair enough.

To be honest, there's not a great deal to see in the city hall itself. I have a look around the oak-beamed rooms, lined with portraits of severe-looking prince-bishops, and politely admire the wrought-iron candelabra, because the attendant points it out especially.

If it all seems too distant in time to care about – and I think that's a reasonable view, at this remove – Osnabrück's City of Peace tag has a more contemporary resonance, too.

It was the birthplace of Erich Maria Remarque, author of *Im Westen nichts Neues* – 'Nothing New in the West' – which you'll know as *All Quiet on the Western Front*. There's an archive centre and library devoted to him and his work, and I spend half an hour there, accidentally discovering all sorts of things that fascinate me but have nothing to do with his books.

He had affairs in the 1930s with both Hedy Lamarr and Marlene Dietrich, for example, while documents on display indicate that Remarque not only had a stonking wine cellar, but also owned scores of original works by the Impressionists. They are all valued on a handwritten account – fifteen thousand dollars for a Cézanne, twenty-five thousand for a van Gogh, or a Degas 'woman in bathtub,' a snip at a grand. If you wanted to piss off the Nazis, who had long dismissed Remarque's books as 'unpatriotic,' this was definitely the way to do it – by collecting what they saw as degenerate art and swigging vintage Bollinger.

It comes as a jolt to find that although Remarque escaped Nazi Germany, and found fame and wealth, not all his family were so lucky. He lived in Switzerland and the United States, died in 1970, and was buried back in Switzerland. But his sister, who had stayed in Germany, was arrested in 1943, subjected to a sham trial and executed – beheaded – for her anti-Nazi stance.

There's a similarly sombre mood at the Felix Nussbaum Haus, a Daniel-Libeskind-designed gallery, which holds the largest international collection of the Osnabrück-born painter murdered at Auschwitz in 1944. The building itself makes a real statement – angular boxes of wood, glass and steel, with jagged, shard-like windows and polished concrete corridors and galleries. "If I perish, do not let my pictures die," said Nussbaum, and here they now live in a remarkable setting.

In the end, this is all rather more than I was expecting from Osnabrück. It could have been dull, or a dump, but it's neither. True, it's a little nondescript and modern in some parts, and a bit manicured and pristine in the old town, but there's a reason for that.

Founded as long ago as the eighth century, and a city since the twelfth, it suffered the same fate as a lot of historic German towns and cities – bombed to pieces by the Allies during World War II, and painstakingly rebuilt afterwards. The British maintained a garrison here – the largest British garrison in the world – until 2008. You wouldn't know any of that now. It's done well for itself: come back from the ashes of war, styled itself as a modern, go-ahead German city.

Let's not get carried away. You wouldn't come here on holiday. I mean, *you* wouldn't. I have, obviously, and it was a bit of a stab in the dark, but it's turned out all right.

I've got a hotel for the night, around the back of the cathedral. We'll see how sensible that is when the midnight bellringing starts. All that remains now is to find out which restaurant serves the best schnitzel (it's a trick question – ALL schnitzels are the best), and where I might get a beer.

It turns out that it's the same place, the estimable Rampendahl Hausbrauerei, where I spend a happy couple of hours eating deep-fried things and drinking cloudy homebrew. It's exactly the sort of split-level, wood-beamed German brewpub of my dreams, with copper pipes running above the bar and tankards hanging from the ceiling. I turn down the 'Wedding Soup' (beef broth with 'custard royale,' no thank you), but can thoroughly recommend the waffles with ice cream and chocolate sauce for dessert.

I idly contemplate a nightcap elsewhere, but with clubs called things like Neo and Hyde Park, I suspect that Osnabrück's nightlife is modelled on that of my hometown, Huddersfield, circa 1980. Huddersfield being another place that you wouldn't go to on holiday, though in a parallel universe there's probably a travel writer concocting an improbable tour of Europe where the lines cross at a reasonably attractive, former textile town in northern England.

Good luck to them finding a schnitzel there.

NORTH
HAMBURG TO NARVIK

∾

Hamburg-Copenhagen-Stockholm-Mora-Östersund-
Gällivare-Kiruna-Narvik

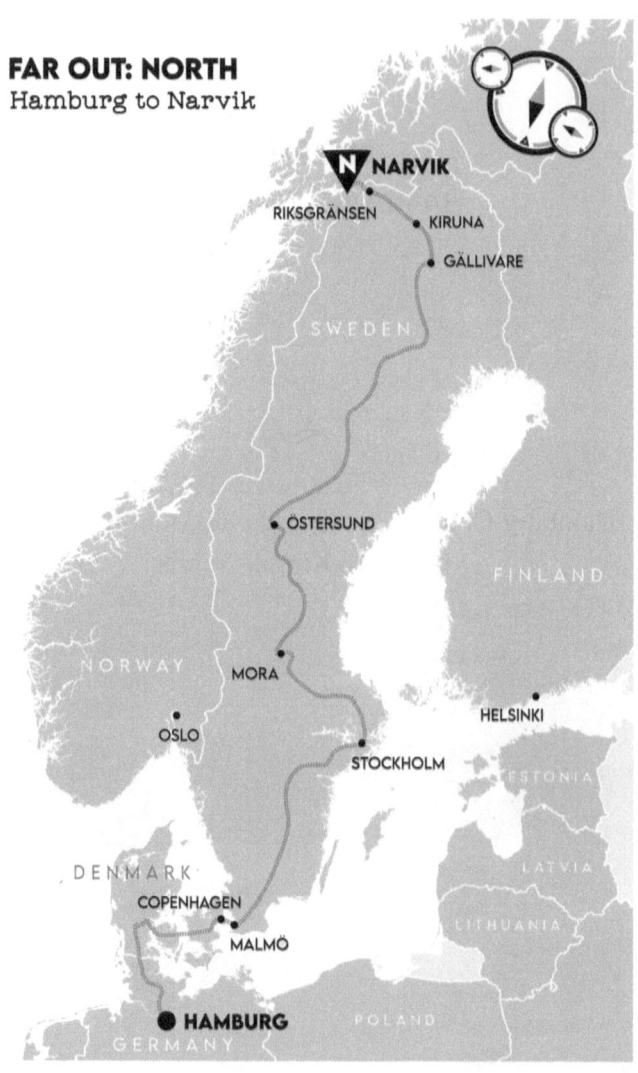

CHAPTER 3

OSNABRÜCK TO HAMBURG

Thus far, heading to my first real destination, the northernmost train station in Europe, I am shocked – shocked, I tell you – to discover that I have been travelling southeast at best.

York to Newcastle to Amsterdam to Osnabrück is not the route a polar explorer would choose, put it like that. However, I take my inspiration from Ernest Shackleton. There's a photograph in one of the many histories of his Antarctic expeditions, with Shack on a train in London, surrounded by trunks, chests, boxes, skis, sleds, and coils of rope, the picture captioned, 'Well on the way.'

The man was going to the South Pole, but was definitely en route, as far he was concerned, on the 09.13 from London Victoria.

Accordingly, even though I have gone backwards, I

am well on the way to Narvik – despite it still being almost three thousand kilometres away. More to the point, I'm finally turning north at Osnabrück.

If I just kept going, the absolute quickest I could get to northern Norway by train would be two nights', three days' travel, culminating in the direct night train from Stockholm to Narvik. If I carried on at that rate, though, not only would it be exhausting, but this book would finish on about page forty-five.

"Boy, it really was just a pamphlet about Narvik, Uimaharju, Algeciras, and Praia das Maças," you would all exclaim, before firing off a complaint and demanding a refund.

To forestall any unpleasantness, rest assured that I shall be stopping many times along the way – not always in places you'd expect, or necessarily even want to read about, but I can't help the geography or the lie of the railway tracks.

The first stop, however, Hamburg, is entirely planned, and while it's only two hundred kilometres and a couple of hours along the route, I think it's worth the effort.

The last time I was here was in the summer of 1980, on my first ever Interrail trip, so there's an element of visiting for old times' sake. Not that any of it rings a bell, even the rather impressive station, with its vast iron-and-glass canopy. Second-busiest station in Europe, apparently, after the Gare du Nord in Paris, where the Eurostar arrives, so over the years I've knocked off the top two without even trying. (Enters the rabbit hole of 'busiest railway stations in Europe.' Discovers eleven of the top twenty are in Germany. Decides no one will read a book about that.)

I'm only here for one reason, Miniatur Wunderland, the world's largest model railway. This didn't exist back in 1980, and I wouldn't have gone anyway, model railways then being on a par with disco, folk music and knitting to the hip, young, punky gunslingers we all thought we were in those days.

But now I'm all grown up, the idea of over sixteen thousand metres of track, twelve hundred trains, and twelve thousand rail cars in fourteen themed layouts seems strangely compelling. Plus, I'm writing a book about train travel, so it would be rude not to go.

It was the idea of twin brothers, Frederik and Gerrit – surname Braun, excellent choice – and their friend, Stephan Hertz, who planned it to be the world's largest model railway from the start. Because they weren't completely bonkers, they did plenty of due diligence, including a survey asking thousands of visitors which attractions they would visit in Hamburg. Their as-yet unfulfilled idea of Miniatur Wunderland came in third, which made them think they were onto something, though – and this is the bit I love – "with female voters it fell into last place." You don't say.

It opened in 2001 in one of the palatial, red-brick warehouses that still line Hamburg's waterways, and honestly, it's a joy to visit. Even for ladies, as long as they don't have a fit of the vapours in the close company of so many gentlemen railway enthusiasts.

What they got right from the outset is that it's not about the trains, or at least not completely, which is an odd thing to say about the world's biggest train set, but it's true. The themed 'worlds' on several floors in two buildings – Germany, Switzerland, USA, Patagonia, and so on – are the clue that this is a fully realised vision, backed by extraordinary model-making and design skills.

Each world is enormous and works on several levels – so it's not just trains in motion, but also subways, cable cars, cruise and cargo ships, trucks, gliders, hot-air balloons, and planes.

It's difficult to describe how magnificent this is. I shuffle around with scores of others in astonishment, noting – almost at random – a working cement factory, a stadium with twelve thousand individual spectator figurines, a full airport with landing planes, a six-metre-high mountain, a Rio de Janeiro favela, Las Vegas lit by thirty-three thousand LEDs, a cog railway up the Matterhorn, Swiss ski resorts, Mount Rushmore, the Grand Canyon, and Patagonian fjords and ice floes full of penguins.

All are rendered in exquisite miniature on dramatic dioramas that span entire floors of the warehouse building. You can peer inside and around corners to see the inner workings of the train sets, and marvel at the painstaking construction of the scenes themselves, from a Scandinavian harbour with an actual tide to the marble quarries of Italy.

The detail is perfect and often hilarious – press a

button at the Sistine Chapel, and you can see Michelangelo leaping inside on a trampoline, the only way he can paint such a high ceiling. Another button launches a teeny bungee-jumper, while every fifteen minutes Mount Vesuvius blows and spews lava onto a lavishly recreated Pompeii. There are jokes and surprises at every turn, notably a fantastically self-reverential bit of humour in the Hamburg section, where there's a model Miniatur Wunderland building, with the world's smallest model railway inside that – shrunk to a 1:7,569 scale.

Two hours goes by, just like that. I've probably seen a twentieth of it properly, and there are hideaway scenes and details that I might never find in multiple visits. Checking the website later, for example, I'm gutted to find that I missed the arctic ghost ship, and the fully-accurate-I'm-sure Area 51 display, complete with basketball-playing aliens.

You'll note I haven't much touched upon the trains themselves, the varied track systems, the drive mechanisms, the 3,454 switches, and the 1,380 signals, and that is for the very good reason that I don't know anything about them. Those matters are best left to the railfans and modellers who find joy in the mechanics and logistics of building model-railway lay-outs so that people like me can go, "Ooh, look, a little train coming out of a tunnel!"

Afterwards, I take a short walk along the river to the alluringly named Portugiesenviertel – the Portugal Quarter – on the internet promise of a cheap lunch in a Portuguese restaurant. There are quite a few in the neighbourhood, courtesy of those who came here as harbour-workers in the 1960s and '70s, but the Portuguese were hardly the first.

Hamburg has a long history of trade and immigration, from the Vikings who sailed up the River Elbe in the ninth century – big on pillaging and looting, less so on trading – to its medieval heyday as part of the Hanseatic League. There are reminders of its cosmopolitan heritage everywhere: not just my grilled sardines, rice and salad for lunch at the Olá Lisboa restaurant, but a Swedish church at one end of the street and no fewer than three seamen's churches at the other, Danish, Norwegian and Finnish.

Keeping to the river, heading east, and then striking inland, it's another twenty minutes on foot to perhaps the most notorious area of Hamburg – the infamous Reeperbahn in the St Pauli neighbourhood. Once the home of Hamburg's ropemakers, it became – still is, to some degree – a red-light district for the sailors from the nearby docks. And then in the 1960s it shot to prominence when an unknown English band started to make their name on the dive-bar circuit.

I'm here in the mid-afternoon when nothing much is open, and there are just a few tourists wandering around, like myself, pondering days gone by. I suspect it's a bit livelier, not to say provocative, late at night, if the signs for five-euro vodka bombs, sex shops, and strip bars are anything to go by.

When Elaine first met me, she harboured some

doubts, because – as a travel writer, always on the move – she imagined that I had a girl in every port. Places such as Hamburg, she surmised, were like catnip to the younger Brown. I could have been up to all sorts, and she wasn't sure that the kind of wagon she wanted to hitch herself to.

Once she got to know me better, the very suggestion of past adventures came to be the cause of immense – and continuing – hilarity.

"Cup of chamomile tea in every port, maybe," she'll snort. "Date with a hot history museum, more like."

If I object – "I could have if I'd have wanted" – she only laughs harder.

Rude. Anyway, I did have a date once, in Portugal.

"Ah yes, the famous port sisters."

"I never said they were sisters."

They were working at one of the port-wine tasting houses in Porto, when my travel friend, Tyler, and I rocked up one afternoon for the free tour and drinks. Tyler was blond, rugged, and Australian. I was me. I forget how we'd become acquainted – presumably in some hostel or other as I backpacked my way through Portugal.

We got chatting to the two Portuguese girls pouring the drinks – presumably Tyler did the chatting, me being me – and the upshot was that we ended up with a date that evening in one of the classier riverside bars in Porto, after the girls' shift finished.

I don't know what they were expecting, though

Tyler's surf-boy physique must have done some preliminary heavy lifting. Possibly, they were expecting that we would scrub up for an evening out, and be in a position to buy them drinks at a classy bar.

But frankly, Tyler and I had already been as dressed up as far we could, in order to go to the port-wine tasting, given that we had both been living out of backpacks for several weeks. And buying rounds of drinks in classy riverside bars was also not a realistic option for backpackers on about ten quid a day. I rather think our presence at the free, middle-of-the-day wine tasting had been a clue.

Anyway, we had one drink, which we each paid for ourselves, and then, wouldn't you know it, but the girls suddenly remembered that they had a family party to go to, and with that, my travel-writing dating career was over.

Elaine is usually beside herself at this point of the anecdote. The words "eejit" and "chamomile tea" are occasionally to be made out, among the rasping laughs. She roars even more if she remembers the coda to the anecdote, which is that Tyler turned out to be multi-directional in his attentions. I know this because about a week later he made a pass at me one night, in a hotel where we had been forced to share a double bed because he told me that was the only room they had left.

"A boy in every port, as it turns out!"

"All right, laugh it up."

The only way you can stop her coughing up a lung

is to point out that she did, in fact, choose to marry me. That puts a stop to her gallop, though I do then have to sit through a litany of reasons – including the words "raw material" – that usually finishes with the phrase, "Anyway, I could see you were harmless," which, in Elaine's native Ireland, is less complimentary than it sounds.

What this all means is that I'm allowed to go to places like the Reeperbahn. Encouraged even. Because while there is table-dancing at the Pink Palace Sex House, for example, and untold pleasures available at the Titty Twister Bar, Elaine is correct in her assessment that the mere sight of either will have me flushing like a Victorian vicar who's just caught a glimpse of an uncovered piano leg.

I fetch up instead at the true target of my walk, a disc-shaped plaza off the main Reeperbahn where the Fab Four, The Beatles, are memorialised in stainless steel cut-out form.

Actually, here in Beatles-Platz it's the Fab Five, because when the band first came to Hamburg in 1960, it was pre-fame, pre-hysteria, pre-everything. At that point The Beatles were a callow five-piece – the teenage Lennon, McCartney and Harrison, with Pete Best on drums and Stuart Sutcliffe on bass.

It was Sutcliffe's arty German photographer girlfriend, Astrid Kirchherr, who gave them their early black-clad, mop-top style. Sutcliffe died of a brain haemorrhage in April 1962, and Ringo replaced Pete Best in August the same year. So while the drummer figure in the plaza can be taken as either Best or Starr, Stuart Sutcliffe stands poignantly away from the others, bass pointing down at the ground, the eternal Fifth Beatle. I think that's rather sweet, to remember him like that.

From the plaza, I walk up the narrow street, Große Freiheit, where many of the clubs are now techno and dance places, but others still have names redolent of the Sixties – the Dollhouse Beach Club, Olivia's Show Club, The Bunny Burlesque, and Susi's Show Bar (where, on the photo outside, someone appears to be enjoying a champagne enema.)

At the prompting of a Liverpool promoter, The Beatles came to Hamburg in August 1960 and played their first gig here at the Indra Club, at Große Freiheit 64. It's still there, with a Beatles plaque on the wall. There's also a plaque at the site of the old Star-Club, one of their later haunts, which I find eventually by ducking through the archway at number thirty-nine to the courtyard behind at the Highway Club.

It was at the Kaiserkeller, though, at number thirty-six, where they perfected their craft. It's still a music venue, with a roll call of bands across the ages scrawled on the façade, but for a few months in 1960 The Beatles played there every night.

Their contract with the club owner is reproduced on the wall, and it's brutal – playing for up to eight hours at a time, until two or three in the morning, with half-hour breaks, all the while living in an old, unheated storeroom at the back of a dodgy, nearby cinema.

The writer Malcolm Gladwell popularised the notion of the ten-thousand-hour rule in his book, *Outliers* – the idea that, beyond natural skill or even genius, greatness requires the investment of enormous time. That the key to success in any field is practice – and huge amounts of it.

I think about this often. It's one of the reasons that, after forty years, I'm an all-right travel writer and not, as I might have wished, a professional footballer. I did not do my ten thousand hours on the football pitch – and I was rubbish at it anyway – but I have travelled hundreds of thousands of kilometres, and written millions of words, and that's all added up to something.

And what does this have to do with Hamburg and The Beatles? Quite simply, it's where they put in their ten thousand hours.

It often seems like they came from nowhere – debut single, 'Love Me Do,' a Lennon-McCartney number, released October 1962, and the rest is history.

But by the time they were done with Hamburg, in that same year, they had already played together for thousands of hours. They weren't a garage band or a bedroom sensation – they were honed professionals who knew exactly what they were doing, with a look and a sound that they had perfected in a grungy Hamburg backstreet.

Obviously, McCartney couldn't write a travel book

to save his life. Horses for courses, Paul, horses for courses.

I end the day in the Schifferborse, a restaurant opposite the main station, which I found by the simple expedient of typing 'schnitzel hamburg' into a search engine.

It turns out to be a sort of dine-in galleon – like someone converted the set of *Pirates of the Caribbean* into a restaurant – with a real ship's anchor at the entrance, and wooden ships sticking out of the wall. Only it's not really a themed restaurant either, just a good old German fish and schnitzel emporium, with decent food and a loud, buzzy atmosphere even on a gloomy Wednesday night.

Tomorrow, it's Scandinavia – Copenhagen, to be precise – and the start of the long journey north. I have a ticket to ride, and I'll be going helter skelter on a magical mystery tour, and…

No, fair enough, I'll stop now.

CHAPTER 4

HAMBURG TO COPENHAGEN

The train from Hamburg barrels due north towards Kolding on the Jutland peninsula, where it's going to take a sharp right for Copenhagen.

For a long time, there was a more direct route to Denmark involving a train-ferry between Puttgarden and Rødby, which would have been fun but the spoilsports discontinued it in 2019. If you want the same rail-sea experience, the last one still in operation in Europe runs from Calabria to Sicily in Italy. It is quite something to sit in a railway carriage as it rolls onto a ferry and sets sail, the driver throwing his hands in the air and going, "Look, no rails!"

The Puttgarden-Rødby train-ferry link is being replaced by what will become the world's longest road and rail tunnel, the Fehmarn Belt fixed link, crossing the eighteen-kilometre strait between Germany and Denmark. But the estimated completion date is 2029 at the earliest, and I'm not hanging around for that, so the long way round it is.

It's hardly second-best, given that Denmark spreads across a peninsula and an archipelago, which means encountering rail bridges galore across sparkling Baltic waters before we reach Copenhagen. Even if they do finally dig that eighteen-kilometre tunnel, I know which route I'd rather take.

It also means an initial leisurely ride through the small towns, fields and farmland of Schleswig-Holstein, the long-disputed part of the northern German-Danish borderlands. If you had a British education, and suffered interminable history lessons about events you couldn't care less about, you will at least recognise the name. Apologies in advance if you are German or Danish.

The convoluted status of the two duchies of Schleswig and Holstein boiled down to a matter known famously as the Schleswig-Holstein Question – are you paying attention, Form 3B? – which occupied some of the finest minds of the nineteenth century. Namely, what would win a fight between one cow-sized Schleswig spider and a hundred spider-sized Holstein cows?

Count Bismarck, the German chancellor, got involved and sent a crack team of investigators, and the question was only finally resolved in 1919, when the

Treaty of Versailles called it for the spider, and northern Schleswig became part of Denmark. I may have got some of the details wrong, but that's basically the gist of it.

I don't have long in Copenhagen – half a day, one night – before I move on, so it's probably best to lower expectations in advance. It's going to be the same in Stockholm, too, my next destination, because the trip is all about the journey north – the long, and hopefully spectacular, train ride through the wilds of central and northern Sweden, and then the pan-arctic traverse to Norway and Narvik.

Consequently, major cities and country capitals will come and go, and if you're after a full appraisal of their attractions, with genuine historical and cultural insight, you really should have bought a guidebook.

But if it's random sights you're after, between train changes, I'm your man.

As it happens, I have been to Copenhagen exactly twice before, but I'm not sure either visit will help inform today's brief excursion.

Once was forty years ago, when I did what every backpacker did in those days – got off the train and walked straight to the Carlsberg brewery, where the free tour ended with a bacchanalian, free-for-all beer tasting. Memory of that event, and of Copenhagen itself? Zero.

I toy with the idea of revisiting the brewery, but the free tour is now an exhibition 'experience.' If you add on a tasting of just three beers – 1980s backpackers would be rioting at the point beer four failed to materialise – the whole thing costs a scarcely believable forty-two quid. So, that's a no.

My other visit to Copenhagen – also scarcely believable – was to attend the final of the 2001 Eurovision Song Contest.

I used to write travel features for the *Daily Mail*, and perhaps should have examined the small print when the offer of the press trip came in. Generally, travel press trips are great. Someone else organises and pays for everything, even the drinks. You stay in nice hotels, and have a cheery press officer on hand at all times to take you to interesting places and pay for even more drinks. And at the end, all you have to do is write eight hundred words about how lovely it's all been.

I saw the words 'You are invited,' 'Copenhagen' and 'Press trip' and that was good enough for me. But the whole point of this invitation-only Copenhagen press trip was the Eurovision Song Contest final, which I know lots of people love, but I can take or leave.

It is famously camp and entertaining if you watch it on TV, and duck in and out for half an hour at a time.

Instead, we were taken to the Parken football stadium in the late afternoon, where we sat through the opening act from the previous year's winner, the songs from twenty-three nations, the interval act, the intermediate chat, the voting, the calculating, the declaration of the winner, and the repeat performance of the winning song. Bravo, Estonia with 'Everybody', performed by Tanel Padar, Dave Benton and 2XL.

It must have taken six hours, and most of us had had enough after two. The press officer, sensing a mutiny, kept getting the drinks in, and when we all finally left after midnight, none of us could have told you what country we were in, let alone what event we were attending. The UK, I understand, acquired a plucky twenty-eight points and finished fifteenth, Lindsay Dracass' 'No Dream Impossible' proving a sadly inaccurate prediction.

Memory of that event, and of Copenhagen itself? Also zero.

I have, therefore, a blank slate and half a day to fill, and what finer way to fill it than with a long harbour-side walk to a pointless statue?

The Little Mermaid is the only other thing I do remember from my first visit. It's one of those tick-list destinations for every backpacker on the European circuit, and I thought I'd go and say hello again, after all this time.

Quite why it's a tick-list destination is another matter. Who knows how these things emerge as important or unmissable?

It's an iconic landmark according to virtually every source, which may be so, but it's not inherently interesting or even of much artistic merit – a small, overly romantic statue of a naked mermaid sitting wistfully on a rock at the rather far-flung end of Copenhagen's harbour.

It takes me forty minutes to walk from the main station, through the attractive city centre, past all the colourful boats and cafés at Nyhavn. On I trudge – with an almost grim determination not to stop, have a coffee and enjoy myself – along the harbour and through the park, until it's clear I have arrived.

There must be a hundred people here already, milling about on the promenade, waiting in turn to get close enough to take a picture. A crammed tour boat swings by, with another hundred on board, who all whip out their phones en masse. More people come and leave, the whole time I'm here. I'm genuinely surprised, I thought it would be me and a handful of others, though I later see that there's a tour-bus drop-off point just around the corner.

The small bronze statue was put up in 1913, a gift to the city from the Carlsberg founder, Carl Jacobsen, who had been much taken with the fairy-tale of the little mermaid by Hans Christian Andersen. Jacobsen commissioned sculptor Edvard Eriksen, whose wife gamely modelled for the sculpture, making this one of the earliest genre examples of what I like to think of as the Modern Nordic Nude.

Take it from me, if you've never been to Scandinavia, they are not shy when it comes to public works of art reflecting the male and female form. There's barely a town without a commissioned statue that the city authorities requested of the sculptor, "That's great, now do them without clothes. And make *that* and *those* bigger, while you're at it."

Never mind maiden aunts, there are public statues that would make a Scandinavian builder blush – I passed at least one on the way to see the Little Mermaid and had to avert my eyes, such were the terrifying appendages on display.

There is, in fact, also a more recently sculpted Big Mermaid, six metres high, as opposed to the metre-and-a-bit original I've come to see. It was on display here at the harbourside for a while, but the figure's ample breasts – sculpted by a man, of course – were deemed pornographic, which is a bit rich, frankly, if you've seen some of the eye-popping horrors elsewhere in Scandinavia. The Big Mermaid, accordingly, was run out of town, its future currently unclear, though if anyone's looking to landscape a couple of artificial hills for a toboggan run, I know where you can find a base layer.

In truth, it's hard to get that worked up about the Little Mermaid – unimposing is the word – though she gets damaged or defaced now and again, usually in protest about something or other. The poor little thing has had her head sawn off at least twice; she's also been blown up, dressed up, had paint dumped on her, and is occasionally covered in graffiti.

The location, meanwhile, is not overtly picturesque, despite the park and star-shaped fortress in the background. While the harbour waters lap gently around the granite rock base, the statue itself sits opposite a largely industrial skyline that, at my count, consists of four chimneys, one of them belching smoke, seven wind turbines, one derelict windmill, one aerial mast, and at least one crane.

And yet… still they come. As I just have, for the second time. And I can't say I've learned any more about its powers of attraction, except that perhaps every generation has to discover the Little Mermaid for itself.

I note that a recent Google review – one star, "Why is this place the main attraction in Copenhagen?" – gets right to the point, but then digresses with a spectacularly context-free Gen Z take on a statue that's been a big draw since it was erected in 1913. "Maybe some influencer hyped it up," they say. Bless.

To give them their due, contemporary Copenhagen is something of an influencer's wet dream. If beautiful young things aren't draped around Danish design or fashion outlets, they are banging on about new Nordic cuisine, inspired by the likes of Noma, named best restaurant in the world an impressive five times.

The excellent TV show *The Bear* is basically one long homage to Noma and Copenhagen – they filmed a season-two episode here (when pastry-chef Marcus lives on a houseboat and learns to up his dessert game), that's how hot the city is for foodies. Nineteen restaurants here currently have Michelin stars – though if they're not careful they're all soon going to run out of heritage carrot tops to sous-vide and ditches to forage in.

I like all this side of Copenhagen of course, I'm not a complete heathen. But I don't have the time to track down the finest Copenhagen hot dog or strawberry tart, both of which are a thing for bubbly young peeps with their phone in selfie mode.

Instead, I've signed up for a walking tour that promises to shine a light on alternative, counter-culture Copenhagen, in particular the so-called Free Town of Christiania, which I've always been curious about.

It was founded in 1971, when a collective of hippies, artists, anarchists, and activists squatted in an old military base, just across the canal from the city centre.

They occupied the barracks buildings, ramparts and land, hoisted their own flag, and declared Christiania independent of Danish government and laws. They built and renovated houses, raised families, opened shops, businesses, galleries and cafés, worked on communal gardens and allotments, and allowed in a ton of drugs, because, you know, hippies. All this, just a twenty-minute walk from the Danish parliament building.

Amazingly, this was tolerated for a long time, on the look-how-open-we-are-as-a-society basis. It was seen as a social experiment, which in 2012 acquired a legal basis, so that the inhabitants – maybe a thousand of them – now own much of the land and buildings via a community-controlled foundation. You can even buy an honorary share in Christiania.

But the drugs – all illegal in Denmark – were always a problem for the Danish state, and a flashpoint, especially when the gangs moved in after the 1990s. Buying a bit of weed from an old hippie was one thing; a drugs market known as 'Pusher Street' quite another. While the government looked the other way when it was just local dealers on the scene, it was hard to ignore the growing gang-related violence.

A shooting in summer 2023 killed one man and injured another four, at which point the locals of Christiania – some of whom had lived there for decades – decided enough was enough. They closed down Pusher Street, symbolically ripping up its cobblestones, and collaborated with the city authorities and the police in an attempt to keep the drug gangs away. For, despite the problems, Christiania has long been one of the city's top tourist attractions, with the community relying on income from the shops, restaurants, art spaces, and music venues.

All of this information I had to look up later, because my 'alternative' walking tour – specifically devoted to the hippies of Christiania – turns out to be a big, fat dud.

It doesn't start well. "If you're woke, sensitive, or Swedish," says the guide, "you're going to be offended at some point."

Woke. Really? The go-to insult for people with no awareness. This approach is doomed to failure, I can tell him now.

I was once commissioned to update an alternative American guidebook to Washington DC, the premise of which was that it was 'irreverent' about everything, from the world-class museums and fine-dining restaurants to its civic architecture and public parks.

I was only updating it, thank God, but the poor sap who had written it had had to find something irreverent to say – snarky, funny, jokey – about literally every sight in the city. Which includes the Holocaust Memorial Museum. I think he took the piss out of something in the gift shop, but I couldn't even read most of the book, so misjudged was the tone throughout. I checked the opening hours and admission prices, took the money, and said never again.

And yet here I am, as our guide invites any Germans in the audience to raise their arms, and then sniggers and says, "No, better not."

Nazi salutes, see, do you get it? Are you not entertained?

We walk up and down a few streets, and endure some very light-touch commentary, interspersed with jibes about the Swedes, and a few swipes at Americans. And because the guide is determined to be edgy and humorous, they drop the f-bomb a few times, and talk about Christiania via the medium of drugs ("The Danes love drugs!" Do they, though? Any more than anyone else?). And that's about it, for an hour and a half.

You know what, they have done their job. I am offended by the content, just not in the way they mean. It's so lazy, and no robust sense of humour is required because none of it is funny. The historical and cultural insights are shallow and context-free. If you're going to roast the Swedes in the audience, at least tell us why. It's desperately poor stuff, and I could do better with the Wikipedia Copenhagen page and ten minutes' prep.

The tour doesn't venture into Christiania itself, though I can't blame them for that, because the community doesn't want organised tours from outside wandering in. They run their own guided tours, which I wished I'd known about, but because we've stopped nearby, I take a walk through on my own.

From what I've already said, you might wonder if this is a good idea, but Christiania is perfectly safe. People have lived here since the 1970s, and it goes about its business, despite – or perhaps because of – the swarm of tourists which descends most days. There's a carved totem entrance, and then I'm on the main drag that leads down to an open-air hippy market and the first of many small shops and cafés.

I have to say, it's tricky to call as a fly-by visitor, just here for an hour or so. It has a patchwork '70s vibe – the bits I see resemble nothing so much as a festival village – and every building is covered in giant murals and graffiti.

I walk past obviously lived-in apartments, and tended gardens and allotments, even in and around buildings that look unkempt at best and derelict at worst. Handmade cargo-bicycles lean against walls; there's rainbow bunting and flags everywhere.

I spot a jazz club, a wood workshop, a concert hall, and a blacksmith – those are just the businesses I see, though a map details many more shops, plus a dozen galleries and over twenty places to eat. There's a recycling centre and even a post office. Like I said, a safe, thriving community.

But how much you'll like it depends, I suppose, on your tolerance for what we might call 'All that hippy bollocks.' If you wouldn't want to go to Glastonbury or Burning Man – and I count myself very firmly in that demographic – then Christiania probably isn't for you. Scruffy, is what my mother would have called it. Needs a good haircut. Weeds everywhere. Holes in the pavements. I can hear her tut-tutting now.

The drug lords might have gone, but there are still solitary men loitering by stacks of upturned beer crates who I suspect could hook you up with some mary jane, or whatever the young people are calling it these days.

My mother, however, was made of sterner stuff than her outward demeanour suggested. The woman went to Nepal on a bus with my dad, and delivered her first child – it's me! – in a maternity ward in a Ghanaian public hospital. She would have persevered with Christiania a bit longer, so I seek out a café and see what's on the menu.

They are big on vegetarian and vegan food, no surprise, which to a hip, metropolitan dandy like myself is all good.

I have come on a long journey since the 1970s and 1980s when, in Huddersfield at least, a meal in a veggie café tended to be made by people whose beef (apologies) with The Man extended to railing against the capitalist concepts of taste, texture and colour. Vegetarian food was brown and made of beans, and in those days no one liked it.

Copenhagen, though, has a ton of Michelin stars, don't forget. I am keen to see what the chef can do, so I take my place at an outside table that looks like it was bashed together from old hobbit doors and primary school trestle tables.

Chef has suggested the lasagne, together with an assortment of salads, most of which entail a combination of mayonnaise-bound cold potatoes, and grated carrot and cabbage. So far, so Huddersfield.

The lasagne, when it comes, is remarkable, though not in a Carmy-in-The-Bear, minimalist-plate, maximalist-flavour, kind of way. Between the layers of pasta are sweetcorn and kidney beans, which is no one's idea of a lasagne. Although it is the sort of thing Heston Blumenthal would do, and serve as an air-dried dessert, so maybe I'm just not au fait with the current Nordic dining scene.

I think the lesson of a trip to Christiania is, go on one of their own tours, investigate it properly, because I'm sure it's nicer than I've made it sound, and ask if there are any cafés that don't combine the twin cuisines of Mexico and Italy to novel and thrilling effect.

I schlep back across town and retire for the night in the very agreeable Copenhagen Plaza, right opposite the train station, so I can get away early the next day. This is a proper old hotel from 1913 – all burnished wood and polished brass – with an antique elevator that looks so creaky they've put a notice inside it telling you not to be alarmed.

My room looks out over multiple rail tracks, and there's a steady flow of trains, which despite misgivings turns out not to be a problem at all. I find traffic noise – cars and motorbikes – hard to sleep through, but here the soft, rhythmic dah-dum-dah-dum-dah-dum of wheels on track soon does its job.

CHAPTER 5

COPENHAGEN TO STOCKHOLM

My train the next morning to Stockholm first requires a slow rattle over the long Øresund bridge between Denmark and Sweden, and then a quick change in Malmö. The train takes the lower deck, so the views are not as clear as I'd hoped, but it's a sparkling run across waters dotted with nippy sailboats.

Sweden, at last, which is proper Scandinavia, at least as far as I'm concerned.

I first came here in 1986, landing further up the west coast in Gothenburg, arriving on a direct ferry from the UK, a route which no longer exists. I was writing a guidebook for Rough Guides – my first – and knew nothing much about Scandinavia, and even less about writing books. Yet there I was, getting off the Harwich ferry with a guidebook to write, and the entire summer ahead of me to cover Sweden and Norway, while my co-writer took on Denmark and Finland.

I ended up writing three editions of the Scandinavia guide, traipsing up and down for various periods over seven or eight years, before handing the book over to someone else. I was young and it was exciting, being paid – eventually, hopefully – to travel, although when I think back on it now, Scandinavia was a tough first gig. Solo travel over huge distances, in largely rugged country, on the tightest of budgets in the most expensive region of Europe. Swanning around Greece or Spain, it was not.

I know, cue tiny violins, right? But I can only say what it felt like at the time, which was as if it was an audition – in many ways it was – for writing about cheaper, hotter countries that were more to my taste.

It's been well over thirty years since I was last in Sweden, and it would have been satisfying – rounding circles and all that – if I could have started this trip in Gothenburg, too. But a check of the rail timetable shows me it's three hours away from Malmö, which is too much of a diversion. I have an endpoint in mind and a schedule to keep.

The Malmö-to-Stockholm train appeals to me from the start. Wide, woven-textile seats that are reclinable and adjustable, with lots of leg room. A personal table, sockets and coat hook, plentiful luggage space, braille signage if required. The spotless, dare I say stylish, café calls itself a bistro, and has prawn salads available, as well as muffins and a help-yourself coffee urn with free coffee refills. All this in second-class travel.

The first time I travelled by train in Sweden was courtesy of a free rail pass provided by the Swedish Tourist Board in London. The head was a lovely woman called Barbro Hunter, who was that terrifying mix of Scandinavian charm and brutal directness. "How rough is this guide?" she asked, the first time I met her. "Because we only like newspaper articles and nice guidebooks about how lovely Sweden is."

For reasons known only to her, she decided that a gormless first-time travel writer who had never even been to her country before was the perfect vehicle for her largesse. For when Barbro, God bless her, spoke, people in Scandinavia jumped.

The Swedish rail pass was her opening gambit. With it, I could jump on trains whenever I liked, which saved me a fortune.

I gaily boarded the first few trains, enjoying the space and the views, and the free coffee refills, until one day an inspector examined the pass more closely and threw me out of my seat with the never-to be-forgotten phrase, "You cannot sit here, this is a first-class pass. Please move to the first-class compartment."

Barbro – may her name be forever hallowed – had provided a first-class rail pass. I had not read or understood the small print, and had been slumming it in second all along.

She also furnished me with a personal letter of introduction. On headed notepaper from the Swedish

Tourist Board, it said something like, "To whoever it may concern, please afford British travel writer, Jules Brown, any assistance you may be able to offer."

I brandished it at every available opportunity, tentatively at first, then boldly and often. Museums, galleries, boat tours, ski lifts, bus companies, ferry operators, cinemas, concert halls – they all quailed before the name of Barbro Hunter, and I had a far more agreeable time in Sweden than a man with no money had any right to have.

Today, on my own dime, I am seated in mere second class, amidst what turns out to be a tour group of Australians in their sixties and seventies. They have also just changed trains from Copenhagen over the water. Their tour guide is doing her best.

"This is a different country, right?" asks one.

This is the lesser spotted 'If it's Tuesday it must be Sweden' brigade. I really thought they were extinct.

"We're in Malmö," says the tour guide, "now on the train to Stockholm."

They're not all convinced. "We're in Sweden?"

"Yes."

"And we were in Denmark, twenty minutes ago?"

"Yes."

How they all laugh. There is much talk of the Nullarbor plain crossing, and the wilds of Tasmania, and the seventeen hours it takes back home to drive for a pizza.

The tour guide moves onto the many and varied joys of Sweden that they will experience from the train.

The great university town of Lund, the lakes, the castles. It's a tough crowd; they are all still asking about coffee, and is it Tuesday or Wednesday?

"It is also the home of many inventions," she says. "Did you know that Spotify and Skype are Swedish?"

I prick my ears. I did not, madam.

"And then there is IKEA, of course," she adds. "A very clever invention."

Well, the tour group isn't having that. Not that it's not Swedish. They're happy to cede that. One after another, they point out its inadequacies – the missing screws, the nuts and bolts you always have left over, the panels put in backwards by mistake. IKEA, I am hearing, is not a hit in the senior communities of the Australian Gold Coast.

"There is a hotel," continues the tour guide, bravely I'd say, "where you can stay, and all the furniture is from IKEA."

Cue guffaws and uproar at the very thought, though I am rather taken with this as an idea for a future pointless excursion, which is my speciality.

On investigation, the hotel turns out to be in the small town of Älmhult, which we do indeed flash past – also the location of the first ever IKEA store, opened in 1958, which is now the site of the flagship IKEA Museum. And the name IKEA, don't you know, is derived from the initials of founder, Ingvar Kamprad, Elmtaryd, the farm on which he grew up, close to the village of Agunnaryd, thirty kilometres from Älmhult. I mean, come on, there's a whole book in this, surely?

To a background of Australian scoffing, the train continues through quintessentially Swedish countryside in the region of Småland. It's the Sweden of TV, film, and Pippi Longstocking – immediately recognisable as such, even if you've never been.

There are tilled fields and bales of hay, wheat waving in the wind, silver birch by the tracks, pines beyond, and water, water everywhere. Still ponds lie beside isolated farmhouses, followed by larger lakes, each with a boathouse, and rowboats pulled up on the shore. Wooden barns and houses are painted the deepest of reds – the iron-rich colour known as 'Falun Red,' an historic by-product of the country's copper mines and a classic Swedish signifier.

Endless bodies of water come and go, but we're not even scratching the surface of Sweden's lakes on this route. To the west of our current position, for example, is the town of Jönköping, at the southern shore of finger-shaped Vättern, 135 kilometres long from point to point and the sixth-largest lake in Europe.

But that still doesn't make the cut in Sweden, because even further over to the northwest is Vänern, largest lake in the country, largest in the EU, third largest in Europe, twice the surface area of Luxembourg. I know, too many lake-related facts when you're still trying to work out how to pronounce Jönköping – try something like Yurn-shur-ping.

Water, forests, meadows, farmland – this is Sweden in a nutshell, seen from the high-speed train to Stockholm. Small, well-kept towns; waterside houses with white picket fences; parks, jetties, campgrounds, and picnic benches. A deer pops out of the trees as the train shoots past, and scampers back into the undergrowth. Birds rise from wooded islets in the lakes. White clouds scuff across the horizon.

It all looks incredibly wholesome, the sort of place the Famous Five might come on holiday, cycling down lanes with bottles of pop and jam sandwiches, a mystery to solve before bedtime.

I doze against the window, the hours pass, and Stockholm finally appears. We cross even more water on a sparkling final run into the heart of the archipelago in which the city sits, getting a birds' eye view on the right of the old town before pulling into Stockholm Central.

Despite its celebrated charm and beauty, when I first came here to write a guidebook I clearly found Stockholm difficult to like, if the written evidence of said guidebook (*The Rough Guide to Scandinavia*, first edition, 1988) is anything to go by. The city is "self-important" and has "little soul," I told people sternly, and "its fabled beauty palls after a few days."

What a twenty-three-year-old arse I was, confident that, after spending only a short time in one of Europe's finest capital cities, I knew enough to dismiss it out of hand. The shopping streets displayed a vulgar "glut of Nordic consumerism;" as for recommended restaurants, my readers could forget it. I barely had a cooked meal the first time I came to Scandinavia, such was the ferocity of the pricing. I survived off rye crackers and tubes of garish pink prawn paste, supplemented by the occasional frightening hot dog from town-centre kiosks.

The saintly Barbro Hunter didn't know any of this yet, because it took eighteen months of research and writing before the book came out. Which explains why – in anticipation of a nice guidebook about lovely Sweden – she put me up for my first night in her fair capital city in the five-star, waterfront, Grand Hôtel, so posh it has a circumflex on the 'o.'

I turned up with a backpack and snotty attitude, and was led up several flights of stairs and down long corridors by a uniformed attendant, who eventually threw open some doors, sniffed disdainfully at me, and announced, "This is your room, the Royal Suite."

More French doors were opened onto a balcony with views of the Royal Palace opposite; the complimentary fruit platter was indicated; the dinner hour in the restaurant mentioned, where I had been assigned a reservation.

No tip for the attendant, obviously, though that was less to do with my general arse- and snot-ridden attitude and more to do with my enormous embarrassment at all this largesse. I'd never stayed anywhere like this before, or been given a free first-class rail pass – or been given anything for free, in fact – and genuinely didn't know what to do or how to behave.

So I acted as any inexperienced, unconfident, small-town boy would – i.e., went bright red, avoided eye contact, and mumbled "Uh, thanks, I guess."

The kicker, for the hotel, is that the Grand didn't even get a review in the first edition of the guide, it being deemed too fancy and expensive for a Rough Guide crowd.

That was true, I suppose, in the early days. The guides later grew with their readership, as we all got older and better off, and began as writers to realise that you might want to go to a restaurant for dinner and not forage in a market bin. Or, indeed, sleep rough in a Stockholm park, as I seem to have suggested you should consider, while I tucked myself into a nine-foot-wide bed in the Royal Suite and ate chocolate-coated strawberries.

Lesser suites at the Grand, I am tickled to see, currently cost over two thousand pounds a night; they don't even quote a price for the Royal Suite on the website. This I discover while I dump my bag at my accommodation of choice tonight, namely the Generator hostel, whose advertised vibe rings all sorts of alarm bells, but it is at least handy for the train station.

There's music playing at reception – the sort of music that sounds like a plumber banging a waste pipe while a child plinks away on a one-note piano. There are skateboards for rent, and a podcast studio available for guests' use. None of this sounds like I'm going to enjoy it. Barbro Hunter wouldn't have put a travel writer here, I can tell you.

But my room is up on the fifth floor, and it's private, quiet and spacious, with its own desk and bathroom. And on further investigation, the hostel is rather sweet.

The skateboards hang in a line at reception, and they all have names – Myles, Olive, Cole, etc. There are events advertised, which in Prague would be things like 24-Hour Naked Bar Crawl, or Kalashnikov Paintball, but here are a board-game night, quiz night, and movie night with popcorn. True, there are also DJ nights, but the only visible vinyl by the decks is a Kenny Rogers album.

This must be the famous Gen Z sobriety I've read about, layered perhaps with a heavy dollop of irony. Maybe there's a back room I haven't seen where they are all off their nut on Bacardi Breezers and cocaine, but it's rather charming. They'll be running their respective countries in fifteen years' time, and can't possibly do any worse than my lot.

I don't need to walk around Stockholm for old times' sake to know that it's strikingly beautiful, whatever I thought the first time around. Everyone says so, and I'm inclined to believe them. Besides, I don't have the time to retrace all my steps to see exactly how wrong I was. An afternoon now, and tomorrow morning, and then I'm on the train again.

But I do stroll down and cross the bridge to the small island that was once the heart of Stockholm, now the historic old town, or Gamla Stan. I was surprisingly nice about it in the guide, even if I was a bit sniffy about the number of tourists there. (I was writing a guidebook. Who did I think was going to read it?)

It's packed again today but it is strikingly gorgeous, with the Royal Palace dominating the north side, and the rest a crowded labyrinth of tall merchants' houses in red, pink and yellow, with soaring gable ends, and decorated windows and doorways. The slender green spire of a red-brick church pokes above the rooftops, while the skinniest of cobbled alleys lead down to the waterfront, where ferries skid across the water in the distance. I pull up a cane chair at a café for an espresso and a slice of cake, and listen to the contented babble of happy visitors.

All awful, obviously. No soul, beauty palling by the second. What an idiot I was.

There is one other place I do want to visit. I was very taken with it the first time around – best museum in Stockholm, I pronounced loftily – and it has quite the backstory.

Sweden was on her way to becoming a huge imperial power at the end of the sixteenth century. King Gustav II Adolf came to the throne in 1611 determined to make his mark and, beset by ongoing religious wars and struggles for influence, ordered the building of a huge new warship in 1625, known as the Vasa. It was going to dominate the Baltic – almost seventy metres long, with ten sails, sixty-four specially commissioned bronze cannons, and over seven hundred carved and brightly painted statues, heraldic devices and decorations, designed to project shock and awe on all who were met in battle.

It was a beast, the largest warship ever built, and emerged from a Stockholm shipyard, close to the Royal Palace.

And then, on her maiden voyage, on 10 August 1628, the Vasa sailed for just thirteen hundred metres, listed badly under a strong gust of wind, and sank quickly, still within sight of the shipyard. The ship went down in thirty metres of water, in front of thousands of onlookers; thirty people on board died. Gustav Adolf, naturally, was livid, but a subsequent inquest basically found no one was to blame – given that the king himself had personally approved all the plans.

The ship lay in the mud and silt of Stockholm's inner harbour for over three hundred years, largely undisturbed, until it was rediscovered in 1956. It was eventually lifted from the mud and moved – under water at first – reappearing from the deep in 1961, and then displayed at a new dockside shipyard and museum.

That's the whole ship, by the way, which was mostly intact. Not just bits of it – not simply a wreck. Over ninety-eight percent of the original structure survives, making it easily the best-preserved seventeenth-century vessel in the world.

It's an extraordinary story, far more convoluted than my brief account allows, while the salvage and ongoing preservation of the Vasa is another fascinating matter altogether.

Since my day they've built a new museum, while the ship itself continues to be assessed for the best way to maintain and present it. But the sight of it, up close, in a supportive cradle in a purpose-built display hall, remains as thrilling as I remember. There really is nothing else like this anywhere in the world.

The Vasa's huge bulk towers overhead. It's more than fifty metres from the keel to the top of the main mast, and the curved timbers bulge outwards, obscuring the view of the heights. Fashioned from over a thousand oak trees, the ship is so vast you can almost fancy that it breathes. It was designed to carry hundreds of people, not just sailors and soldiers, but their wives and children, too.

The blackened wood has a soft shine from the various treatments it's been subjected to, and while the paint and gold leaf has gone from the sculpted elements, they are as detailed and expressive as the day they were carved. Roman emperors, Greek heroes, Biblical figures, gargoyles, lions, mermaids, and angels – all designed to intimidate and impress.

I'm blown away, one more time, by how ineffably cool this is – that the survival of the Vasa has given us a window into the seventeenth century. The surrounding museum extrapolates an entire world from the rescued ship and its contents.

But I'm also questioning something for the first time, standing right underneath this whale of a ship.

It's how anyone ever thought it would float in the first place.

Agreed, I don't know much about the art of seventeenth-century ship building, but even I can see that this is too top-heavy, too narrow in the beam. The lowest gunports are just a metre above the waterline –

I'm standing on a platform where I can look directly inside, through the large square holes for the cannons. The merest gasp of wind, a tilt of the ship, and in would flood the water – as duly, and you might say predictably, happened.

At the time, according to the records, it seems the shipwright was asked, "Why did you build the ship so narrow, so badly, and without enough bottom that it capsized?", which gets straight to the point. And while the inquest came to no conclusion, probably because everyone involved was implicated in one way or another, I can offer an answer. It's written right there on a museum information panel.

"Ship drawings were unheard of," it says. The master shipbuilder simply used "experience and dead reckoning," which is probably fine for a rowing boat but, I would venture, not ideal if you're building a twelve-hundred tonne warship. Just a thought.

With time on my hands after seeing the Vasa, but no real idea what to do with it, I turn to one of my favourite websites, Atlas Obscura, which always has unusual and offbeat ideas for anywhere you might go in the world. Give it a whirl next time you're somewhere with an hour or two to spare.

Hello, what's this? Someone has calculated the exact geographical centre of Stockholm, working it out from the cardinal points of the official city boundaries.

Is it anywhere interesting or attractive? Of course not, it's a traffic circle by a random housing estate in the suburbs, but this someone is clearly cut from the same cloth as myself. His canvas is merely Stockholm, and not the European railway network, but I applaud his effort. Even so, what kind of eejit would actually go and have a look at the entirely uninteresting geographical centre of Stockholm?

An hour later, after a metro ride and a dusty walk, I am standing at a traffic circle by a random housing estate in the suburbs.

There is an information panel, though it's in Swedish. It's almost as if they don't expect any tourists to come out here. There's also one of those signposts with signs pointing every which way. They usually say things like, "Rome, 2,550 km," though this one points to loads of places in greater Stockholm I've never heard of. The city hall, I note, is four kilometres *that* way, so that's something.

You do have to be a bit odd – no, let's say focused and determined – to come up with an idea like this, and then see it to fruition. Persuade the city council to recognise your mad notion. Get them to put up a panel and a signpost at a suburban traffic circle.

I'm all for it, of course, but then I am quite an odd man, too.

I jump back on the metro and delve back into Atlas Obscura, which you shouldn't get the wrong idea about, because it has all sorts of good stuff, too. Like the Bergianska Trädgården, where I end my day.

The waterside botanic gardens are a few kilometres north of the city centre, and they are everything the geographical centre of Stockholm isn't. Worth going to, for starters.

I wander along mown grass paths and stony foreshore trails, happening on a hideaway Japanese garden, with weeping willows, moss-covered rocks, and arched bridges. There are a couple of glasshouses, in one of which are some gargantuan waterlilies – two metres and more across – as well as a few alarming plants that appear to have actual tongues. Not going to lie, I sidle past those with a wary eye.

Outside, hay has been cut. There's an orchard to wander through, and a reed-fringed wetland to sit beside and watch the dragonflies. It's a calm and peaceful spot to say farewell to Stockholm.

With apologies to the city for all the snark, when I didn't know any better.

CHAPTER 6

STOCKHOLM TO ÖSTERSUND

The quick way to Narvik and the Norwegian north is, counterintuitively, up through Sweden, on the overnight train from Stockholm. A nippy eighteen to twenty-one hours, depending on the service: urbane Nordic capital to fjordside arctic port, just like that.

That isn't the way I'm going.

Instead, I'm taking the famed but slower Inlandsbanan, or Inland Railway, straight up the middle of Sweden through a vast wilderness of forests and lakes, one of Europe's great train journeys. That takes two full days and only gets me as far as Gällivare, above the Arctic Circle, where I'll re-join the main railway route over the mountains to Narvik.

Tell me that doesn't sound like an adventure?

The entire Inlandsbanan route is thirteen hundred kilometres long, starting at Kristinehamn, a small port on the immense Lake Vänern. But the connections are much easier if you miss out the first three hundred kilometres, which is why I find myself speeding towards the town of Mora this morning. I'll stay the night and pick up the Inlandsbanan proper from there – first to Östersund and then on to Gällivare, a thousand kilometres of rail travel in total, spread over two long days.

It takes four and half hours from Stockholm in any case just to reach Mora, another scenic ride past lakes, forests, meadows, and yet more lakes.

We're entering the fabled, central county of Dalarna, regarded by Swedes as the nation's heartland, rich in culture and tradition. The ubiquitous red paint colour on every house was originally derived from a pigment from the Dalarna copper mines in Falun, while pagan folklore hangs heavy in this part of central Sweden, especially around the time of midsummer.

Let's just say the makers of horror hit, *Midsommar*, didn't have to look far for inspiration for their fictional, human-sacrifice village – about fifty kilometres from Dalarna, in fact, to Hälsingland, the next province over.

At Rättvik on Lake Siljan, there's a sandy riverside beach, and jetties, gardens and ice-cream stalls. Some occasional heretic didn't get the memo from the local council and has painted their house in yellow, but that's as unsettling as it gets. A white, wooden church pops up its tower on the far shore, while rustic camping cabins and a large caravan park stretch down to the water.

It all looks very inviting and outdoorsy on a hot day,

with seemingly everyone in view from the train window either on a bike or a stand-up paddle board. Top pro tip: never do both at the same time.

Finally, the train hugs the lakeshore on its way round to Mora, passing huge woodyards as we enter town, with water being sprayed over thousands of stacked, sawn trunks. As late as the 1960s, the whole bay bobbed with floating timber from three local sawmills, though the waters are recreational now and there's a gentler, garden-village feel to Mora.

I take a turn round town in the early evening, walking past a freestanding, tapered, red-timbered bell tower that looks like the top half of a Buck Rogers rocket. Further along there's a typical wooden church with a quiet graveyard, while pedestrianised streets with coffee shops and bike racks lead down to a tree-fringed water's edge. There's a small summer fairground here, plus moored boats and the chatter of voices from a restaurant terrace.

It's another of those unheralded places that looks so inviting – let's move here! – but I know me. The chill winters and dark days would eventually grate. And – three hundred kilometres from Stockholm, an hour and a half's drive from the nearest decent-sized town – being a teenager here must suck, big time.

I like my hotel in Mora, handy for the station, and this time also featuring a proper Scandinavian breakfast. Although I warmed to the Generator in Stockholm, the art-house breakfasts left a lot to be desired. No one wants toast with a sixty-five-degree egg, cooked sous-vide for forty-five minutes, or a smear of Nutella in their hand-rolled granola. We want a buffet, and especially a Scandinavian hotel buffet.

I can't tell you what a novel experience that was back in the 1980s, when muesli was about as daring as breakfasts got. My first time in Scandinavia, I spent the first few days navigating the groaning tables with a suspicious eye. None of it looked like an English breakfast.

There was bread, but it wasn't white and square, and it had nuts and seeds in it. In fact, there were six kinds of bread, which just seemed like showing off.

Cheese with holes in it that wasn't cheddar, which you sliced off with a hitherto unknown tool, the cheese plane.

Herring in mustard, rollmops, pickled cucumbers, liver pâté – all recognisably food, but being served at the wrong hour.

Oat milk? That would be, what? Milk with oats in it? They're going to be serving this in coffee shops in forty years' time? They were just messing with me now.

There was also something called 'blueberry soup' among the juice selection, and there was an honest-to-God salad bar, with both lettuce and sweetcorn, the chef obviously still drunk from the dinner service.

These days, of course, I'm familiar with the modern breakfast buffet, and much more health conscious, so before heading off for the day I just have my usual small bowl of natural yoghurt with seeds and fresh fruit. Then a plate of sliced cheese and salami, a bowl of cornflakes, a full cooked breakfast, three muffins, some cake, a chocolate croissant, and a smoothie. Come off it, you know you all do the same.

The Inlandsbanan train is waiting at Mora station, for the once-a-day summer service to Östersund, 320 kilometres up the line, a journey that's scheduled to take six and half hours. This is genuinely slow travel – there are sixteen stops en route, and the maximum speed is eighty kilometres an hour, though down to fifty at times. You don't come this way if you're in a hurry.

The line had been planned as early as the 1850s, to open up the rich timber resources of central and northern Sweden. Shorter, private lines came into being, but construction of the entire route started in 1907. It was built in stages, with heroic navvies cutting a line through forests, bogs and winter snows, and raising bridges across rivers and lakes. Interrupted by war, and then the financial crisis of the 1920s, the Inlandsbanan wasn't completed until 1936, and saw its first traffic the following year.

It played a significant role during World War II, transporting timber, iron ore and soldiers for the Nazis through ostensibly neutral Sweden. After that, it shuttled timber, passengers and cargo up and down the length of the country, connecting tiny settlements and logging towns.

However, it's always been a challenge to keep it going, especially as the road network has improved. Many of the depopulated villages are now shadows of their former selves. There's still a fair amount of freight traffic on the line, but passenger services are down to one a day in each direction on the two longest sections, from Mora to Östersund, and Östersund to Gällivare.

The train itself is something of a rarity, a single, twin-diesel, railcar of a type only otherwise in use in the Balkans and Uruguay – a standard-gauge Y1, originally made by Fiat in Italy, but later modified and produced in Sweden for the Inlandsbanan.

I've put all that in for the rail buffs, though I can't imagine many of them made it past the Reeperbahn sex club/Little Mermaid/buffet breakfast content, but if you're still here, welcome on board!

For the rest of us, what this means is that it's a teeny red-and-cream train, with a combined engine and single carriage. There's a toilet on board, and coffee, water and snacks available, and even a few charging points, but otherwise it's fairly basic. The carriage has seventy seats, and there are only ten of us on board today, though the train guide, Clara, says it was full the previous day.

And with a toot of the whistle we're off, pulling away from the yellow-painted station at Mora, past a very long series of stationary timber wagons.

The line immediately cuts a narrow swathe through pine forest, with the train hemmed in on either side. We hover on a bridge at one point, with a view of a thundering waterfall, pouring brown water after rain overnight.

The whistle blasts keep coming. Anders, the driver, has a hair-trigger train-toot finger, and every road and track crossing – however minor and un-trafficked – gets a blast. Anders, you suspect, didn't yearn to become a train driver, so much as a man paid to be in charge of a large, mobile whistle.

Clara, meanwhile, battles against the toots to keep up a running commentary about places of interest. This is hard going, because this early section of the route is not overly dramatic – there's a restored water tower here, a remote, indeed invisible, fire-warning tower over there, and some random stone carvings by the side of the track. Fair play to her, Clara works with what she's got, but when I tell you that my notes for this part of the journey go – Treeeeeeees. Greeeeeeen – you'll understand her difficulty.

Seventy percent of Sweden is covered by forest, and it's coming right up to the train tracks. It takes a full hour before we get any kind of horizon, and even then it's just a distant ridge of trees on a tree-fringed skyline, with more trees in every direction. If you were plonked down in the middle of that, I dare say you'd be lost in ten minutes, bloodied from brambles within the hour, and dead in a day.

Case in point. Not too long into the journey we reach the highest point on the whole line, over five hundred metres above sea level. It's at a place called Björnidet, which, according to Clara, means "Where the bear is sleeping." Or, once they've heard you crashing around, shouting for help, "Where the bear is chasing."

We continue through vast plantations of spruce and

pine, the slender trunks marching away in arrow-straight lines, with distant flashes of lake water in the distance.

It's not quite true to say there's nothing out here, but it definitely falls on the feck-all side of the ledger. Where there is an occasional, solitary cabin – "You want it here, sir? Are you sure?" – you can't help but feel for the long-suffering partner who agreed to a holiday home but didn't make further enquiries about the location. It's a bold choice, certainly, as any film with 'cabin' or 'woods' in the title will attest.

Our first scheduled stop, after two hours, is at Fågelsjö, a clearing in the woods with a Wild West air, where the train tracks disappear both ways into dense forest.

There's an abandoned wooden house, and a stall outside it run by a fella with a beard and waistcoat who looks like he plays mandolin in Mumford & Sons. We have a twenty-minute halt here, where we're told we can buy homemade lemonade and one of his famous cinnamon buns.

They call this having a 'fika' break, and honestly, you hear this all the time in Sweden, because, obviously, they invented cinnamon and buns. Before the concept of fika was established, no one had ever met someone in a café for a coffee and some cake. It's like hygge, which is just Danish for sitting around in your pyjamas drinking hot chocolate, but thank goodness we now have the words for both activities.

The scenery picks up thereafter, as I start to spy huge, moss-covered rocks scattered amongst the trees.

The ground between is carpeted with lichen, which, along with the moss, is reindeer food – they scrape away the snow in winter with their hooves to get to it.

This seems a long way south to me for reindeer, but apparently Dalarna county is their southernmost range. They stay in their mountain-grazing grounds in summer, but if you take the Inlandsbanan train in winter, when the reindeer have been brought down to the forests, you sometimes see them scamper across the tracks in front of the train. Not always successfully.

I glimpse the very occasional settlement across a valley or small lake. Most of these villages have lost their schools and their shops, the houses now mainly used for back-to-nature holidays. I suppose it depends on your view of mosquitoes and bears, but I would take some persuading to get off the train.

On it trundles, past the excellently named Sveg, a timber town with an airstrip, and the only place of any size we have passed so far. Population, two and a half thousand, childhood home of crime writer Henning Mankell, and where every business seems to have Sveg in its name: Sveg Camping, ICA Supermarket Sveg, Circle K Sveg filling station, Dollarstore Sveg, and the Svegsbadet aquatic centre. I think it must be surprisingly easy to get lost in Sveg if you don't specify exactly which type of business you require.

Looking out of the train window at any point today, it's not hard to see how Ingvar Kamprad of IKEA lighted upon an abundant material to use for his flat-pack furniture. In fact, there's more wood in Sweden now than there was a century ago, thanks to a thriving forestry industry. They plant four hundred million trees a year in Sweden, and only harvest one percent of the forest area. There are, they say, eighty-seven *billion* trees in the country, although after a few hours on the Inlandsbanan, I reckon that's an underestimate.

There's even a Swedish town in the far north, Skellefteå on the Bothnian coast, surrounded by half a million hectares of pine and spruce, where everything is made of wood, because why wouldn't you? Apartment buildings, schools, bridges, multistorey carpark, airport control tower, and a twenty-storey cultural centre and hotel 'plyscraper' – all made from bonded, cross-laminated timber. You can see the attraction: quick, cheap, sustainable construction. The practicalities, however, must have been immense. How do you get a town hall onto a trolley and into the back of a Volvo?

After five hours, the trees begin to subside as we hit an arm of Storsjön, the Great Lake. It's more agricultural here, with farmed fields running down to the water's edge, and white-baled hay laid out in neat rows. Östersund is on another arm of the lake and is large enough to have suburbs with lake views, which we enjoy as the train runs right alongside the water into the centre of town.

This is easily the biggest place so far on the route, and it's the end of the line for today. After six and a half hours, we pull in at eight-fifteen pm, a little over five minutes late. We would have been on time, except

Anders felt he had to do some extra tooting on the way in.

I decide to give myself an extra night here and a day off, seeing as the morning Inlandsbanan departure north is at a displeasing seven-thirty. I've been travelling non-stop for four days and it's time for a rest in an attractive lakeside town, which would be a grand idea, if on my day off it didn't decide to rain – heavily – all day.

Trudging through wet streets, I'm hardly seeing Östersund at its best. It's also twelve degrees out, when it was twenty-five just three days ago. I'm not only wet, I'm unexpectedly cold, too.

I persevere with a soggy walk for an hour or so. There's an austere, modern main square, though older streets arrow off to either side, and these are rather pleasant – coloured sails above, hammock chairs hung from the trees that line the streets, and terrace cafés, empty today.

Apparently, the lake has a monster – the Swedish Nessie – that resembles a rippling serpent with "eyes as big as plates." Sightings date back four hundred years and yet – hard to believe – there's no photographic, video, physical, biological or chemical evidence that such a creature exists.

What does exist is a swimming lido, unsurprisingly empty and lashed by rain. I make a dash instead for the park café, where I hunker down cosily with a warm coffee and cinnamon bun in a daring hygge-fika hybrid move. A solitary Jet ski zooms past in the distance, a brave choice for today.

This is hardy, outdoors Sweden for you. Decent summer weather is a bonus, rather than a given, and they don't care anyway. A poster in the park advertises frankly aspirational warm-weather activities: beach volleyball, live music, boules, wakeboarding, and outdoor yoga, none of which are in evidence today. Although I bet if I turned up at the beach volleyball court, there would be enough fresh-faced locals waiting around in the pouring rain for a game.

The gig posters, meanwhile, promise only two types of music. You can go and see HammerFall – tattooed, vintage power-metallers in studded leather – or wispy, blonde, soft lads and lasses in wheat fields plucking banjos.

On any other day, I'd head to Östersund's major attraction, the open-air Jämtli museum, the sort of place where costumed locals wander around demonstrating traditional midsummer activities like milking bears, whittling pitchforks, and throwing American backpackers off rock ledges. However, the heavy rain has now turned into a deluge. At Jämtli they will doubtless be enjoying the traditional country pursuit of cowering in a turf cottage, wishing they lived in Greece.

I buy a ticket instead for the meditative Ingmar Bergman triple-bill showing in town, investigating the human condition in a world of pain and struggle.

Pauses.

Waits to see if anyone has been paying attention to my disappointingly low-brow cultural preferences.

Bergman? Are you mad? *Jurassic World: Rebirth* is on, in English, at the cinema a block over from the hotel. I am done for the day. Let the dino-chomping commence.

CHAPTER 7

ÖSTERSUND TO GÄLLIVARE

Breakfast the next day is a rushed affair, given the early start to catch the train. It's one explanation for a new first for me – possibly the world – when I contrive to pour yoghurt into my coffee.

Look, there are – I count them – twelve cartons of what appear to be various milks on the buffet counter. All the writing is in Swedish and because of this I go carefully down the line, discounting most of them as obviously flavoured, until I reach a regular looking, green-and-white carton that claims to be just three-percent fat. It is, only it's pourable, three-percent yoghurt. That is not a coffee combo Caffè Nero is going to run with any time soon.

When I find the actual milk selection there are still six candidates, including only one that appears to be semi-skimmed milk from a cow, and not made from oats or puréed American backpacker. Eighteen yoghurt and milk products on one small breakfast buffet in one small provincial Swedish town, and it's my fault I put yoghurt in my americano? I know you're here for the travel tips, so: mjölk, milk; mellanmjölk, semi-skimmed milk; filmjölk, the devil's fermented milk product.

With all due respect to Clara, today's train guide, Nils, is an altogether slicker proposition. Waistcoat, branded Inlandsbanan shirt, tie pin, and flawless English, though with a tendency towards the archaic – men are 'chaps,' someone has a 'gander' at something, and in one anecdote, two people put their 'noggins' together.

Everyone I've met so far has flawless English, if not the Edwardian variety that Nils favours. It's just as well because the Nordic languages are often impenetrable to foreigners, until the occasional, bizarre time that you can understand perfectly what's going on. I refer you to the public notice seen on a road, where I did a double-take and then took a picture, so improbable was it that I could read it. 'All tippning av snö förbjuden,' it proclaimed clearly, in Swedelish.

Today is going to be one long ride. It's seven hundred and fifty kilometres from Östersund to the end of the line at Gällivare, with thirty stations on the way, including six scheduled stops for us. That's thirteen and half hours on the train, during which time we're going to cross the Arctic Circle.

This is exciting stuff, and Nils is up for it. He is nothing if not helpful. Talking of the request stops on the way, he says, "If you want to be thrown out in the middle of the woods, I'll make that happen."

Woods there are, of course, with gorgeous spreads of delicate, white anemones carpeting the ground between the trees. And lakes, lots more of them than the other day, which makes for a more interesting ride, yesterday's rain having given way to bright sunshine. There's the glint of reed-fringed waters on either side of the train, bobbing with the small crowns of waterlilies erupting from hand-sized green bases.

If Sweden has all the trees in Europe (though I can hear Finland saying, "Hold my coat"), it also has ALL the lakes (Finland: "And my shirt"). There are a hundred thousand of them by one count, as well as over a quarter of a million islands, a good proportion of these inside the lakes. Sweden is very much Europe's lake and island supremo, which is interesting enough on its own, but that doesn't stop Nils from wheeling out some barrel-scraping facts when he feels our attention is slipping.

"We are now on one of the longest islands in a lake with a railway on in Sweden," he says at one point, somewhere north of Hoting. Maybe it's more impressive in the original Swedish.

After three hours, just shy of the campsite station halt of Dorotea, we pass a sign saying we have entered Lapland, traditional home of the Sami people, who range across the Nordic regions. Vast, empty lands lie ahead – Lapland takes up a quarter of Sweden, with just one percent of its population.

This feels momentous. Over five hundred kilometres from where I started, in Mora, I'm finally in what can be described as the north of Sweden, although there is still a heck of a way to go. Nils, meanwhile, is trying to drum up interest in Dorotea, where he says there is a caravan museum – "If you're interested in caravans, and full respect if you are," he adds carefully, unsure of his audience.

Lunch is an hour's halt at a woodland clearing by the lake at Vilhelmina, where Bergmans restaurant has its own smokehouse and serves salmon wraps at rustic outdoor tables. I stretch my legs and bask under a warming sun. This is more like it.

The other day's dinner stop, before we reached Östersund, was at an unmemorable buffet attached to a ski centre and shop, where I had a ski shop schnitzel, and try saying that in a hurry.

Today's catering is better all round. Later, at Sorsele, a simple café sells us tubs of ice cream made from their own milk. And later still, at Arvidsjaur, Nils calls ahead with our orders and I pick up a smoked reindeer wrap for dinner from a local hotel, which has sent down a van to meet the train.

The first leg of this journey had the advantage of novelty, and was thoroughly enjoyable to boot. Today's, in truth, is better if far longer.

For a start, there's more to see, as the scenery opens out. Not just trees right up to the track, but huge reaches of water, open marshland, small settlements, occasional sawmills, and old station houses – many now privately owned after being sold off by the state railway over the years.

Don't get me wrong, the trees haven't gone anywhere. Ten hours into today's ride – sixteen overall on the Inlandsbanan, since I started – I can still see a fair few of those eighty-seven billion. You don't need to worry about nodding off and missing anything, put it that way. It's mesmeric, after a fashion, but also slightly overwhelming. Unnerving, even.

Elaine is very hot on forest bathing and walks in nature, it being extremely beneficial for your mental wellbeing. She often takes me on a stupid walk for my stupid mental health, which I enjoy as much as the next man forced to open the curtains and put down his phone. My point being that this would be right up her street, despite the evidence that we're all going slightly mad in this carriage.

Even Nils is not immune. I say, even Nils. The man has been going up and down this line for weeks since the season started. He's showing clear signs of forest madness. His anecdotes are becoming rambling. There's one about a man with a hat on a mountain, and no punchline, which passes us all by. In another, he claims to have gone to see Santa Claus who told him to go away because he was on holiday. He's only prevented from running amok with the ticket machine by a scheduled stop at an isolated halt, which contains a small museum about the navvies who built the Inlandsbanan.

This is fascinating, with plenty of old photos, tools

and dioramas shining a light on what was a horrible job. The navvies were plagued by lice and mosquitoes. They slept in their work clothes, there were no toilets in the camps, and everything froze solid in winter. Would it surprise you, though, to learn that they had a woman to do all the shopping, cooking, cleaning, and laundry, who worked longer hours than them, and didn't get a day off? I thought not.

Outside, a man with a guitar is doing his best with some self-penned train- and tree-related forest folk music, which he is singing to a crowd of zero.

This is the very definition of a tough gig – two trains a day, no one has any cash to buy his CDs, and we've only got twenty minutes before we're all herded back on board. But he cracks on, belting out one folk banger after another. If you do this trip, take a hundred Swedish crowns in cash, and remember the name – Johan Piribauer, the man's a legend, though perhaps advised not to give up the day job just yet.

At around seven-thirty in the evening, and with still a way to go, the train makes one final halt at the long-awaited Arctic Circle, so we can all grab the requisite photos.

According to a weathered billboard, it's 2,611 kilometres from here to the North Pole, and 17,389 to the South Pole, and you might expect them to make a bit more of a song and dance about all this.

Full disclosure: I have been here before. In my Rough Guide days, and enabled by the tourist board, I rode a few short sections of the Inlandsbanan, including this stretch across the Arctic Circle. I was unimpressed then – "godforsaken" was my considered judgement – but even though I was ungracious about it, I still think I had a point.

There's a line of painted white rocks that curves around the hillside, and a white clapboard that says 'Polcirkeln,' or Polar Circle, and not Arctic Circle. If you're wondering what the difference is, there are two polar circles, the Arctic and the Antarctic, and they are banking on you knowing which one you're at.

We all take a picture and then get back on the train, Arctic Circle seen, done and crossed. You can even buy a certificate on board to commemorate your visit.

Here's the thing, though. We're at about 66° 34' N – that's sixty-six degrees, thirty-four minutes north of the equator. It's the southernmost latitude at which the sun doesn't set after the summer solstice in June (the midnight sun) or rise after the winter solstice in December (polar night). That's why we mark the Arctic Circle, because north of here it never gets dark from late-May until mid-July (or, similarly in winter, never gets light). The further north you go, the longer the effect.

But it's that 'about' 66° 34' N that's important, because – inconveniently for the Arctic Circle station stop – the Arctic Circle isn't fixed. Earth has a tilt, which fluctuates marginally but significantly over thousands of years, meaning that the polar circles actually drift: the Arctic Circle is currently moving northwards about fifteen metres a year. Which in turn means that whenever they marked out the polar circle here in these underwhelming white rocks, it definitely isn't here anymore. Even the mapping on my phone agrees: it thinks we haven't quite got there yet.

The train has to stop somewhere for the tourists, I understand that. It's just that I find the technicalities all rather interesting, but there isn't so much as a simple information panel to explain it all. Just some rocks in a now random location, and a certificate to say that you have visited said random rocks. And now I'll stop complaining and ruining the moment.

At a little past nine pm, the train pulls into Gällivare station, and that's the end of the line for the Inlandsbanan.

Two solid days, twenty hours' train travel in total, a thousand kilometres from Mora – that's some journey, one I'm glad I've done, though perhaps wouldn't repeat. One-and-a-bit times in a life is probably enough, though I still haven't done it in winter, which is supposed to be magical, and I didn't see any of the wildlife that others wax lyrically about.

The website promises wild animals next to the railway track, if not bouncing up and down by the windows, then at least making themselves available and visible for train travellers. It's not just bears that live in central Sweden, but wolves and lynx, too. Elk and reindeer – guaranteed. Beavers in the rivers, circling birds of prey – absolutely, can't miss them.

Except I didn't see a single thing apart from the trees, despite hours of straining my eyes through the window, trying to catch a glimpse of something on the move. There was an elk at Arvidsjaur, where we stopped to pick up dinner, but it was sculpted from wood. The best live sighting I managed was a dark shape, bouncing away from the track into the forest. Could have been an elk, I suppose, and that's what I'm going with.

I might simply have been unlucky, but I suspect I'm just not very observant. I have form for wildlife-spotting in Sweden, having once been taken deep into a forest on a dawn 'safari' with a big, bearded, lumberjack-style wildlife guide. He kept holding his finger up for quiet, and then pointing into the undergrowth, and all I had to show for it two hours later were flies and mosquitoes in every orifice. You couldn't open your mouth to speak, without it filling with a zillion insects, which you could only get rid of by swilling down a warm beer from the boot of the vehicle. At six am. I was not happy.

We all wave goodbye to the Inlandsbanan train, and say tickety-boo to Nils, who has been a spiffing fellow for the entire journey. I make my way to my overnight accommodation, a few minutes' walk from the station.

I don't sleep well, partly because I'm stiff from the long train journey, but mostly because of the midnight sun. Here in Gällivare in the early summer, a hundred kilometres above the Arctic Circle, it's permanent daytime. There are blinds in the room, and I have brought an eye mask with me, but there's a sort of craze that descends after a while when you're in a place configured like this.

The mask helps, but it's disorientating: you wake bolt upright, pitch black behind the mask, thinking you've slept for nine hours. Take the mask off, and it turns out to be the middle of the night. Or day, I suppose.

I open the blind. One-thirty am. Broad daylight. Not even twilight. Just the regular daylight going about its business. You could do daytime stuff, no problem – play golf, read a book, sunbathe at one-thirty freaking am. I sigh and close the blinds.

When I finally wake up again, groggily, at eight am, I feel like it's still one-thirty and I've not slept at all.

An hour later, this place has made me grumpier still. The accommodation is hideously expensive, which – this far north, and with not much choice – I can forgive. But for my money, I've had a single room, with a shared bathroom so far down the hall it might as well be in the train station. Paper thin walls, booming wooden floorboards, heavy, creaking doors, and the poorest breakfast so far on the trip – though, I note, I still have to play dairy product roulette with my coffee, there being no fewer than ten choices next to the cheese, salami, and sliced bread.

To cap it all, a sign in the bathroom asks me to clean the toilet and shower myself after use, with the cleaning products, mop and brush provided. Do you know, I rather thought that might be their job?

The note ends, "Please treat the place as you would

treat a friend's house." That's much more like it, so I steal into their private lounge, raid the drinks cabinet, switch on the 65-inch 4K TV that Elaine won't let me buy, and fall asleep on their sofa.

I didn't see anything of Gällivare last night, and I only have a couple of hours this morning before my onward train, but that's enough time to give it a whirl.

Let's start with the name, which I know you've been struggling with every time you've seen it thus far. It's pronounced Yell-i-var-ruh, which is going to save you a lot of time at the ticket office, if you're ever heading this way.

Originally a seasonal reindeer-herding site for the indigenous Sami people, the town has long been subservient to its mining industries, with iron ore found here in great abundance in the seventeenth century. There's been large-scale mining since the 1880s, and the town still supports one of the biggest iron ore mines in the world. While I wait at a level crossing, a freight train passes, the engine pulling no fewer than sixty-eight filled wagons.

Gällivare, then, is not what you'd call a looker, railway station aside, which is a rather splendid black-and-terracotta-coloured wooden building, flanked by enormous goods yards. The big visitor attractions hereabouts – advertised in the station – are tours of the nearby Porjus hydroelectric plant, and of Aitik, Sweden's largest (and the world's most productive) open-cast copper mine, which tells you something about Gällivare's mindset.

Actually, they sound pretty interesting. If I had the time, I'd probably sign up for one of them.

I'm less taken by the offer of a three-hour, winter ice-fishing experience. "Have you ever fished in a frozen lake?" says the flyer. The answer, surely, is in the question. But wait – "Swedish fika included." Well, that makes all the difference. I'll be sure to tell the nurse there's a cinnamon bun in my pocket as she surgically removes fishing rod from fingers.

The small town centre, meanwhile, is a dull grid of apartment blocks and buildings that looks exactly like what it is – a housing estate and business district dropped into a wilderness. According to a town map it conceals "well-known stores stocked with popular brands, and unique boutiques."

Challenge accepted.

A walk around the block, including the town's main street, reveals three pizzerias, one Chinese restaurant, a barber's, two beauty centres, a discount clothes store, flower shop, photographic studio, and a couple of corner shops. There's a massive, modern, red building with a grass roof that turns out to be a high school, and a white, wooden church on a little hillock. Popular brands and unique boutiques, not so much.

It's easy to poke fun at places like this. It's also not very fair. I didn't do Gällivare any favours in the original Rough Guide either ("a steely grey mesh of new streets best walked through quickly"), given that I had the same short time to have a look around before moving on. Remember that, next time you read a guidebook saying somewhere is dull and unremarkable, and not worth a look. The writer probably never got beyond the railway station. Guilty as charged.

So, still with an hour before the train leaves, this time I have a closer look. And you know what? Gällivare is all right.

Don't get me wrong, I wouldn't want to live here, but there are some older residential houses in the trim streets surrounding the church, all with manicured lawns, plunge pools, saunas and hammocks – the Swedish dream, you might say. Meanwhile, a bridge over the rail lines leads me down to a lovely riverside walk, where reeds rustle in the breeze. Stately houses on the other side have closely mown gardens that reach to the water's edge.

A tiny, wooden, eighteenth-century chapel, barely bigger than someone's lounge, occupies a quiet spot above the river.

The Lappkyrkan, or Lapp Church, one of the town's oldest buildings, was "mainly built for the Sami as they became Christians," says the notice pinned outside. That word, 'became,' is doing a lot of heavy lifting for a people with a history dating back thousands of years pre-Christianity, and with a highly developed cultural and belief system of their own. The Christian missionaries could have just left them to get on with it, is all I'm saying.

If I had more time, I'd hike to the top of Dundret, the flat-topped local mountain that I can see over the river. Get me some fika in the summer café, do some fly-and-mosquito wildlife spotting.

But the train is due, and if you think Gällivare has been a strange destination, just wait until we get to the next stop.

CHAPTER 8

GÄLLIVARE TO KIRUNA

I could reach Narvik in one five-hour train ride from Gällivare, and the northern leg of my trip would be over. But there's a stop on the way that I really want to make – at the town of Kiruna – and it's going to delay me for a couple of nights. I think it will be worth it.

That means only a couple of hours on the train today, for which my rear end thanks me heartily. The Inlandsbanan train was basically seventy bus seats on wheels. Today's is only a regional, Swedish Railways service, nothing fancy, but it still feels like a free upgrade.

Beyond Gällivare the scenery changes, dramatically so, starting with huge boulder fields, relics of the retreating ice ten thousand years ago. While there are still plenty of trees, the landscape is no longer dominated by spruce and pine, but by the less dense mountain birch. Large expanses of prairie-like grassland open up to either side, and in the far distance above the tree line there's snow on the higher mountains. Bare hills are studded with wind turbines. The rivers are wider and wilder, the horizons bigger.

The rail line, meanwhile, snakes off into the distance, on an elevated embankment that's cleared of growth on both sides. I've not taken either trip, but this train feels like it could be speeding across Canada or even Siberia.

And then, abruptly, we glide from the wilderness into Kiruna between monumental rifts and mountains, none of them natural. These are the heaped dunes and deep valleys of mining spoil, dust rising in the air as diggers shift the rubble and stone around. The train chugs on through a dark-grey desert, past snaking pipes and rusting machinery – the arctic lair of road-warriors, Mad Max and Furiosa.

I get off at Kiruna station, a series of open platforms sited way out of town, and set a course for the centre – which is not as straightforward as you might think, because Kiruna is a deeply odd place.

The old town that I arrived in the first time I was here no longer exists. The original train station, city hall, and surrounding wooden houses, have all been razed to the ground. There's now parkland where the streets I followed from the old station used to be; the new station is twenty minutes' walk further out.

The reason is the town's mine, the largest underground iron-ore mine in the world. You can see it from anywhere in town – the long, scarred mountain opposite, stepped like giant Inca terraces. Grey, brown, black, throwing shadows across the small lake at its foot.

LKAB, the mining company, has been extracting iron ore from the mountain for over a hundred years, but for decades no one appreciated the effect that was having on the town itself.

The iron-ore seam – four kilometres long, up to two hundred metres wide – stretches beneath mountain and town, and a century of mining operations has caused dangerous subsidence. The deeper they mine, the more the land above collapses – and the cracks at the top are now spreading eleven centimetres a day, which means huge swathes of the town are living on borrowed time.

Walking into the old centre, it's immediately obvious what's happening to Kiruna. On one side of a demarcated line, there are empty houses and apartment buildings awaiting demolition. Other sections have already been cleared, and wide gravel expanses await landscaping. Schools, hospital, sports hall, fire station, shops, and businesses are all going to have to be moved; when I walk past, construction workers are taking down the old, brown, Scandic hotel floor by floor. It won't be there by the time you read this.

Nor will the church, the jewel of Kiruna, a Sami-inspired vision in painted red oak that was a gift to the town in 1912 from LKAB. It's not being demolished, but instead moved to a new site – the entire thing, all seven hundred tonnes of it, transported on trailers across town.

It's still there on the day I'm in Kiruna, and I peer over the fencing to see the building jacked up on steel girders – the last survivor in place of the town I visited forty years ago. (It's worth searching for video of the church move, which finally happened in August 2025. Thousands lined the streets as it crept at half-a-kilometre an hour to its new site. It took two days to reach it.)

And all this is because the mine is so valuable, and Kiruna so integral to the mine, that LKAB and the town authorities have simply done the obvious thing, and moved the entire town centre. Three kilometres to the east, in fact, where a new residential and business district is rising from previously undeveloped land.

A new town hall and cultural centre was unveiled in 2018, a monumental, circular building known as Kristallen (The Crystal), or the Toilet-Roll Holder, depending on who you talk to. There's still a lot of residual trauma about losing much-loved buildings, like the old town hall, which was called 'Kiruna's living room' by many. At least the original metal-lattice belltower was saved, and it now stands sentry next to the new town hall. The moveable church, meanwhile, has been relocated to the cemetery, halfway between old and new town.

It's all happened incredibly quickly. A replacement Scandic hotel opened in 2022 – a kind of Nordic ziggurat to go with the toilet roll – followed by another four-star hotel in 2025. Brand new apartment blocks march off down streets that end suddenly in waste ground currently occupied by diggers and dumper trucks. There are shopping malls and coffee shops, boutiques and restaurants, a bookshop and a gallery. But if you plonk the little yellow man down on Google maps, the streets are too new to register – he just gazes out over a massive construction site. It will look different again in two years, and unrecognisable in ten.

Meanwhile, original Kiruna feels centre-less, unmoored – increasingly cut off from the new development. It's slated to be abandoned entirely sometime in the 2030s. (The same thing, incidentally, is happening in Gällivare, where the land under the town is also compromised by their mine. They have their own blueprint for new development.)

I take a long walk between the two Kirunas, ignoring the bus, experiencing the reality of the move the town has had to make. Picked up and put down again. Old to new. It's an arresting story, and I'm not sure what I think about it.

Kiruna always had a frontier feel – Sweden's northernmost town, well inside the Arctic Circle – but it's more than that. It's a company mining town that's been shaped entirely by the demands of the industry, with nature forced to bend to its will. Not everyone here agrees with what's happening, but you can't argue with a sinking town. Homeowners in the affected areas were offered good deals to move, and many have taken the keys to new downtown apartments. But that doesn't mean there isn't a divide here – that there aren't dissenting opinions.

To find out more, I'm booked onto a tour of the mine itself, LKAB being remarkably open about the issues that iron-ore mining has caused here. A large group gathers the next morning at the tourist office, and we're loaded onto a bus, where the advance safety briefing is thorough and not at all reassuring.

If there's trouble – unspecified – we are to wait for the evacuation team. If there's real trouble – no further details – we should make for the underground cinema where "there is always air." If there's smoke in the mine – hang on, what do you mean, smoke? – then we should grab a hazmat helmet and follow our guide. And if our guide is incapacitated, someone should call the emergency number using her phone – at which point she shows us where her phone is, side jacket pocket, while we all whimper.

Everyone now thoroughly freaked out, the bus takes us on the ten-minute drive to the main mine entrance, where we simply drive into the black depths of the mountain. There are, incredibly, almost a thousand kilometres of road down here – junctions, signposts, traffic lights, parking, the lot. We go deeper and deeper, to a depth of over five hundred metres, and pull up in front of the visitor entrance, where we disembark and grab a hard hat each.

We're not going in the actual working bit of the mine, you understand? We don't get a go with the drills or anything. But we are in excavated caverns half a kilometre underground for a tour of the visitor centre, museum and display machinery, and it proves to be an entertaining if relentless recitation of mind-boggling facts.

The iron ore here is sixty-five to seventy percent pure, which is what makes it so valuable. On first discovery, they just dug it from the outcropping rock on the surface with pick and spade. By the 1960s, they were mining underground. Now they are down to 1,365 metres deep, using fifty-metre-long robot drills to get at the ore. There's a restaurant at that level for the workers, and whereas they used to have a wooden rescue sled for emergencies, now they have ambulances and a fire engine stationed underground in the mountain.

They blast at night. If you live close enough to the mine, apparently you can feel the tremors in the early hours, at one-thirty am every day. The ore skips, holding forty tonnes at a time, zoom up one-and-a-half kilometres to the surface in a matter of minutes. Outside, in the immense marshalling yards, each sixty-eight-wagon iron-ore train fills in twenty minutes, a hundred tonnes in each wagon, and then travels by rail north to Norway, or south to the Swedish port of Luleå. Enough iron is shipped out every day to build thirteen Eiffel towers.

This is awesome stuff, as is the blue-lit tunnel with enormous examples of boring and drilling machinery. Any other time I'd go for the 'boring machinery' joke, but I'm having too much fun clambering on, and even walking through, these behemoths.

Meanwhile, the museum displays vintage tools and

photographs, recreated navvies' quarters, and anything from old buckets and ventilator masks to a full-sized trolley car once used to ferry workers to the mine. There's a haunting photograph of a working family – husband, wife, granny, and six kids, outside a lean-to shack that looks barely habitable. They're dressed like they've come straight from the pioneering American West; they look miserable as hell.

Tricky questions aren't avoided either. For example, the contemporary refining and production process is heavily reliant on fossil fuels, so LKAB is developing carbon-free processes, including something called sponge iron, which does sound cuddly and green. But this will require huge amounts of electricity – up to fifty percent of Sweden's annual production – which in turn will mean building new nuclear power plants. There are trade-offs everywhere: shifting the entire town of Gällivare is only part of it.

What we hear several times on the tour is that mine and town are inextricably linked. Iron ore was first found in the area in the seventeenth century, and first extracted in the eighteenth. And until LKAB started its operations in 1890, there was nothing else here. No mine without the town, no town without the mine, is the refrain.

Only, that's not strictly true. The church that the mining company kindly paid for – the one shifted across town – was originally erected on the site of a seasonal Sami tipi encampment, used as they moved their reindeer across the northern lands.

The name Kiruna is a Sami word meaning ptarmigan, the game bird. The iron-ore mountain, Kirunavaara, was their hunting ground, below which was a lake teeming with salmon. The lake that the mining company later drained because of fears that it would seep into the mine. There are no longer any salmon in the part of the lake that survives.

The Sami people have lived in these lands for thousands of years, fishing, fur-trapping, and reindeer-herding. What we perhaps see as an empty wilderness – or a source of raw materials – they regard as a living, cultural landscape.

Here in Kiruna, in Swedish Lapland, they are part of a wider, indigenous region known as Sápmi, with the Sami spread across Sweden, Norway, Finland and Russia: as many as forty thousand people in Sweden consider themselves to be Sami. But, as with other indigenous peoples, their light touch on their traditional lands made them both invisible and expendable when progress came calling.

Some of this I'm discovering at my hotel in Kiruna, the Samegård, a modernist, 1960s interpretation of a Sami dwelling, built of square, squat blocks, with external supporting beams and a central skylight shaped like the top of a tipi. It stands right on the border of the town demarcation line, and may have to move or be demolished, which will be a shame, because it's delightful. I like staying here – a taste of older Kiruna, handy for the station, with a homely B&B feel, and a kitchen where I can make myself a cup of tea.

It's been a part of the Sami community since the sixties, and doubles as a cultural centre where their stories can be told. These both celebrate and bear witness to the Sami experience, because Sami culture has been under siege since the nineteenth century, their custodial lands exploited and damaged by what they regard as Swedish colonialism. The mining at Gällivare is a classic example: it's fragmented the land and made reindeer-herding more difficult, negatively affected the wildlife, and polluted the local water sources.

There's a small museum in the basement of the hotel, a counterpoint to the giant machines on display at the mine. The contrast is fascinating, if poignant: beautiful textile work and embroidery, carvings, tools, clothes, shoes, hunting gear – even a leather baby's crib that could be hung from a tree. It's human workmanship on a different scale.

On my last day in Kiruna, I follow the 'Midnight Sun Trail' around the base and then up the flank of Luossavaara, the smaller mountain on the other side of town from the mine. It's scarred – cleft in two – by an earlier period of opencast iron-ore mining, but it's been largely reclaimed by nature, making for a quiet walk among low, spindly trees, alpine flowers, and spreading heather.

As the path climbs, there are ever-widening views across nearby lakes, and to distant snow-covered mountains. On the top, by the chair lift of a ski run, the views are all-encompassing – the railway line and vast marshalling yards, the residential suburbs, the landscaped parks, and the towers of the new town.

The Sami and their reindeer have followed tracks across this mountain for thousands of years, yet it's also a threatened landscape.

LKAB have discovered the largest concentration of rare earth elements in Europe, and even more iron ore, this time with a high phosphorous content (used to produce mineral fertilisers). They will start mining in the next decade, and it's being badged as strategically vital for the post-carbon economy and the world's food production. There will be reindeer eco-corridors and amelioration schemes, but the mining will happen. Things will change, because there's no mine without the town, no town without the mine.

Ultimately, Kiruna is both a wild place and a monument to human ingenuity. The scale – the technological knowhow – is breath-taking. There are robot miners, for goodness' sake, two kilometres under the earth I'm standing on.

And eventually?

In another hundred and fifty years, or a thousand, maybe the Sami will move their reindeer herds through abandoned twenty-first-century towers?

Perhaps they'll camp in tipis on the wild parklands, gone to seed when the ore and minerals ran out; or became too expensive to extract; or when the world simply turned away from such exploitative human activities?

CHAPTER 9

KIRUNA TO NARVIK

Finally. The train to Narvik. Next stop, Europe's northernmost railway station.

It leaves Kiruna at three-thirty in the afternoon for a three-hour run across the mountains separating Sweden and Norway. If I'd caught the night train from Stockholm the day before, this is the service I'd be on.

Instead, it's taken me six days and six nights to get this far. It's starting to feel like a true wilderness adventure, and once we leave Kiruna's ore heaps behind, the scenery decides to join in. The train makes straight for the snow-spattered mountains, on an increasingly spectacular route.

The railway was opened in 1903, enabling ore to be shipped from Kiruna to the port at Narvik. Before the road was completed, as late as 1984, train was the only way you could travel directly between the two towns.

One follows the other closely, the twin-lane E10 highway visible below as we trace the edge of a long tract of water, Torneträsk, in Abisko national park.

Mountain slopes and screes – and snow patches – reach right down to the shoreline. If I could lean out of the window, I'd be able to touch the snow at times. We flash across rivers that freeze you to the marrow just to look at them – furious grey and white water, straight off the mountains. I can see a single boat in the distance, perhaps someone out fishing from one of the isolated lakeside cabins that dot the landscape? Parking areas contain a surprising number of camper vans and RVs, braving the remote drive to Sweden's wild edge – over thirteen hundred kilometres from Stockholm, eighteen hours' solid driving.

At Abisko itself – a tourist station in high wilderness – large numbers of spry, muscled visitors disembark, toting backpacks like leaning towers, bristling with poles and draped with ropes. Apart from a few cabins and hikers' hostels, there's nothing except the wild outdoors here. "Tough and uncomfortable," says my old Rough Guide of hiking in the Abisko national park; not to say "downright treacherous."

I must have been surmising and extrapolating, because there's no way I got off here the first time round, and it's not happening today either. Half of the men on the platform look like Darryl Dixon from *The Walking Dead* – like they could kill and skin a moose if they had to. The women look like they could kill and skin the men. A bear or a wolf could probably hold their own, but you wouldn't want to be, I don't know, an arctic fox or a hare.

Forty minutes later, Riksgränsen – lake view, snow caps, even a hotel – marks the Swedish side of the border, and Bjørnfell, a couple of kilometres away, the Norwegian. It's no exaggeration to say that once we get into Norway, the scenery changes – I was going to say, for the better, but that's not quite right. It's been dramatic if bleak on the Swedish side; heading into Norway, it becomes truly stunning.

The train swoops across a bare, weatherworn, highland plateau dotted with small lakes and wooden cabins. The man on his deck, sunning himself in his underpants, legs akimbo, has no concerns about the occasional passing trains. Let's face it, it's why he does it, and we all give him a cheery wave.

The track then hugs steep, forested mountainsides, high above a rocky canyon – a lost world, swathed in trees, with the glint of a snaking river far below. A simply humungous view slowly unfolds past the tiny summer hamlet of Katterat – waterfalls cascading from precipitous cliffs, snow caps in the distance. The train swings round again, revealing an alluvial plain and, finally, the deep, glassy water of Rombaksbotn, a classic, curving, steep-sided fjord, with tumbling screes and sheer rock faces.

What a ride this is. For another half an hour, we enjoy sparkling water views, as the train takes a flat line around the valley heads, high above the fjord, the slopes and trees reflected in the water far below. Higher peaks, dark in shadow or glistening white with snow, roll into the distance on all sides.

We pass one final, dramatic suspension bridge, curve round into Narvik, and here I am – at the northernmost passenger railway station in Europe, all caveats and objections duly noted.

I snap celebratory photographs – the words 'Narvik Stasjon' emblazoned on a yellow-painted building, the train at the platform, and an old steam loco displayed under a canopy. After the effort involved in getting here, I feel I should stick around at the station for a bit, but it's getting on for seven pm so I walk into town to find my hotel.

There's not much to Narvik, the centre being only a few streets deep, though there are suburbs and houses dotted around the harbourside hills. It's backed by snow-capped mountains, while beyond is the wider Ofotfjord, which slinks all the way out past fractured peninsulas and islands to the Norwegian Sea.

It's this location that is all-important – a deep-water, ice-free port, with access to the North Atlantic sea lanes, connected by rail to the iron ore mines of Kiruna and Gällivare. When war broke out in Europe, the tiny town in the far north suddenly became a huge strategic prize.

If you controlled Narvik, the railway and the mines, you had control of Europe's iron ore, and with it, the material for guns, tanks, submarines, and ships. At the start of 1940, a significant part of the Allied war effort was devoted to defending Narvik from the

German forces already encamped in northern Sweden.

The conflict was brutal for the town, which was largely razed to the ground. Local people endured terrible hardship, or fled as guerrillas into the hills. Bombs carpeted the docks; ships were sunk in the fjord; thousands of soldiers and sailors from both sides died, and are buried in local cemeteries. When the Allies later withdrew, to redeploy troops elsewhere in Europe against the Nazis, Norway fell to the Germans.

It's almost a hidden part of the history of World War II, at least as far as most British people are concerned. It doesn't resonate in the same way as touchstone events like the Battle of Britain, Dunkirk or D-Day. But for Norwegians, Narvik remains as a symbol of endurance and fortitude.

It was settled in the first place, under near-impossible conditions, by the navvies who built the cross-mountain railway. After what later inhabitants went through in the war, everyone would have been forgiven for turning their backs on the town. But the reason it was fought over so viciously is also the reason it was rebuilt – as a strategic port for the iron-ore and mineral industry. The modern town – population around fifteen thousand – is not what you'd call attractive, but it is resilient and strikingly set.

It's not getting dark here any time soon – not for weeks – so I take a late evening stroll down to the harbour to have a gander at the boats and container ships. LKAB, our old mining friends from Kiruna, operate the cat's cradle of chutes and conveyor belts that deliver the ore from the trains into the storage sheds and onto awaiting ships.

Up in the centre, there's a steel shard sculpture poking into the sky, and – unlike the feeble effort I encountered in Stockholm – a proper multi-directional signpost showing the kilometre distance to various cities. 'Hamburg 2210,' it says, which seems about right for the most direct route by road, though I've travelled further on the train. 'Nordpolen 2407' is the eye-opener: I'm almost halfway to the North Pole.

I'm staying a block away in the Wivel Hotel, which fancies itself as that now meaningless descriptor, a boutique hotel. My box room with a skylight, up on the third floor, is small, I'll give them that, but their breakfast is fantastic – best of the trip so far.

And that, you would think, would be that. Mission accomplished. Narvik ticked off.

Unfortunately, however, there has been an incident involving some idle sleuthing on one of my recent train rides, during which I went down the wrong rabbit hole and allowed a little man on the internet to sow doubt in my mind.

Oh no, said the little man, on some Reddit thread, it's not Narvik at all. Schoolboy error. It is in fact the Swedish border halt of Riksgränsen that is the northernmost passenger railway station in mainland, continental Europe excluding Russia, Belarus and Ukraine.

Well, how I laughed. And then applied myself to the matter.

If true, it isn't disastrous, seeing as I passed through Riksgränsen only today on the way to Narvik. I have technically 'been' to Riksgränsen, and will pass through again on my way back into Sweden on the next leg of the trip.

But I didn't get off the train at the station, so does that count?

I don't know why I'm asking you. I made up the rules. But it is certainly a grey area.

The first thing is to determine if the little man, curse him, is correct. And Wikipedia, I'm happy to report, says he can go and get stuffed. The latitude coordinates have Narvik station at a whisker further north than Riksgränsen, so it seems I am saved.

But there is a nagging fear that the sort of little men who think about these things probably won't let it lie. They'll point out that the platform juts out a bit further north at Riksgränsen, or that there's some other abstruse reason why they are right and I am wrong. To give you a flavour of what I'm talking about, the Wikipedia entry for Riksgränsen station says that because it's only a train stop with a platform and single track, it is not technically a railway 'station' at all. If also true, that works in my favour, obviously, but you can see the sort of über-nerd bamboozlement we're dealing with here.

Now, tomorrow I could go and visit the Narvik War Museum, have a coffee in the seamen's church, take lunch in the old fish market, and ride the cable car up the mountain for the views. That would be a day well spent in Narvik.

Clearly, however, the better use of my time is to take the morning train from Narvik, get off an hour later at Riksgränsen station, in the absolute middle of nowhere, and then – six hours after that – catch the only return train back.

To be on the safe side. Cover all my bases.

At this point, the universe intervenes. While accepting that the little men, bless them, have their place, don't do that, says the universe. Do this instead. And the universe throws open a tourist office brochure, where there's a double-page spread advertising the opportunity to 'walk across Norway in a day.'

What they mean is that the distance from the Norway-Sweden border at Riksgränsen to the head of Rombaksbotn, the fjord I passed on the train coming in, could be construed as the narrowest point of the entire country. The fjord is an arm of the larger one that Narvik is on, which eventually empties into the sea. That narrow pinch of land between border and fjord enables you to say you've walked across the country. Have a look at the map: you'll see they have a point.

What's more, there's a signposted path, the old navvies' trail, dating from the days when they built the railway. It's sixteen kilometres long, following mountain tracks and ending with a descent to the fjord where, it is said, a speedboat will be waiting to whisk me over the water for an onward taxi back to Narvik.

I'm not overly concerned about the hike itself. I can

still manage sixteen kilometres easily enough, though I'll ache at the end of the day.

The logistics, though, are a worry. I'm booking a return slot on a speedboat, via a website, and am starting my hike sixteen mountainous kilometres away from that eventuality, from a station with no facilities. You could call that entire location remote, but that would be being charitable.

Who's to say this isn't one elaborate joke? If there's no waiting speedboat, there's no other way of getting back to Narvik – the clue to Rombaksbotn's road-free inaccessibility being the fact that there's the suggestion of a speedboat in the first place.

The next day, I am reassured by the number of people who get off the train with me at Riksgränsen, all apparently on the same mission, because there's no other reason to disembark here. I feel that if there is a steadily increasing number of corpses at the water's edge in Rombaksbotn, and a phantom speedboat operator laughing with a stage cackle somewhere in Narvik, news would have filtered through by now.

I immediately fall in with two Norwegian men, Lucas and Oskar, who kindly ask if I would like to walk with them. This removes any shred of doubt from my mind, because they look like they know what they are doing. Over the following half an hour, on our way to the first stop, I have the opportunity to examine our relative suitability for this mountain hike in rough terrain.

Between them, Lucas and Oskar have: serious backpacks, army-issue boots, waterproof trousers, easy-breathe undershirts, wraparound glare-proof shades, additional wet-weather gear, an emergency bivouac, a gas stove lit with a flint, army meal rations, walking poles, enamel cups hanging from their packs, a wicked-looking knife, a hammock, some rope, and very possibly a fold-up kitchen sink. Lucas also has a pair of tight-fitting gloves hanging from his backpack, the sort you might use for gardening. I daren't ask what they are for – they are probably his rabbit-strangling gloves.

Now, let's turn to me. I do at least have proper hiking shoes, and a pair of lightweight hiking trousers. That's as good as it gets. Working on the basis that the current dry but overcast weather might change, and that layers are always good, I have my Marks & Spencer's wool jumper and a Uniqlo shower-proof jacket. That's it. Also, two bread rolls and some cheese that I filched from the breakfast buffet, an apple, and the chocolate from my pillow in the hotel.

"I thought this was supposed to be a relatively easy hike?" I say.

"Yes, but we are always prepared when we go into the mountains." Oskar raises an eyebrow, which I take to mean: look at the state of you.

"I've got some nuts, too," I say, helpfully.

"We can have them when we have our coffee," says Oskar.

Coffee! Up a mountain! They are not kidding about being prepared.

Both have served in the army, as every Norwegian

has to do national service for eighteen months and then remain active and trained until the age of forty-five. They are delightful, the pair of them – clearly honour-bound by Norwegian military code not to let a stupid foreigner die on one of their mountains. I am eternally grateful to them for their service.

When we sit down, for occasional water breaks or lunch, conversations go like this.

"Seating mat?"

"I have my fine-weave English woollen jumper, but thanks anyway."

"Bug spray?"

"Oh, yes, thanks."

"Antiseptic hand cleaner?"

"Why not."

"Wet wipe?"

"How kind."

"Reindeer?"

"What?"

I mean, I wouldn't put it past them. I didn't see any hooves sticking out of the pack, but who knows what they are capable of? But what Lucas means is reindeer jerky, and he cuts a slice off with a knife that you could shave a bear with. It's chewy and caramel-like, and while it doesn't go with pillow chocolate, it's just another reason to thank my lucky stars I ended up on this hike with them.

Riksgränsen turns out to mean 'national border,' which makes sense, and the first section of the walk runs the short distance across the rocky plateau to where a yellow signpost says 'Norge' on one side and 'Sverige' on the other. That, my friends, is a photo opportunity – it's not every day you get to cross a national border on foot.

Another few hundred metres and we're at the first station on the Norwegian side, Bjørnfell – 'Bear Mountain,' if you've been keeping up with the Scandinavian language lessons, and absolutely nothing to worry about, I'm sure. A trail sign here points us the right way, with Rombaksbotn a clearly marked 16.2 kilometres away.

The trail is the railway builders' final legacy. Over a few short years at the turn of the twentieth century, an army of five thousand itinerant labourers hacked, dug and carved a forty-three-kilometre-long railway from Riksgränsen to the port at Narvik. The Ofotbanan was the last piece in the iron-ore jigsaw, opening up the full route to Kiruna, Gällivare and beyond. When it was completed in 1902, it was the northernmost railway line in the world, though subsequent lines in Russia robbed it of the title.

The navvies lived and worked along the route in conditions I don't even want to think about. It's bitter winter for eight months of the year here, and they were working at five hundred metres up a mountain with picks and shovels, ponies and ropes.

Their base was down at the Rombaksbotn fjordside, where materials came in by steamship and a booming construction town developed. And the workers' trail from Riksgränsen down through the Norddalen canyon to the fjord is what we're walking today – in the full knowledge that they had to walk *uphill* to get to work and even to collect their wages.

When the railway was finally completed, the old access route was abandoned to nature. Now restored as the Rallarveien, the Navvy Road, it's a stunning trail with magnificent views, especially during the first half, as we keep to the same precipitous contour as the railway. I stand on rock bluffs that look out on sheer, tree-covered slopes, frothing waterfalls, the darker clefts of distant valleys, and the encircling range of snow-covered mountains. I still haven't encountered so much as a squirrel, but there are birds of prey circling above and banks of wildflowers on sheltered hillsides.

Now and then, a fully laden iron-ore train trundles by in the distance; while at one point we stop to watch workers in high-vis gear hanging off ropes to shore up a rockfall. Modern-day trains, modern-day navvies, same job, same route. It's humbling.

I'd hesitate to say that even I couldn't get lost on this trail, but it does seem to be very well maintained and signposted. Even so, I stick closely to my new friends, though they are keeping up a Norwegian army pace, while these days I have more the athletic gait of a man ambling round the pastry section in Lidl. The day is getting warmer, so I jettison the Marks & Spencer jumper. Oskar and Lucas appear to be putting more layers on, rather than the other way around, but whether they have insider knowledge, or this is just them being prepared for the mountains, I couldn't say.

When it comes, the descent into the Norddalen canyon is both welcome and magical. We drop into a shady glen of mountain birch, with swathes of tight, white wildflowers between the trees. There's a bridge over a thundering waterfall, and steep banks of moss-covered, glacial boulders. Tumbled stone walls are the remnants of old buildings associated with the workers. At one such site, a hundred and thirty years ago, someone looked around at the icy waters and slippery rocks and said, "You know what this place needs? A café."

The woodland path finally ends at the sandy shore at the head of the fjord. Off come the shoes and into the water for a soothing foot bathe – it's so cold, a couple of minutes is all I can stand before my feet start to turn an alarming red. The fjord spreads out in front of me, hills on both sides climbing out of the water at a forty-five-degree angle.

This was the site of the navvies' Klondyke-style settlement, where previously there had only been one isolated farm. At its height it was a town of five hundred people, with shops, businesses, warehouses, hotel, police station, post office, and working harbour. All gone today, though I spend some time picking through the surviving stone foundations and reading the information panels.

I make my way to the quayside, where people are being helped onto – be still, my beating heart – a high-performance RIB. The speedboat exists!

In a few minutes it will run us across the fjord, stopping briefly at the rusting hulk of a German destroyer, the Georg Thiele, sunk during the 1940 battles for Narvik. We'll hear of a fight so fierce that, after the war, locals said that fish from the fjord tasted of engine oil for years.

But for now, it's enough to dangle my legs from the quay and savour the whole experience of the last two weeks, since leaving Hamburg.

The long days on trains. The thrill of reaching Europe's northernmost railway line and station. The aches and pains of travel.

The knowledge gained from putting one foot in front of another on one of the most thrilling walks I've ever undertaken.

And the life lesson learned – that in the event of societal breakdown after a cataclysmic meteor strike, find yourself a couple of fighting-age Norwegians and never let them out of your sight.

EAST
NARVIK TO UIMAHARJU AND HELSINKI

Luleå-Haparanda-Kemi-Uimaharju-Joensuu-Helsinki

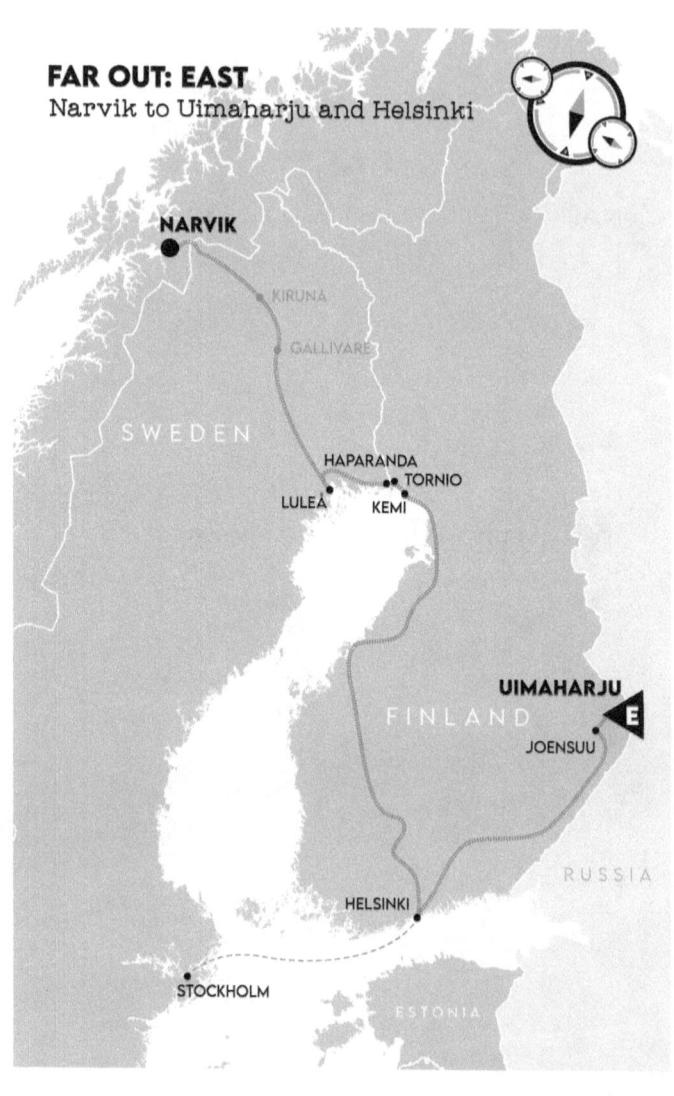

CHAPTER 10

NARVIK TO KEMI

If you check out where Narvik is on the map, and are aiming for your next railway stop to be in Finland, the correct response is, "Good luck with that."

I had hoped to avoid any backtracking on this trip if possible, but by train there is only one way in and one way out. The next nearest station in Norway is two hundred and fifty kilometres to the south, and while a five-hour bus ride from Narvik would put me back on the main Norwegian and Swedish rail network, it would then take another four or five days to get where I wanted to go.

That makes about as much sense as the premise of this entire book – in that, you could do it, but why would you?

Yes, I realise I've said that out loud.

Backtracking it is then, which means the daily

morning train from Narvik back down the line, at least for the first five hours. Hello Riksgränsen – for the third time, no less – and bonjour Kiruna and Gällivare. It's just as enjoyable in reverse, and I choose to feel lucky to have the opportunity to see the scenery again rather than be annoyed by riding rails only recently travelled.

At Gällivare in the mid-afternoon, where the main line meets the Inlandsbanan, we steer south for the Bothnian coast, the first new stretch of the route for me. Somewhere, still a long way down the Inlandsbanan, people with tree-crazed eyes are counting the hours until they reach the bright lights and fleshpots of an arctic mining town.

My destination for the night is the port of Luleå, still three hours away. In truth, this part of the journey is little different from any of the long Inlandsbanan stretches. If you wanted to start a tree-based business in lower Norrbotten county, you'd be all right for raw materials.

Checking the timetable, there's a prick of recognition at the name of an upcoming station, Boden.

If you've spent the years I have, surrounded by bales of fabric, stacks of sewing patterns, and tottering piles of fashion catalogues, some of it is bound to stick. I screenshot the timetable, circle the town, and send it to Elaine. "Isn't this, you know, that catalogue place?" I say.

"Well done, you!" she says, with a smiley face. "You could nip off the train, get me a sample or two?"

Is she being serious? She might be. I did once have

to go to Milan and eschew the famous sights in favour of standing outside a suburban fabric shop for about three hours while she negotiated the purchase of what appeared to be Italy's entire supply of Loro Piana cashmere.

I stay put. There isn't another onward train today, and Elaine – I'm whispering this bit – is not the boss of me.

Boden comes and goes. I do a bit of internet searching to pass the time.

The Boden clothing retailer, with its iconic catalogue, is British. Started by a British entrepreneur called Johnnie Boden. Headquartered in Acton, London. All of which Elaine knows, obviously.

Trolled by my minx of a wife. Entirely prepared to see me walk around a random Swedish town on the hunt for non-existent fabrics. That is very well played, I have to say.

A bit more searching reveals that Boden wouldn't have been the worst place to spend the night. "A pleasant surprise," according to my Rough Guide, with an "exciting military history," according to the tourist website.

In the spring of 1917, on his way back from exile to foment a revolution in Russia, one Vladimir Ilyich Ulyanov changed trains here. Never mind the fabrics, it's surely worth getting off in Boden just to repurpose Ken Dodd's finest joke – what a lovely day for going to the train station, knocking on the door, and saying, "Is Len in?"

We reach Luleå at around six-thirty, after an eight-hour ride that's swapped arctic wilderness for the gentler scenery of the Bothnian coast, the gulf of water that separates Sweden from Finland. We're still a long way north, though, well inside Swedish Lapland. The reason the railway was extended to ice-free Narvik was because the port of Luleå, the original rail destination for the iron ore, couldn't be guaranteed not to freeze in winter.

I like it immediately, even on just the short walk from the station into town.

The whole place sits on a little peninsula, surrounded by the harbour waters of a fractured coastline. There's a red-brick church with a tall steeple, and any number of wooden, clapboard houses laid out in a grid pattern. Luleå was first settled in medieval times, and has been a busy port since the seventeenth century, but it has the unfortunate habit of burning down. Most of the town, and its layout, dates from the last time that happened, in the 1880s.

There are wide streets, all freakishly clean, leading down to a handsome waterfront square, despite the cranes and tankers of a working port. Here, there's a summer beach, with volleyball on the sand and a queue at the ice-cream stall. Over on the north harbour, site of the original town, are cruise boats, waterside restaurants, and a boardwalk with views over to wooded islands and promontories.

Maybe it's the wooden houses, the manicured streets,

the picket fences, but in many ways it reminds me of an archetypal American town from TV or the movies – say *Happy Days*, or where Marty McFly lives in *Back to the Future*. There's even a low-slung convertible doing the rounds of town this fine evening, though instead of Biff or even The Fonz it contains four, portly, Swedish thirty-somethings blasting out hip-hop and looking very pleased with themselves. I'll say the car's a Chevrolet, I have no idea, but it's pink and you know the type.

Luleå has that wholesome vibe I've got from several towns so far on this Scandinavian leg of the journey. There would be something very fine about sitting with a seafood platter in a waterside bistro, watching the light dance on the water on a summer's evening. If only the seafood platter wasn't seventy-five quid, and I didn't keep feeling the need to jump on trains to the four corners of Europe. Pizza it is, and an early night, because tomorrow is another long day.

To reach Finland on the train, I have to travel around the northern end of the Gulf of Bothnia. It's a couple of hours' forested ride from Luleå to the border town of Haparanda, where things are slightly complicated by the fact that the Swedish and Finnish rail networks don't join up.

They run on different gauges, Finland mostly using the broader Russian gauge, which makes sense when you appreciate that the Russian empire used to start just across the river from Haparanda. Tornio, the adjacent Finnish town, was part of the Grand Duchy of

Finland until 1917, an autonomous state under the ultimate control of the Russian Tsar.

What this means in practice is getting off at Haparanda station, making my way the couple of kilometres to the transport terminal on the Swedish side, and picking up a bus for the half-hour ride to Kemi in Finland. From there, I'm booked on the overnight sleeper to Helsinki.

It sounds relatively straightforward, and I have around six hours to make it across the border and reach Kemi, thirty kilometres away. The border isn't the problem – you can just walk across the bridge from Sweden to Finland, no worries.

But the promised joined-up transport, into town and on to Kemi, leaves much to be desired. There are bus stops outside Haparanda station, but no sign of any buses. I could walk, but it's going to take forty-five minutes and it's a hot day.

Eventually, a taxi pulls up, disgorging passengers. The driver is persuaded to take me and another couple of travellers the short distance into town to the transport terminal. She quotes the entirely humorous sum of fifteen euros for a four-minute ride, but one which gets us to the bus departure point at least. Here, we're promised a bus at quarter to three in the afternoon, directly to Kemi station, and so we wait. And wait.

It's not like there's nothing to do in Haparanda, he says, hastily scrolling through his phone. For example, almost interestingly, it is the easternmost town in Sweden.

Wait, there's more. Haparanda is the Swedish transliteration of the Finnish name Haaparanta, meaning 'aspen shore.' Aspens are in short supply in the neighbouring traffic circle and car park, though I note there is an IKEA directly opposite. And what about this for a fact? That IKEA, just across from Haparanda bus station, is the world's northernmost IKEA store. Worth coming here for that alone.

Time drags, and just when I'm contemplating nipping over the road for the world's most northerly plate of IKEA meatballs, the Kemi bus finally turns up. In the last hour or so, more and more people have descended upon the bus stop, so now there's quite a queue. Very orderly, it being Scandinavia, but with a certain amount of twitchiness given the lateness of the service.

Why the bus company decided to send a minibus is a matter known only to them.

Stern looks are exchanged as relative queue positions are examined. There's a slow procession onto the minibus, during which it becomes clear that not everyone is going to get on. I'm all right, middle of the queue, but I still have to stand wedged in at the back with a couple of others as the bus departs to a gentle, apologetic muttering, which is the sound irate Swedes make when they're furious.

However, that's the end of the drama and across the bridge we go – into Finland and on to Kemi. The Nordic country of Finland, I am reminded, when I choose to post about my experiences later that day in a railway travellers' Facebook group. Nordic, not Scandinavian, Finns are very keen on the distinction.

I daren't tell them about the *Rough Guide to Scandinavia*, which includes Finland *and* Iceland, which is also apparently not Scandinavian. This is on a par with foreign visitors saying gaily that Scotland is in England, or the brave people who insist to her face that Dublin-born Elaine is from "southern Ireland."

I generally stand back and watch with enjoyment as the touchpaper is lit on those occasions – it's a thing of rare beauty to see Elaine say smartly that there is no such place, only to be met by further bumbling insistence that she, an Irish person, must be wrong, or perhaps they meant Eire, and anyway it's all part of the UK, isn't it?

It is a salutary reminder that we need to be careful how we refer to other peoples' lands. And I'm talking as someone who comes from Yorkshire, which can only be said with the suffix, 'God's own country,' and where the word 'Lancashire' is a dire insult.

I reach Kemi station with two hours to spare in the end, where a terrace café serves me reindeer quiche and a slice of blueberry pie. Ahead, a first night for me on a Finnish sleeper train, and then the final run out tomorrow morning from Helsinki to the easternmost railway station in Europe.

This is the quickest leg of the whole trip by far, or at least the part with the fewest stops. Even so, I've come seven hundred kilometres from Narvik in a day and a half. Crossed two national borders. Seen the world's northernmost emporium of flatpack furniture. Eaten some reindeer.

No one can say this isn't proper travel – even if it is a barmpot enterprise, as we say in Yorkshire, God's own country.

CHAPTER 11

KEMI TO UIMAHARJU

I have an ambivalent relationship with night trains.

I respect their existence and the service they provide. With a growing network and better connections across Europe, they are the future if we want to cut down on short-haul flights. They are undeniably a good thing.

They are also terrible, at least all the services I've ever been on. The romance of a night on the rails fizzles out sharpish in a cramped four- or six-berth couchette shared with strangers. Access to your narrow bed is by vertical ladder, and the compartment door opens and closes all night as one by one your fellow inmates pad down the corridor to the shared toilet and come back whimpering in horror. Water is the best thing it's going to be sloshing around on the floor, put it like that.

I'm not talking about the luxury Orient-Express, or private sleeper cabins on the newer routes. Or even buying out the whole couchette, which is a recommended tactic in train-travel circles if you don't want to share. I know there are better, more expensive, alternatives to be had to the usual grim misery, if only you could prise the credit card from my dead, cold fingers.

My experience, like many train travellers, is at the budget end of the scene. Travelling overnight to save money, compared to a hotel. I only want to go the lengthy distance from A to B as economically as possible.

Kemi to Helsinki, case in point. It's a seven-hour daytime ride, meaning a prior night's accommodation somewhere I don't particularly want to stay. No offence, Kemi.

Or travel overnight on the eleven-hour sleeper, with a useful connection from Helsinki first thing tomorrow morning.

The sleeper train wins, and here it comes, arriving bang on time at Kemi station.

If you can board a train jauntily, that is what I do. Springing up the steps with a breezy whistle, patting small children on the head, pinching the cheek of the ticket inspector.

And why so jolly, given all that I have said?

It's because I have seen the website photos, and have conducted a lengthy conversation on the phone in English with a charming employee of VR, the Finnish railway company.

For the Helsinki sleeper is more like it. With an Interrail pass discount, I've got a private cabin with en-suite bathroom for a shade under fifty euros. Even at twice that price, it would be a bargain compared to a comparable trip and train cabin elsewhere in Europe.

I even get to go upstairs to bed, because the train is a double-decker and my cabin is up top. It's a cosy space with two bunks, and there's a little fold-out padded seat next to the window so I can watch Finland go by from the comfort of my cabin. The bed is properly made up with sheet, pillow and duvet, and there are towels provided.

It's the bathroom that's the clincher, though. Anyone who has ever taken a night train and had to use the public facilities will know what I'm talking about. I've got my own toilet, handbasin, and shower, plus soft toilet roll, soap dispenser, and mirror. All mine, mystery liquids on the floor entirely down to me.

There is even a handheld bidet shower-spray, which for a few terrible moments I assume to be the shower itself. Brandishing it in one hand, and contorting myself experimentally, fully clothed, I come to the conclusion that there is no way that I'm going to get *that* to reach *there*. And even if I do, the ceiling is going to get a soaking.

And then I depress a lever almost by accident and the entire bathroom swivels. It's like I've gone through the wardrobe door, but instead of snow and a lion – I mean, thank God there's no lion – I'm in a fully formed shower cubicle. A protective side wall keeps the water off the loo and basin, and there is the actual shower head, with hot and cold running water. The butt cleaner will not be required.

Still fully clothed, I depress the lever a couple of times, just to get the hang of it. I'm not what you'd call handy. My shelves are hung at a variety of angles, not all of them conducive to expecting things to stay on them. It would be in character for me to get stuck in here, and I'm not calling home to admit that.

Shower fully mastered, and the train now on its way, I set off for the restaurant car, which is another big thrill for those of us used to eating crisps horizontally in a top bunk and calling it dinner. It's modern and sleek, with window seats and buffet tables, and there is real food available – meatballs or salmon on mash, and traditional salmon soup. This is all very enjoyable, and I settle in for an hour or so watching the trees as we make our way down through Finland.

If you're looking for a rundown of the route, I'm afraid you're out of luck. It is daylight all night, and on any other sleeper train I might have been awake long enough to describe the railway yards and industrial areas of places like Oulu, Kokkola, and Tampere.

But I have my own cabin, a window blind and eye mask, and the next thing I know it's gone six in the morning and we're approaching Helsinki.

Finland is not somewhere I know. Apart from Helsinki itself, which I have been to previously, the most time I've spent in Finland would be the few hours getting to, and then waiting at, Kemi station.

I'm breaking new ground here, and my first fully conscious train ride in Finland is going to be the 06.54 from Helsinki to Joensuu, where there's a change for Uimaharju. The far eastern reaches await.

Train announcements thus far have all been in three languages, Finnish, Swedish and English, and the Joensuu service is no different.

"Passengers are reminded not to drink their own alcohol on board the train" says the guard.

It is seven am. That is not an announcement you'd expect to have to make on an early morning commuter service, but no judgement here. Whatever it takes to get through the day.

I settle in for the four-and-a-half-hour ride to Joensuu, which takes us northwest into the forests and lakes of Finnish Karelia.

It's a region of great cultural and historical significance, part of a much wider area that spreads across into present-day Russia, though disputed long before that by Sweden and imperial Russia. The border was fixed after World War II, much to the chagrin of Finland, which lost traditional Karelian territory to the Soviet Union.

All this is to pay tribute to the place that Karelia holds in Finnish hearts. For a foreign visitor, looking out of the train window, the pulse remains steady.

If you've never seen trees or lakes before, fill your boots, what a treat. If, however, you've spent the last ten days seeing ALL the trees and ALL the lakes, then there's not a lot to occupy you. Except, that is, for the railway line's astonishing – not to say alarming – proximity to the Russian border.

At the town of Lappeenranta, just two hours from Helsinki, St Petersburg is only two hundred kilometres away. If the road was still open, and you were allowed to drive there, you could be in the Hermitage museum within three hours.

The Finnish-Russian border is even nearer, and the train edges ever closer. Between the stations of Simpele and Parikkala, the track crosses a bridge over an arm of the Simpelejärvi lake. Look to the right, and the water and woods beyond are Russian, an angle in the national border lying almost within touching distance.

Both railway line and Finland's Highway 6 shadow the border for several hundred kilometres, a useful reminder for flippant visitors that, in Europe, we live our lives with different threat levels. I'm looking out of the window, thinking, "Cool, that's Russia." I suspect the Finnish armed forces currently have a different view about that. The two countries share a thirteen-hundred-kilometre border, and Finland has long been prepared for war with its neighbour. The 2022 invasion of Ukraine certainly hasn't put minds at ease here.

I make a swift change of trains in Joensuu. Half an hour later, the railway line makes a final curve eastwards, the train coming to a brief halt at Uimaharju before moving on.

It's an isolated, country station, hidden behind a stand of birch trees. The red, wooden station buildings are closed, and there are weeds growing up the steps.

The sort of lonely halt where only a fool would get off the train.

A fool gets off the train. That would be me. It's not like I was going to come all the way here and not get off. It is indisputably the easternmost railway station in the European Union. And, for the purposes of this book, the easternmost passenger railway station in mainland, continental Europe.

I could do a little jig of celebration if I wanted. It's not like there's anyone here to see. Instead, I put down my backpack and take some photos, to add to my collection of photographs of random stations that only mean anything to me. Dinner parties are fun at our house, I can tell you.

The town centre is a few hundred metres' walk away. It's little more than a four-way roundabout with a triangular cairn in the middle, and a tiny, adjacent strip mall containing a small supermarket, bakery, and pharmacy. What there are lots of, though, are signs pointing to other small crossroads towns, fifty kilometres away in all directions, and logging trucks thundering past.

Uimaharju – pronounced something like 'Oo-ee-mah-har-yoo' – translates as 'Swimming Ridge,' but don't let that mislead you. What it's big on is timber for construction, and the production of something called dissolving wood pulp, which is used to make textiles and all sorts of other products.

Once I knew I was going to Uimaharju, I didn't look too closely at its potential attractions and charms. Not because I didn't want to spoil the experience, but because I could already tell what it might be like, given its location – nowhere, middle of – and the nature of the station – unstaffed, weeds.

No point in putting myself off, I thought. I have to go, it's the rules. Although I did waste more time than strictly necessary acquainting myself with the fascinating properties of dissolving pulp, which apparently can be made into fibres used for sausage casings or the red wrap of a Babybel cheese.

However, with admirable foresight I did make the eminently sensible decision not to spend the night here.

So, that's the good news. I don't have to sleep in the dissolving wood pulp capital of eastern Finland. The bad news is that there's only one train back to Joensuu, and it doesn't leave for another four and half hours, giving me plenty of time to explore Uimaharju.

I look at the roundabout.

Right, that's done.

A couple of hundred metres up the road, my phone says there's a 'pub.' It's a low-lit roadside saloon and, when I duck my head inside, it appears to be popular with the sort of patrons who would benefit from the 06.54 warning about drinking their own alcohol on the morning train.

Next door is a more promising café, in that it's a café and it's open. The two ladies inside speak not a word of English, but they gesture me to the buffet – school-dinner like, but I am in no position to quibble – and charge me the princely sum of ten euros. I am quite the attraction, I can tell you, as people come and go. A foreigner with a backpack, here in our town? In the café, bold as brass? Whatever next?

That takes up about forty minutes of my four and half hours, and then, as I sit outside with yet another coffee refill, wondering about the life decisions that brought me to this point – salvation! Or a bus, which amounts to the same thing.

It's going the wrong way, I grant you, but the chirpy, English-speaking driver assures me that if I stand on the opposite side of the road for another twenty minutes, a bus will take me back to Joensuu. Away from Europe's easternmost town with a train station excluding Ukraine and Russia. Away from the meatball stew in Uimaharju's finest dining establishment. Away from the convenient roundabout-situated pharmacy. Away from it all.

Away from it by bus, admittedly. I feel bad about that for maybe ten seconds – as the hydraulic step lowers, and the bus driver taps the ticket machine.

On the one hand, the glory of riding every inch by rail when I can. On the other hand – well, look around. Uimaharju – it's been grand to know you, but I have to go.

None of this is to throw shade upon Swimming Ridge. They didn't know I was coming. It's not their fault I plucked them off the map and decided to visit for no good reason. But the nature of a trip like this is that some town or other is going to get it in the neck sooner or later. I'm just hoping there's not a bookshop in Uimaharju with an English-language travel section, or that the internet hasn't got here yet.

By way of contrast, Joensuu turns out to be a lovely surprise, a charming, riverside, university town, with everyone eating and drinking at outdoor restaurants, and generally having a fine old time. Doesn't have the wood-pulp interest of Uimaharju, but you can't have everything.

I have a beer by the river, and later grab a decent bowl of ramen and write up my notes. North and east, done. That's two of the cardinal compass points down, and two to go.

But it's a long way to the far south for the next one, and my route there starts from Helsinki.

CHAPTER 12

HELSINKI

I've been waiting for a truly magnificent railway station to come along, and Helsinki is it. Amsterdam, Hamburg, Copenhagen and Stockholm have their good points, but all pale beside Helsinki's iconic central station.

I didn't get the chance to see it on the dawn switcheroo between Kemi and Uimaharju but, allowing myself a couple of days in Helsinki, I now have time to appreciate it. And it really is something else.

Designed in an Art-Nouveau style known as National Romantic, it opened in 1919 as the main station of the newly independent republic of Finland. Every centimetre of its grandeur should be seen through that lens, from the beautifully detailed, cathedral-like, wooden entrance doors to the vaulted ceiling and chandeliers. There are moulded floor-to-ceiling decorative reliefs around massive arches, and brass-clad escalators to take you down to the lower level.

You feel like you should be checking in to a five-star hotel suite rather than looking for a departure board. And that's just the interior. Outside is the mighty clocktower – the clock allegedly set one minute early to give people time to catch their train – and the four, giant, 'Stone Men' sentinels, granite figures grasping globe-shaped lanterns.

I absolutely love it, and take more photographs than dinner-party guests can comfortably be shown.

A few hours later, after a long walk through the city centre and around the harbour, Helsinki is my new favourite city.

There are structures that could be buildings, or could be public art, and turn out to be both, like the curved and tapered Kamppi chapel. Made from spruce, alder and ash (the wood of Finland's forests) and standing twelve metres high in an open plaza next to a shopping centre, it looks like nothing so much as a gigantic – I don't know what, actually. Half a boiled egg? A throne? A toilet bowl?

It's closed when I pass by, so I walk the ten minutes across town to another landmark church, Tempelliaukio, which is a circular hole in the ground hewn from solid rock. Light pours in from a skylight surrounding a reflective copper dome, and the whole effect is transcendent – served up with a background dose of convivial tourist chatter and Richard Clayderman piano sounds tinkling away in the background.

These two buildings alone, along with the railway station, are enough to tell you that Helsinki has thought long and hard about how it presents itself to the world. Indeed, the part of the city between railway station, parliament building, public library, and Finlandia Hall exhibition and events centre has to be one of the finest urban spaces anywhere in Europe. Human, not monumental in scale, which again tells you much about Finnish social priorities.

A traffic-free park, with benches, playgrounds, sports courts, and wildflower meadows, stretches down to a recreational inner bay. From the terrace-café at Finlandia Hall – another iconic landmark of Finnish design – I look out over a beach with a rank of kayaks, a church in the distance, a Ferris wheel and roller-coaster rides, and a tram running along the far shore.

It resembles one of those dioramas at Miniatur Wunderland, as if a kid has drawn up the blueprint for a model railway scene. Yet it's a capital city. Those kayaks to rent are an eight-minute walk from parliament.

The city library, meanwhile, defies definition. It's called Oodi, which means Ode, and occupies a building almost alien in design – sinuous, floating layers of frosted glass, steel, and spruce. There are books, sure, but when the city asked its residents what they wanted from a public library, it turned out they wanted *everything*. You can come in and use the studios to record a podcast, play the drums, or do a fashion shoot. There are console-gaming rooms, 3D printers, vinyl cutters, and engraving machines. A kitchen hosts cooking classes, there's a pop-up events area, story spaces, and work desks, and an entire case of electric guitars you can borrow.

Not surprisingly, Helsinki scores highly whenever anyone produces an index of the world's most liveable cities. At the time of writing, Finland has topped the World Happiness Rankings (there is such a thing) for eight years in a row. You can see why, just by walking around. They design nice stuff for people, stuff that people want, and they make that stuff safe, welcoming, and accessible.

Here's another example that you notice the minute you start to explore Helsinki. There are bike and pedestrian lanes everywhere, with city traffic kept to thirty kilometres per hour. That's not so different from many capital cities, but street design is baked into public infrastructure here, and bikes, pedestrians, and drivers are largely kept apart.

Where they do meet, cyclists and pedestrians respect the crossing lights, and the drivers give way, mostly gracefully – even to the flock of a hundred barnacle geese I saw paddling across the open space in front of the library to a nearby pond. And while this might seem anecdotal, and not particularly noteworthy, do you know how many traffic-related deaths Helsinki had in 2024/25?

Zero.

The most recent comparable figures for London are ninety-five, or eighty-seven in New York.

I know where I'd rather be a goose, waddling across the city centre.

Down at Kauppatori, the harbourside market square, I pick up the waterfront trail that runs around the central city peninsula. In just ten minutes, I'm past the ferry terminal and rounding the headland for a view of wooded islets, reflective waters, and crisscrossing ferries and sailing boats. There are people sunbathing on the flat rocks, and plenty more geese marching through the traffic into the adjacent park, displaying the zero fucks that Helsinki wildfowl do not give.

My aim is a café called Mattolaituri, about which I've read a curious thing – that it's built next to a traditional rug-washing pier. Of all the things I've discovered so far about public-spirited Helsinki, this seems the most unlikely, but as the café comes into view, there they are: household rugs draped over rails, drying in the sun, with patrons enjoying a waterside beer or a coffee.

I'm not entirely convinced these aren't just props, when a car turns up, a man gets out, opens his boot, and grabs a handful of rolled-up rugs. And he's not a man like me, with time on his hands, told by his wife – let's call her Elaine – to take those rugs down to the specialist rug-cleaning shop and have them coddled in the finest fabric conditioners. A man who might say, sod that, I'll run them down to the lake, give them a quick rinse, save myself two hundred quid, she'll never know.

No, this is a young man, clearly in touch with his carpet-cleaning side, who has done the entirely normal thing of rolling up his household rugs and driving them down to the municipal pier for a good wash, and a thrash with a birch twig. It's the only language Finnish rugs understand.

I treat myself to a chamomile tea, watch the boats for a bit, and ponder how it takes all sorts to make a world. Conversations drift in and out of earshot, mostly in Finnish of course, but some in English, as I'm not the only tourist come to see the designer rug-and-Prosecco bar.

I'm not stickybeaking, but inevitably I overhear the couple at the next table. It's the lot of a solo traveller, and I often like to imagine other people's lives as they talk freely about people I don't know and places I'll never go.

These are two American women, in their thirties I'd say, tourists by the sound of it, talking about their trip.

"I don't understand these people who say they can't poop in a public toilet," says one, which is the point at which I tune in fully.

Say what, madam?

"If I'm going to poop, I'm going to poop. You know what I mean? I'm not going to hold it in."

Dear Lord.

"On a rafting trip I didn't poop for like five days. And then when I finally went, I clogged the toilet. It was a mess, you know what I mean?"

The other woman nods. Presumably, like me, unable to find the words. Then a man turns up, clearly known to Poop Woman. Husband, maybe?

"Dave, you want another coffee?"

Dave considers this proposal. "No," he says finally, "I'm waiting for this one to kick in."

This *has* to be the husband. Lid for every pot, and all that. Because Dave, it seems, has primed the poop pump with his first morning coffee, and is just waiting. Because if he's going to poop, he's going to poop, you know what I mean?

Anyway, lunch?

Because the other thing I've read about is a rather special restaurant out on one of the islands in the archipelago. Serendipity working the way it does, it featured in an online travel article the previous day, as I was on the train to Helsinki, and I made a reservation there and then.

The ferry leaves from the market square, which itself is a tent city of food stalls selling slabs of cooked wild salmon, sausage-and-potato hash, fish burgers, and punnets of summer blueberries and strawberries. Fast food, but nice fast food. Inside the old market hall, it's a bit more upscale, with cafés serving things like cured reindeer, bear carpaccio, and shucked oysters. Also, if you want a reindeer-skin car-seat cover, this is very much the place to come.

But I have my eye on even finer things, namely the three-course set lunch of modern Nordic cuisine on the tiny island of Lonna, a ten-minute cruise away.

I am the only person that gets off the ferry, which is giving me strong Uimaharju vibes. And at first sight, the island does little to suggest a good time is going to be had by all – or even just by me.

It's a little squashed circle of a thing, which I walk around in its entirety in exactly five minutes. It had a fortress on it in the eighteenth century, and later served as a gunpowder store and then a base for loading mine-carriers. Up until the 1940s, underwater cables laid around Lonna were used to demagnetise ships that would otherwise blow up on contact with a sea-mine.

Some of the old red-brick military buildings still survive; in the courtyard of one is the Lonna restaurant. There's also a popular waterside sauna here, but the whole place is quiet when I arrive, though it does fill up as ferries drop off more diners throughout the afternoon.

If this is my farewell to Helsinki, it's perfectly in keeping with the city itself – fun, quirky, stylish, well-judged. Even affordable, in a country which isn't always: thirty-nine euros for a lunch of grilled summer vegetables with a light, smoked-cheese foam; poached sea trout with cauliflower espuma and pea purée; and a wild cherry sorbet with dark chocolate mousse and a pickled rose petal. I'll put my travel-guide writer's hat on briefly – the food is mostly organic and locally sourced, the restaurant is open May to September, and I can't recommend it highly enough.

With no one to eavesdrop on, it's my own thoughts that occupy me as I work my way through the menu. Don't worry, they're poop-free.

Looking back, it's easy to see that I didn't appreciate the Nordic countries when I first came here, in my early twenties.

Of course, I was excited to have a job that involved travel, and I got to write and publish a book that other people would actually read. But I'm not sure I ever loved Scandinavia – though perhaps Finland would have been a different matter, if I hadn't been allocated Sweden and Norway.

I was young, and I lived in London at the time, which was the greatest city in the world as far as I was concerned. My haunts were the pubs and clubs of Soho, and I went to gigs and gallery openings, ate in Chinatown, and played football on Clapham Common. I couldn't imagine a better place to live, and didn't for many more years after that. I see the same thing today in my eldest son, who has taken to London life like his father before him, and – also in his early twenties – can't conceive of a better, cooler, more invigorating place to live.

All the things that were – are – great about Scandinavia, the things I now appreciate, were just not on my radar at twenty-three.

It's clean, quiet, and ordered. The streets are largely free of litter. Things work. Public spaces are designed by and for people, not corporations. Cafés give you free coffee refills, and provide blankets if you're cold and drinkable water that you don't have to pay for. Transport is affordable and reliable. Train buffet cars serve salads and soup.

Kids can play in the city centre in parks that are

thoughtfully designed. There are public benches, and cycle racks, and kayaks, and hammocks, and none of them are broken or graffitied. If you want to make a pin badge, hem a dress, or design a logo, you just go to the city library.

None of these things seemed like reasons to love the countries of the far north of Europe when I was young and foolish.

Now, they seem like part of some utopian dream, especially if you're from a country like mine where the public realm is crumbling and public discourse is increasingly angry. All that was needed, it seems, was for me to get older, in order to fully appreciate Nordic Europe's charms.

But look, I still couldn't live here. The eight-month winters would kill me. I don't do winter sports, and the very idea of a public sauna is deeply worrying. They'd have to tow Helsinki a few thousand kilometres south, and park it next to Spain. And cut the price of wine by three-quarters. Then I'd consider it.

For now, though, this is where I leave you. I'm booked on tonight's Viking Line ferry to Stockholm, that being the most direct way to put me back on the main European rail network. It will get me across the Baltic in sixteen hours, but I don't expect it to be plain sailing.

For example, there are twelve decks on the Viking Cinderella, numbering down from twelve at the top. My cabin is on deck two. There is no deck one. I am – alarmingly – on what's known as the 'Anchor Deck.'

There are two levels of cars and trucks above me, never mind the several decks of entertainment and dining. I am basically going to be a submariner; for the price I've paid, I probably have to be in charge of weighing the anchor or discharging the bilge.

From Stockholm, I'm heading back to Copenhagen, on a route already travelled. Then Hamburg and Amsterdam, and finally on to Paris, where I'll start the real journey south.

I'm not stopping anywhere, except to change trains or stay the night where I have to. There's nothing new to see, and you don't need to do this bit with me.

Honestly, it's fine, go and have a cup of tea. I'll see you in a few days.

SOUTH
PARIS TO ALGECIRAS AND TARIFA

Paris-Perpignan-Villefranche-Latour de Carol-
Ribes de Freser-Núria-Barcelona-Valencia-Ronda-
Algeciras-Tarifa

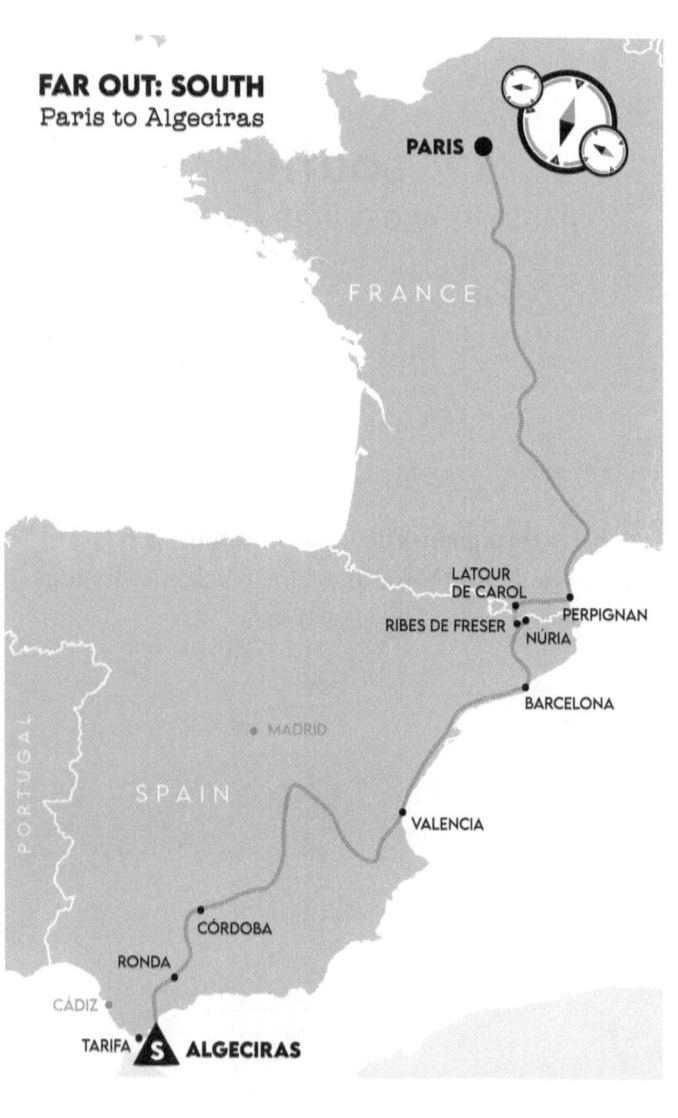

CHAPTER 13

PARIS

My way by train to Europe's far south lies through Paris – city of enlightenment and love. And also of stations, whose names – gares du Nord, d'Est, de Lyon, d'Austerlitz, Montparnasse – speak of romance and travel, and journeys to scores of European cities.

I come in at the Gare du Nord, and I'm due to leave on the night train to Perpignan from the Gare d'Austerlitz. That gives me a few hours in a city I've visited a few times before, but can hardly say I know, and it's not like I'm stuck for options when it comes to famous sights and blockbuster attractions.

Even just the straightforward walk between the two stations, which would take around an hour, passes through the fashionable district of Le Marais and ends up at the River Seine near the Notre-Dame cathedral.

But as the great Anthony Bourdain once wrote,

"Nothing unexpected or wonderful is likely to happen if you have an itinerary in Paris filled with The Louvre and the Eiffel Tower."

Paris itself might be unavoidable – at least, if I want to catch tonight's train to the south – but St Anthony has given me permission to skip all the tourist sights. And so it is that I have plans to do just two things during my few hours in the city – go to the toilet, and then have dinner. But Paris being Paris, I'm going to do them in style, indeed you might say with a certain *je ne sais quoi*.

First, though, I have to contend with the Gare du Nord, Europe's biggest and busiest railway station. It dates from the 1860s and, while it's not as flamboyant as London's St Pancras, the long, monumental façade does that very Parisian thing of turning a public building into a statement of intent.

"You want a main entrance?" went the architect, "I'll give you a main entrance," and then designed a majestic palace of soaring arches, rifle-straight stone columns, rooftop statues and ornate medallions, topped by a French flag and a robed figure of a woman representing the city of Paris. You could simply catch a train here – hundreds of thousands do every day – but if the president decided to move in, they'd only have to hang some curtains and take down the departure boards.

I step back to take a wider look and to snap a photo, which turns out to be a very bad idea. My time in northern Europe has clearly lulled me into a false sense of security. In Sweden or Germany, for example, there are government sharpshooters stationed on high buildings at every intersection, with orders to take you out if you step into the road before the little man turns green.

In Paris, you exit the Gare du Nord onto what appears to be a wide, green pavement, where I turn round for a last look at the station façade. There's a whooshing sound and a strangled cry from behind me as something clips my backpack, and I leap about a metre into the air and stagger as I hit the ground again.

That'll be a cycle route then, between the actual pavement and the road, and several more Parisians are currently storming past at speeds I might previously have thought impossible for bikes and scooters. The riders shout and gesticulate – "Welcome, sir, to our fair city," that sort of thing – while I lurch to safety, heart pounding.

After much performative map-checking on my phone, buying time while I stop having palpitations, I make my way across the main avenue and duck into a side street. This also isn't the wisest move, the Gare du Nord being the sort of old-school station that Europe used to specialise in. By which I mean that the surrounding streets are populated by people who I'm sure love their mothers, own cats, and put out their recycling, but are involved in various enterprises that it wouldn't surprise me to learn aren't entirely legal.

Along the length of one short street, I'm offered many things in guttural French that I don't understand. I'd like to be charitable – could be spare opera tickets, or some free tai chi lessons – but I suspect they are more likely to involve something going up at least one orifice.

I really thought, by my age, I would no longer look like the sort of person that dodgy people in dodgy streets offer dodgy things to, but it hasn't happened yet.

Eventually I hit wider residential streets and then boulevards as I make my way towards Place de la Madeleine. Not only am I finally going to go to the toilet when I get there, you're going to come with me, because this is France's first ever public convenience we're talking about – the Lavatory de la Madeleine, dating from 1905.

I saw a newspaper article about it when it reopened in 2023, and it's since been all over Instagram, which means there are already more people taking photos there than taking a dump. But I've got time to kill in Paris, and Anthony Bourdain said it was all right not to go to the Louvre.

As with the railway stations and other major buildings, la belle époque France went big on the décor in its public toilets. Comfort and luxury were the watchwords, and hang the expense. This one is hidden away in Place de la Madeleine, outside the landmark Madeleine church – tucked underground because it would have been unseemly to erect a loo outside a church.

It's reached from behind obscure railings, down a mosaic-lined, spiral staircase, and I stump up two euros for entry – the subject of much ire on TripAdvisor by people who just wanted to spend a penny and were outraged by the inflationary demand.

It's a rather extraordinary art-nouveau jewel in a city not short of such things, and I have a good look around, at my convenience, so to speak. If hipsters had got hold of it, they'd doubtless have turned it into a kombucha bar, but you'll be relieved to know the city authorities saw the value in retaining its use.

Half a dozen carved and polished mahogany cubicles with stained-glass detailing hide the business elements of the operation. The rest of the space is a spectacle of mirrored pillars, brass fittings, and ornate tiling, plus an antique attendant's cabin. The best bit is the original shoe-shine throne, empty chair in place, roped off between brass rails like an art exhibit.

The whole thing is a museum piece, beautifully restored and well looked after, and it seems a shame to – you know. But I have paid my two euros, and walked forty minutes here from Gare du Nord, not to mention the sphincter-stretching bike-lane experience. I need this, so bear with.

That's better.

I'm hoping dinner is going to be a similarly gratifying event. My night train leaves at nine-twenty-five, and I know from experience that there are no catering facilities on board. Eleven hours on a train without snacks or drinks? Go cold turkey without any turkey? That is what the young people call rawdogging, and I will have no part of it.

Instead, I've bookmarked a meal in Le Train Bleu,

the celebrated railway-station restaurant in the Gare de Lyon, which is just a ten-minute walk across the bridge from my departure station, Austerlitz.

I can't claim any credit for unearthing a Parisian secret. This is another one of those in-the-know places that everyone knows about, and I found out about it from the excellent Man in Seat 61 train-travel website. It first opened in 1900 as the Gare de Lyon station buffet – when railway companies still cared about catering facilities – and is named after the pioneering 'Blue Train' that opened up the French Riviera to visitors from the capital in the late-nineteenth century.

Because I know how these things go, I tried to reserve a table in advance via email, as the restaurant only opens for dinner at seven pm, which doesn't give me a lot of room for manoeuvre. No reply, obviously, because I wrote the request in English, which never goes down well in Paris, though I did get an automated reply with a shrug emoji that just said, "Bof."

As it turns out, Le Train Bleu can accommodate me just fine, because it is the size of several aircraft hangars or one medium-sized principality. I trot up a flower-filled, wrought-iron staircase above the platforms, negotiate a table for one in French by holding up one finger and looking quizzical, and am left alone with the menu.

At this point, I see that I have been dining in entirely the wrong sort of places all my life. If the Madeleine toilets were magnificent, this restaurant is truly astonishing. Every centimetre is painted and gilded, with vast murals that wrap around the vaulted ceilings. Chandeliers glisten, brass rails gleam, and plaster cherubs cling to golden arches. I imagine someone from the railway company went to Versailles and said, "We'll have some of that Louis XIV bling. Yes, in a station restaurant, what's your point?"

The only thing bringing the tone down is, frankly, me, with my backpack hoisted onto the adjacent leather banquette.

There's a fleet of waiters buzzing around – waistcoats, bowties, terrifying demeanour – and this could go one of two ways, because I'm already flummoxed by the pristine and elaborate table setting. There are about nine glasses per diner, and an array of knives and forks of ascending size, which look like I'm covered for everything from a snail to a stuffed swan.

None of this would work, of course, if the food wasn't any good, but the website and menu make much of Le Train Bleu's executive chef, Michel Rostang, who has Michelin stars under his belt. The roast leg of lamb, carved at the table, is his signature dish, accompanied by a potato gratin that Michel says is made with neither cheese nor eggs. A matter for him, of course, but I'd have said that a potato gratin minus cheese or eggs is just 'potato,' but as he's the one with the Michelin stars and not me, I'm going to trust he knows what he's doing.

A waiter appears and suggests – with a raised eyebrow and the slightest of nods – that my choice is approved. I haven't even looked at the prices. Or rather, I have, but stopped reading when I saw that the first of two digits for my meal was not a one or even a two but a five.

It's too late now, I'm all in. I'm not slinking out of a decorated French chef's restaurant – not with the access he has to sharpened blades. Besides, I've seen his picture on the website. Big Mich might have white hair and wrinkles, but he looks like he's buried a few sous chefs in his time.

Consequently, when the wine list arrives, I'm almost giddy. I point randomly at a French red that's served by the glass, noting in passing that the double-digit price starts with a two. How I laugh. At this point, it's like spending Monopoly money. I'll just style it out. Hell, I'll have a second glass if I feel like it, and *that'll* show 'em.

After a short wait, and a five-euro sip of wine, the waiter returns with a trolley and a silver tray with a leg of lamb on it. There's some flashing-blade business – Big M must put them through their paces every night after service – and then a plate is layered with very pink carved lamb, topped with whole roast garlic cloves and a deeply coloured gravy. The potato gratin is served separately in a volcanically hot ceramic dish.

I eat. I take in the surroundings. I slowly relax, and listen to the happy sound of contented diners.

Someone across the way is having crêpes Suzette flambéed at the table with what looks like half a bottle of Grand Marnier, and we all stop eating to watch. One day, surely, a waiter is going to set someone's hair on fire, but disappointingly that day is not today.

As for my meal, I have notes, not that I'd dare give

them to Michel. The lamb is too rare and barely room temperature, and there's not a lot of it. On the plus side, the gratin has had a barrel of cream tipped in it, so he got that right, and you do get a very prettily served fruit meringue for dessert.

By the time the wine has done its work, and the waiter comes round with the final bill, I'm thinking fondly of the whole experience. I should imagine he thinks fondly of me, too, in his reflective hours, seeing as I manage to miss the fact that a hefty service charge has already been included. Accordingly, I lay down entirely unnecessary wads of cash on the table as I leave, resulting in the waiters forming a guard of honour and singing La Marseillaise, while banging trays and lighting dessert blowtorches with vintage Cognac.

Over the bridge I toddle. The night train to Perpignan beckons. My journey south begins in earnest, and I'm going to shake the northern dust from my feet and wake up to Mediterranean sunshine.

CHAPTER 14

PARIS TO LATOUR DE CAROL

The less said about the night train, the better. Remember lovely Finland, and the cosy, en-suite cabin for one? The Narnia shower and all-night bistro?

Yeah, it's not like that.

The Intercité de Nuit services that run from Paris to the south of France are on the cheap and basic side, and you're slotted into six-berth couchettes (four in first class), each with about as much room as you'd get in a mortuary cold-cabinet.

Sleep obviously costs extra, because I don't get any. The stiffs on all sides of me splutter, snore, groan and fart all night, which is annoying but, I suppose, not as alarming as it would be if this actually was a mortuary.

I don't so much wake up to southern sunshine as surface in a daze, after hours of restless confinement. That, I resolve, is very much the last journey I shall ever take in a zombie-filled, second-class, night-train couchette. I drive a dagger into the head of each of the other compartment occupants – they don't die unless you kill the brain – and step into the corridor, as the train rattles past Narbonne.

Whereupon the Mediterranean does its thing, and good vibes are restored.

The train skirts giant saltwater lagoons that stretch all the way to Perpignan, now just an hour away. Sunlight through high clouds is reflected perfectly in the still waters, and there are flocks of pink flamingos feeding in the morning sun. At one point we have flamingos on one side of the train and the glistening Med on the other, and life on a train doesn't get much better than that. A few scattered smallholdings flash by, with tethered horses and planted vineyards, and behind, is a glimpse of the distant Pyrenees.

I've rushed through France overnight to take a more leisurely route through Spain to the far south, and I'm going to start with an historic train ride into those very mountains.

It's not the obvious way to go. The high-speed service from Perpignan puts you in Barcelona in an hour and twenty minutes, or four hours if you take the traditional cross-border coastal route via French Cerbère and Spanish Portbou.

Back when I first started coming to Europe by train, the coastal approach was the major eastern route into Spain, where the tracks changed from the European standard gauge on the French side to the wider Iberian gauge – meaning everyone had to pile off one train and get on another.

If you travel this way today, you still have to change trains at the border, and the magnificent, if dilapidated, station at Portbou (otherwise, just a small seaside village) reflects its former importance as a cross-border freight and passenger terminal.

But I've got another plan in mind, which is to ignore the standard rail routes from France to Spain and make a long detour into the mountains, starting with a trip on the Train Jaune, the famous 'Yellow Train' of the French Pyrenees.

This runs up the Têt valley into the Cerdanya region that straddles the eastern Pyrenees, the route a remarkable feat of engineering completed in the early years of the twentieth century. It's on every train buff's bucket list, and I'd like to find out why, but it does mean spending the night in Perpignan and catching a connecting train first thing the following morning.

Given my lack of sleep the previous night, this is fine by me, and I have a decent, reviving night in the hotel opposite Perpignan train station. I'm on the concourse at seven the next morning in plenty of time to catch the train to Villefranche Vernet-les-Bains, departure point of the Train Jaune, when – naturally – it's cancelled at the last minute.

"There is a replacement bus instead," says a railway official, and waves his hands vaguely. He says this in French, of course, which I can just about understand, but he isn't forthcoming about which of the four station exits this bus might depart from. In, ooh, let's see, six minutes' time. And if I don't catch this bus, my plans are scuppered because the day ahead relies on some tight connections.

Many years ago, we had a French exchange student come to stay in our house for a week, which was the usual mix of embarrassing and excruciating for all concerned. His English was as bad as our French, but he did at least make an effort – including the memorable anecdote he told one day about a lunchtime mishap involving "the sausage of my teacher," which has gone down in Brown family lore.

The French being a sophisticated lot, and the English being brutes, I'm sure it sounded entirely wholesome to him, despite the disgraceful sniggers. I bear this salutary tale in mind as I race around Perpignan station accosting total strangers and demanding information in my best, saucisson-of-my-teacher, French.

Miraculously, I find the bus, and it deposits me an hour or so later in Villefranche, with another hour before the Train Jaune departs. This gives me time to stroll the few hundred metres from the station to the tiny, neighbouring town of Villefranche-de-Conflent, a handsome-looking place that's entirely contained within mighty seventeenth-century defensive walls.

I wander through the imposing town gate and along narrow streets with tall, buttoned-up, stone houses, looking for breakfast. The place is deserted. Every café and bar is resolutely shuttered and closed, 'de-Conflent' being French for, "We like a lie in, even though we have a top tourist attraction on our doorstep."

While I've been away on the fruitless search for a wide-awake café patron, things have developed back at the station, where there's now a long queue for the first Train Jaune of the day. It's sitting there on the platform – bright yellow, as advertised, with a jaunty red trim – and looks altogether like a scaled-up version of one of those Noddy road trains that trundle around tourist resorts.

I'm somewhere near the back of the queue, which is frustrating because although I have a pre-booked ticket, it's unreserved seating and there are only two open-air carriages, which fill quickly. I have to settle for a seat in a regular carriage and hope that won't detract from the experience, because by all accounts this is one of Europe's most dramatic railway lines.

There's a spectacular sixty-three-kilometre ride ahead of me, via twenty-two stations at remote villages and hamlets, deep in the French Pyrenees. The electrified line was built on a narrow, one-metre gauge to cope with the twists and turns as it climbs from 427 metres at Villefranche to the highest point of 1,533 metres at Font Romeu. After three hours, nineteen tunnels and forty bridges – including the oldest railway suspension bridge in France – the Train Jaune ends its run at the French-Spanish border, where I'm going to change trains and head further into Spain.

There's a whistle and a lurch, and we're off, almost immediately winding through narrow gorges and negotiating a series of stone bridges and viaducts. The line bends around chiselled rock outcrops, hugging the hillsides, with views at times across steep, tree-covered slopes.

There are stops at occasional stations – rundown, graffitied halts for the most part – where, inexplicably, people alight and stride off confidently into the wilderness. They all have towering backpacks, filled – it's to be hoped – with high-tensile rope, dried rations and bear spray, because I'm not seeing any signs of civilisation out there. My Norwegian friends, Lucas and Oskar, would love all this. They'd be skinning squirrels and brewing up coffee in a heartbeat.

I'm travelling on a warm, sunny day, but the train provides year-round access to this mountain region, whatever the weather. It's still the only way supplies can get into the upper Cerdanya after heavy snow. They have a snowplough on permanent standby, and a team of workers whose task it is to get up in the middle of the night and walk the forty tunnels to clear the icicles. I'll bet that part of the job was never mentioned in the recruitment interview.

More people get off the train at Font Romeu, a couple of hours into the journey – a mountain resort so high that it has an altitude training centre for France's Olympic athletes.

The scenery is fully alpine now – with wooden chalets and ski runs – and then for the last hour we scoot through rolling wildflower meadows with far-reaching views to much higher surrounding mountains, capped by white clouds. Occasional patches of snow gleam in the distance, while huddled villages and solitary houses cling here and there between the crags.

These views are what the lazy travel writer would call vistas, so vistas they are – sweeping too, and panoramic to boot. Maybe even majestic. You're getting your money's worth here on adjectives, I can tell you.

As the train has been making its slow, rattling way up the mountain, I've been rethinking the carriage situation. The two open carriages, I noticed, had hard, slatted wooden seats, while my regular carriage has padded seats and big windows that fully open, so I haven't missed out in the slightest. I've had a comfortable ride with great views.

But now and again, the train careers around a sharp bend or crosses a curving viaduct and I get a view of the open carriages behind me, where everyone is having a grand old time – throwing their hands in the air and whooping like they're on a rollercoaster. And I think, that would have been nice, to be a hands-in-the-air kind of passenger. Plus, they get all the cars tooting at them every time we go anywhere near a road or cross a level-crossing, and then there's even more waving and laughing.

Everyone sitting in the open carriages is basically on a three-hour version of the Grand National at Blackpool Pleasure Beach, while I am tut-tutting like a disapproving maiden aunt who's been terribly disappointed in her life choices and wishes she had accepted that marriage proposal from the South African diamond-miner.

As you can see, I am fully committed to the maiden aunt role. Then again, I am not cooked like a lobster by the time we arrive, so that's a small victory.

Anyway, my advice for what it's worth, is to sit inside on the righthand side (direction of travel) for the best views. And then jump out at one of the stations when it's thinned out a bit near the end, and switch into an open carriage for the last half an hour.

Thus it is that I arrive – carefree, wind in my hair, married at last to the diamond-miner – at Latour de Carol/Enveitg, one of Europe's most remote train stations.

We've descended a little by now, but we're still at over twelve hundred metres high and, let's face it, miles from anywhere. Even so, this is a station of some renown among the sort of people – no judgment – who stand at the end of platforms with notebooks full of serial numbers.

It sits between two French villages (hence the double name), a couple of kilometres from the Spanish border and twenty-five from Andorra. The first clue to its importance is the size of the station. It's far bigger and more impressive than it has any right to be, given its isolation, with no fewer than four platforms, which seems to be three too many at first glance. And it's because it's one of the few stations in the world where three different track gauges meet: the narrow 1.0-metre gauge of the Train Jaune; the standard 1.435-metre

European gauge used in France; and the wider 1.668-metre Iberian gauge.

So what, you are thinking? And, very possibly, give the gauge talk a rest, will you, we came here for light-hearted travel writing, not a maths lesson.

But here's the amazing thing about Latour de Carol/Enveitg station – because of the gauge variations, from here there are direct French trains to Paris, and Spanish trains to Barcelona, no changes required. You can get on at Latour, where all you can see are mountains, snow-caps, and goats, and be on the Champs-Élysées in twelve hours or the Ramblas in four, and that's surely remarkable?

I'd note it down in my little book, if I had one, but I settle for taking photos of the three trains currently in the station – my little yellow Noddy train, a smarter red-and-grey SNCF number, and a shabbier orange one that I take to be the Spanish service.

Even that's not quite right, because heaven forbid you make the mistake of thinking anything about this region is Spanish, or indeed French. It's considered to be Catalan on both sides of the border, which you can tell from the local place names – Enveitg among them, which looks nothing like Spanish or French.

Accordingly, the very French-sounding Latour de Carol is down on the timetable in Catalan as La Tor de Querol, and the orange train at the station is badged – rather disarmingly – as a Catalan commuter service to Barcelona. Mind you, it's three and a half hours each way, so you'd only have time for lunch before you had to come back home again, which sounds like my kind of job.

However, I've still got one more diversion to make before I reach Barcelona. I'm not yet finished with the Pyrenees, and an hour down the line from Latour I'm making one final connection today at Ribes de Freser for another tremendous rail ride into the mountains.

CHAPTER 15

RIBES DE FRESER TO NÚRIA

In the years after 700 CE, in a lush, broad valley, under the peaks of the eastern Pyrenees, a hermit named Gil lived and preached among the local shepherds.

He carved a simple image of the Virgin Mary which, according to legend, he hid in a cave during the Muslim conquest of Spain. The statue was rediscovered several hundred years later, and ever since pilgrims have made their way into the mountains to seek blessings from Our Lady of Núria.

You don't have to believe any of that to appreciate the grandeur of the setting – a fertile, glacial bowl under soaring, jagged mountains. As well as a pilgrimage site, the Núria valley is also a major winter resort, with a huge – and, it has to be said, rather ugly – hotel complex that envelops the sanctuary and dominates the valley.

That might not sound the most enticing of prospects, but what elevates Núria is the lack of access. There's no road here – for centuries, pilgrims made their way over the mountains on foot, and many still do. But there is a railway, which runs for twelve kilometres from Ribes de Freser on the main Barcelona line, climbing an astonishing thousand metres in thirty-five minutes, arriving right next to the hotel and sanctuary in the highest of the high Pyrenees.

I know you're here for the full facts, so buckle up – it's the fourteenth highest passenger railway in Europe, the highest outside the Alps, and has a maximum incline of fifteen percent.

I have ridden this route once before, over thirty years ago now, when I came here on a research trip for Rough Guides. Back then – in world-wide-web infancy – the only way to gather information about train timetables and hotel prices in remote places was to visit in person. All I had time for in Núria that day was a quick walk from the station to the sanctuary, a check of the hotel facilities, and then back on the train to Barcelona. I had always planned to return, and maybe stay the night and walk in the mountains.

Decades later, this is my chance. Europe's fourteenth-highest passenger railway, here I come.

It doesn't start well. The mountain train is barely thirty seconds out of Ribes station before it grinds to a halt – literally, there's a terrible grinding noise that drowns out all conversation.

After a minute or two there are some heartfelt

apologies in Catalan and Spanish for the unscheduled stop "for technical reasons." There's a bit more grinding, and then silence again, followed by someone in Catalan suggesting – I may be paraphrasing at this point – that they are going to try switching it off and switching it on again. Which they do, and bingo – we're back in business.

The line is known as the Cremallera de Núria, opened in 1931 and still the only way in and out of the upper valley. It's technically a rack (or rack-and-pinion) railway, with a central toothed rail for traction on the steep gradients – *cremallera* means 'zipper' in Catalan, which makes sense when you see the track laid out with its middle 'zip.'

The train needs all the help it can get, because once we're past the outskirts of Ribes de Freser, it enters serious mountain terrain.

We pass through an incredibly narrow gorge, with cut rock just centimetres from the windows. There's a green carpet of moss and vegetation to either side, and occasional glimpses of the Freser river valley through gaps in the trees. Huge steel nets hang overhead, anchored to the rock by cables, which suggest that rockslides and falling boulders are entirely possible.

The line remains hemmed in as far as the village of Queralbs, about halfway, which is the last place in the valley you can reach by road. After here, the route opens out, but only in the sense that the railway now follows a precarious line high above the river valley, with sheer drops below and craggy peaks behind. Deep valleys veer away to the right, as the train climbs ever higher, pulled up on the teeth of the zipper.

Just when you can't see how it can possibly negotiate the sheer bank of crags ahead, the train dives through a long, rising tunnel and emerges into the sunlight and the open spaces of the upper Núria valley. Ahead lies the resort – a plain, brown, four-storey hotel flanking a grey-stone church with a simple spire. The final run in is alongside a deep, green reservoir, crowned by high peaks.

Here we are, at two thousand metres, in a largely pristine landscape. It's stirring stuff, even arriving – with no effort on my part – by train. Imagine walking in, soaking your aching feet in the water, and reflecting upon the majesty of the surroundings? You can see the attraction for pilgrims across the ages.

The hotel, however, is a different matter. It is – how shall I put this? – a little bit *The Shining* in character. There's a touch of 'All work and no play makes Jack a dull boy' about the vibe. Admittedly, it's not peak season, which would be winter, but it's vast and echoing, and hardly anyone else except me has got off the train. Which is becoming a habit.

The strangeness continues. As I check in, I'm told I have booked three rooms for the night. Granted, I'm the man who got on the wrong train at Berlin airport once, and circled the entire city before ending up back at the airport. It's entirely plausible that I may have made multiple bookings by mistake – I wouldn't put it past me.

But on this occasion, I know that I haven't, and I show the reception clerk the booking confirmation: Brown, one room.

She's not having it. "Well, you have three rooms."

"OK."

"Maybe you can cancel the other two, because otherwise you are paying for three rooms."

"Ri-ight." Meaning, I don't think so.

She's persistent, I'll give her that. "You can go to the booking website and cancel the other two now, perhaps?"

Well, I'm not doing that, because I don't have a booking for two extra rooms, and anyway, I don't see how any of this is my problem. I'm here, on my own, and clearly just going to occupy one room.

"Oh, wait."

Here we go.

"Are you Brown, J?"

"Yes, Brown, Julian, as per the passport."

'Not Brown – Duncan? Or Brown – and she flourishes another name that I don't quite catch.

"Nope, definitely Brown, J."

"Good, that all seems to be in order."

It turns out that in the Catalan Overlook Hotel, where the only people present are the confused desk clerk and, presumably, a ghostly bartender with homicidal tendencies, there are three Browns booked in tonight. Literally no one else, but there are three English people called Brown, two of whom she wanted me to deprive of their rooms by cancelling their reservations only five minutes ago.

So, Brown, Duncan, and Mystery Brown, you're welcome, I hope you enjoy your rooms.

There's still plenty of daylight left, so I take the cable car from near the train terminus up to a mountain refuge with a café and a sweeping view. The hotel and resort look less intrusive from up here, as the higher surrounding peaks come into view, ranged along the French-Spanish border. They all top out at around the 2,700-metre mark, which is not too shabby a height for Europe.

I don't have time, or the gear, to scale anything like that, but I follow a waymarked path for half an hour, just to be able to say I've finally walked in the mountains I first glimpsed thirty-odd years before.

I call a halt at a little peak – at 2,418 metres, according to an altitude app on my phone – which is the highest I think I've ever walked to. Wild horses are visible in the distance, and there are vultures swirling overhead, but the further peaks are beyond me, and rain and mist are threatening, so I retrace my steps to the cable car.

That just leaves the sanctuary itself, though at thirteen hundred years' remove it's hard to separate legend from fact.

Our hermit, Gil, later San Gil (or Saint Giles) is said, for example, to have stayed in the valley for four years from around the year 700, and then hid his carved statue in a cave before fleeing persecution from the Muslim invaders. Which is all fine except the advance troops of the Moorish conquest didn't reach the Pyrenees until at least fifteen years after that date.

With Gil long gone, it fell to a Syrian pilgrim – a long way from home – to discover the statue in the late-eleventh century, along with a cross, a bell, and a cooking pot, that Gil had used to summon the shepherds to eat and pray. Those three items are still symbolic today, for reasons that will become clear.

The statue itself, though? That's another tricky one, because the one on display, while undeniably ancient, is not *that* ancient. It's clearly Romanesque, dated to the twelfth or thirteenth century, so it's not the one that Gil carved, if he even came to the valley at all.

Most stories associated with Saint Giles the Hermit are apocryphal at best. There's little in the record about him until the tenth century, when legend reports him to have been from Athens and, later, living as a hermit in what's now southern France. The abbey he purportedly founded, the Abbaye de Saint-Gilles, lies south of Nîmes, three hundred kilometres from Núria. It's a stretch, to say the least, to find him wandering in the remote Pyrenees.

But veracity is never the point in these tales. As a foundational story, it had enough piety and mystery attached to endure, and faith did the rest. A cave hermitage became a stone chapel – still visible in the grounds – and pilgrims began to make their way into the mountains. The sanctuary church is a twentieth-century addition, focus – along with the statue – of pilgrimages and festivals each year on 29 June, 1 September, and the big one, 8 September.

I climb the stairs inside the church and stand briefly in front of the revered painted statue of the Virgin Mary and child.

I realise that I am not the target audience for this kind of thing – I freely admit to zero religious feeling – but this one is a fairly challenging example of the genre. I'm familiar with Romanesque religious imagery, and accept that there were still a couple of hundred years to go before perspective and accurate anatomy wrought their magic upon art. But this statue – supposedly a doting mother and her cherubic child – is clearly of Joe 90 clutching a naked middle-aged man in his lap.

There's an enduring belief that this frankly terrifying statue of the Virgin of Núria can aid fertility, which accounts for the side room featuring a wooden contraption containing a mounted cross, a metal cauldron, and a bell – Gil's utensils, remember them?

If you're looking to get pregnant, the advice is – "with appropriate prayer" – to ring the bell and then place your head in the cauldron. You name the subsequent girl Núria, or the boy Gil.

I can just about accept this. I mean, why not, if you've given everything else a shot? My only scepticism arises from the accompanying notice, which states that the head-in-a-metal-pot-plus-bell-ringing protocol is also a sure-fire method for "the relief of migraines."

I think we can all see where the migraine sufferers of Catalunya might be going wrong.

Over dinner that night, I think back to my only previous visit. Then – as on today's journey – I noticed a rocky footpath winding up from the lower village of Queralbs. It comes in and out of view from the train window. I'd thought back then that it would be a fine thing one day to walk on that path, back down the valley. If that day's not today – well, tomorrow – then when would it be? Because I suspect I won't ever pass this way again.

A check of the timetables shows me that it's possible to hike down to Queralbs, pick up the Cremallera there, change trains again onto the mainline at Ribes de Freser, and still be in Barcelona by late afternoon.

I get up early the next day to find mist in the valley, and the ghostly sight of horseback riders trotting across the grass lawn between hotel and lake. The hotel has an outdoors store and the young guy in there says the mist will clear later, and – looking me up and down – that the walk shouldn't be too strenuous. I feel there is an unspoken, "even for a boomer like you."

First, though, breakfast, where the omelette guy is having a mare. He's cooking them on request, adding ham, cheese, chorizo, pepper and onion, according to choice, but he's either a stranger to the omelette, or perhaps he's just not used to working under these conditions. Namely, being observed closely by a handful of querulous Catalans and three English Browns who want their breakfast and want it now.

There is much scraping and flipping and muttering, until he slops one out onto a plate and then starts the whole laborious process all over again. At this rate, 'Breakfast served from 8 am to 10 am' looks hopelessly optimistic, so I give him a miss and check out the buffet instead, which is up to Scandinavian standards. All the breads, cereals, hams, cheeses, fruit, yoghurt, cakes, croissants, and – double take, yes it's true – a fridge filled entirely with that Catalan breakfast speciality, the Cornetto ice cream.

The walk is well signposted – the Camí Vell, the old way – and starts out high above the river, passing occasional thundering waterfalls. There are glimpses of the train track on the opposite flank of the valley, and a distant noise as the first service of the day makes its steep ascent. At one point, I'm opposite a long, roofed gallery protecting the track, and out whooshes the train, its bright, blue livery standing out against the grey rock.

The mist is still clinging to the valley – thanks for nothing, young guy – which is making the rock path slippery and unreliable. It's slow going, and when the mist does eventually rise I'm not sure that's any better, because now I can see exactly how high and exposed this route is. There are soaring rock faces above me, and tree-studded slopes below. I cross boulder fields from ancient slippages and rockfalls, all the while looking out for the painted stripes that indicate I'm still on the right track.

There are, apparently, mountain goats in the valley,

birds of prey on the thermals, and trout in the distant river, but the only wildlife I see are slugs – big, fat, black ones creeping across the stones. Then again, I've been groaning loudly for at least the last hour, so maybe everything else is steering well clear.

Unlike the old navvies' trail in Norway, this walk is incredibly tough on the knees, ankles, and soles of the feet, descending a thousand metres on rough stone tracks, boulder-strewn slopes, and rock-cut steps. The many things I thought I was concerned about on a high Pyrenean hike – fleas that tease, ticks, leeches, mosquitoes, bears – it turns out I don't care about at all. What I care about is still having knees and ankles at the end of it.

Thirty years ago, I thought this walk looked like fun. It still is fun, in a way, but I am thirty years older. I don't think my mountain-walking days are over yet – I still have the stamina and lungs for it, if not the ankles – but I am aware that there will come a day when this will be too much for me. And unsettlingly, that day is looming into view at a rather alarming pace.

I take a breather at a natural cave by the side of the path. It's been fashioned into a rudimentary shelter in case you get caught by the weather, or just fancy a sit down on a stone bench. I'm still an hour from Queralbs, and it feels like someone has taken a baseball bat to my knees, so resting here for a while has its undoubted attractions.

I once read a news story about a man stranded in the Sahara, who survived by eating tiny bats which he caught, cut their heads off with his penknife, and then stirred the insides before drinking a bat-juice cocktail. He sheltered in a cave and did that for nine days, until he was rescued.

I simply don't have that self-preservation gene. If the ankles and knees are shot, I'm just going to have a little lie down in this stone shelter and be eaten by giant slugs.

But, guess what? Exactly three hours and twenty minutes after setting off, I limp into the village of Queralbs. It was never in doubt, old guys rule, etc.

It's a pretty spot, not a cobblestone out of place, where the houses have wrought-iron balconies, ornate window bars, immaculate stonework and climbing roses. Some are four storeys high, others more modest, and all well cared for. There's a Romanesque church at the top of the village, and posters advertising the annual pilgrimage up to Núria.

The man driving the Toyota Turbo 4Runner down the cobbled main street is not really entering into the spirit of things, but then again, maybe he is. Queralbs has well-to-do winter sports written all over it. This is no longer a simple farming village, where the local shepherds might have welcomed the sound of the bell, and the smell from the cauldron, even if they did have to sit under the cross and listen to the crazy old hermit.

But you can see what this place once was, and perhaps still is when the snow falls. Every house is shuttered against the elements, with alleys so narrow you can straddle them with outstretched arms, and buildings set close to guard against the fierce mountain winds.

Right on cue, there's a toot of a train horn as the Cremallera approaches the station.

That's my ride. Time to leave the Pyrenees behind and make a decisive turn south for Barcelona.

CHAPTER 16

BARCELONA

It's lunchtime and I'm at an outdoor table in Praça Reial. There are a few buskers milling about, and a couple of Senegalese guys trying to offload beaded bracelets onto unsuspecting tourists. If you let them put it on your wrist, you're done. It'll cost you five euros, just to stop the aggravation.

A man with a box to sit on and a sketchpad is stationed about five metres from the restaurant tables, looking up now and again before continuing to draw. There are two or three completed sketches at his feet depicting the arcaded square, its ornate lampposts, and regimented palm trees.

He puts in the time, and doesn't make his move for a good ten minutes. Then he gets up, walks over to the couple at the table next to me – a man and a woman, middle-aged, maybe off a cruise – and lays down a drawing. I can see that it's a half-decent sketch of them, sitting at their restaurant table in a pretty Barcelona square.

"For you," he says.

They look at the drawing and at him.

"No, thank you," says the man. They clearly got the talk on the cruise ship. "We don't want it." The woman looks uncomfortable. Tight smile. Just wants to eat her lunch.

"Ah, no," says the artist. "It's a gift. Look, it's you two. I can't give it to anyone else." He grins.

"Really?" says the man.

"Sure, a gift. No worries, why not?"

The couple relax. The woman allows herself another look at the drawing.

"Have lunch, have a nice time," says the artist. "It's a beautiful day."

"Well, thank you," says the man.

"You're welcome." And the artist moves away. Goes across to the opposite side of the square, stands and sketches. Comes back, shifts his box to another spot, sketches some more, chats to the buskers. The couple admire his drawing, and continue with their meal.

And so it begins. Because there's *no way* that's the end of it.

I've been to Barcelona dozens of times over the years, and Praça Reial has always been like this – a bit of a hustle – though it was considerably hairier back in the day.

As a square, it's delightful, an enclosed, arcaded,

Neoclassical space with a central fountain. Just off the Ramblas, not far from the opera house, 'Royal Square' was developed between the 1860s and 1880s for a burgeoning city bourgeoisie. The decorative lampposts were an early project by a young architect called Antoni Gaudí, later to devote his entire life to the building of the Sagrada Família.

But the square is at the bottom end of the Ramblas, right opposite the former red-light district known as the Barri Xinès – the infamous 'Chinese Quarter' that George Orwell and others knew and wrote about.

In the post-war years, Praça Reial acquired a darker reputation as a haunt of drug-dealers, thieves, prostitutes, and beggars. A Barcelona city council history describes it in those times as a "hotspot for riffraff," which makes it sound quainter that it actually was, given the gang fights and turf wars that erupted periodically.

By the 1980s there was a permanent police post in the square – at which point in the story, enter me.

I first came to Barcelona in 1985, travelling on an Interrail pass up from Andalusia and en route to Italy, via the south of France. I didn't do much more than change trains on that occasion, but I had enough time to head into the city and walk down the Ramblas for the first time.

The whispered entreaties got louder and more persistent the closer I got, and by the time I wandered into Praça Reial itself – oh, that looks nice, I thought, a charming square with some restful benches – I had acquired an entourage. They all seemed to think my name was either Charlie or Ash, because that's what they kept on hissing at me. And being very young, and an idiot, it took several attempts at conversation to understand that I was being offered drugs of various strengths and effect.

If I didn't want any drugs – a concept my new friends couldn't get their head around – then they had other offers and services, if I would just step this way into a dark alley, travellers' cheques would be fine, don't mind the sprawled bodies.

Needless to say, I scarpered and resolved never to return to Barcelona, whereupon I got a job with Rough Guides and they sent me straight back there to research their Spain guide. I later wrote the inaugural *Rough Guide to Barcelona*, and then went back pretty much every year for the next twenty years.

As I slowly got to know the city – especially the old town areas, either side of the Ramblas – I learned which streets and squares to avoid. Praça Reial wasn't totally off-limits – there were some authentic bars and edgy music clubs that a fledgling guidebook writer had to at least pretend he'd visited.

Backpackers had been passing through since the 1970s on the hippy trail to Morocco. By the 1990s, especially after the 1992 Barcelona Olympics, the city was looking to tourism as one way to smarten itself up. Praça Reial had the first of several facelifts, which primarily involved the local police enforcing the Basil

Fawlty "No riffraff" byelaw and shipping out all the undesirables.

By now, I'm on to dessert, as is the couple at the next table with their sketched memento of their visit to Barcelona. The latest busker to do the rounds is an accordion player, who opens his coat to reveal his organ (thank you, thank you, I'm here all week) and bashes out some traditional melody – 'Wonderwall' I think.

This is a mark of how things have changed. If he'd walked into the square forty years ago with a valuable accordion, I can tell you now that he wouldn't have been walking out with it.

And here he comes, the itinerant artist, right on cue, a good half an hour after initial contact.

"You like the portrait?" he says to the couple. It's still on the table, but it's been moved around a few times while they looked at it over lunch.

"Yes, thank you, very kind."

"You keep it, you'll always remember Barcelona. Twenty euros, yes?"

The couple look at each other. The slow dawning. The trap revealed. The beaded bracelet firmly on wrist.

"You said it was a gift?"

"Yes, a gift. But my work, my time, you know. It's good, you like it?"

There's a half-hearted attempt to push the sketch back to him, but this man's a pro.

"It's yours. I did it for you. Ten euros, for a beautiful sketch."

Just to be clear, the time for them to have nipped

this in the bud was at the very beginning, when he first laid it on their table. They didn't ask him to draw their picture. So, don't touch it, keep saying that you don't want it, shake your head when he says it's a gift, and turn away and don't engage.

Anything else – the chat, the thanks for the gift, the tacit agreement – and you've just bought yourself a drawing. The only thing to be determined is the price, which was always ten euros.

And here comes the man's wallet, out comes the note – only slightly grudgingly, because the sketch is fine, and ten euros isn't that much if you're on a cruise – and off saunters the artist. Who, let's also be clear, has set up half a dozen other tourists in the square in the same way. Say, fifty euros for an hour's work.

None of this is a scam, a grift, a swindle. The artist could sit in the square sketching all day, but sales would be slow. As it is, the couple have a competent sketch, and a story to tell. It is undeniably a hustle, but that's about as bad as it gets in Praça Reial these days.

The Ramblas itself can be a bit dodgier, if you don't keep your wits about you. It genuinely was once a destination for locals to have a stroll, buy some flowers, call in at the Boqueria market, and sit down for a coffee and a read of the paper.

Nowadays, it's rammed with tourists, human statues, souvenir shops, vape outlets, overpriced pavement cafés, and opportunistic vendors of the type who want to press lucky heather or multicoloured bangles upon you. The stalls at the front of the market are a huge rip-off, and the crowded pavement kiosks and busker pitches a magnet for bag-snatchers.

I finish lunch, which has been at my usual spot whenever I come back to Barcelona. A restaurant called Les Quinze Nits – The Fifteen Nights – which has linen-and-flower-dressed tables on the square and, usually, no need for a reservation. Three courses and wine at lunch costs around twenty-five euros, which is stupidly good value. You get a ringside seat in one of the city's finest squares, and you've had a history lesson, too, which is my gift to you. No, really, yours to keep, no charge.

I have one more night in Barcelona before the next stage of the journey south, on a slow train towards Andalusia. That gives me the rest of the day to do – what?

I've been here too many times to go and see something famous, just for the sake of it. I've visited every church, monument, historic house, museum, gallery and park in the city, more than once. I've even been to all the museums that no one else goes to (the Gallery of Illustrious Catalans comes to mind – not as heart-stoppingly exciting as it sounds).

The Ramblas is not relaxing, I'm not going all the way up to Gaudí's Sagrada Família church just to see if it's finished yet (spoiler, it isn't), and it's too hot for Barceloneta beach, which will be crammed shoulder-to-shoulder anyway.

Instead, I wander slowly through the narrow backstreets on either side of the Ramblas, partly because of the welcome shade and partly to see if there's anything left of the old Barcelona that I remember from my earliest visits.

There's the cathedral, of course, La Seu, which has been here since the thirteenth century, so isn't about to change any time soon. There are still geese waddling around the cloister, as is traditional, for unknown reasons, an idea I'd like very much to see rolled out to other cathedrals. Buzzards in Notre-Dame, condors in St Paul's, that sort of thing, I'll leave the details up to the authorities.

My favourite church is nearby, Sant Felip Neri, tucked away in an enclosed square. Gaudí used to come here every day for some quiet reflection while working up plans for his masterpiece, and it's one of the few churches that didn't have its guts ripped out by the anarchists during the Civil War. It was, however, bombed by the Fascists, and the dents and pockmarks around the entrance are shrapnel damage. That's the kind of historical detail I like, and that the city preserves so well. The stonework could have been restored at any time in the last ninety years, but then you'd lose a little bit of the city's story.

A couple of the old tapas bars nearer the harbour are still going strong, I'm pleased to see. Proper tapas bars – not ones playing the Gipsy Kings, or with a menu of bloody bao buns and satay skewers.

I catch last afternoon orders at Bodega La Plata, which has been here since the 1940s and only serves four dishes – little fried sardines, anchovies or Catalan sausage on toast, and a simple tomato-and-onion salad.

It's a tiny, hole-in-the-wall joint, so you stand outside on the street and sink a glass poured straight from the barrel. As I lean on the wall, a scrap-metal guy rolls slowly past, pushing a shopping trolley full of cast-offs, junk and bits of old iron, and 1980s Barcelona suddenly seems that bit closer.

Other businesses haven't fared so well or lasted the course. Barcelona sees an incredible thirty million visitors a year, up threefold since the turn of this century. Even the grubbiest, most graffiti-ridden streets have tell-tale key-boxes for tourist apartments, which have ripped the heart out of the older neighbourhoods. Regular people can't afford to live here anymore, and the little corner shops and grocery stores have been frozen out by massively hiked rents – these days they are far more likely to be artisan yoghurt emporiums or boutique brioche bakeries.

The city council has finally responded, after years of complaints by locals, and is now refusing to issue new holiday-let licences. 'Restore Barcelona' is the politest graffiti I spot, but 'Tourists not welcome' is more on the nose. There are a few of those messages around, written on sheets and hung from balconies. In one incident that went viral the other year, protestors even shot water pistols at tourists visiting the Sagrada Família.

You can see their point. I pass one bar called Bollocks, while over in the revamped Barri Xinès – the neighbourhood's now known as the Raval – there's a dining establishment called My Fucking Restaurant.

This is what we do, us tourists. We kick out all the old ladies from their longstanding homes, pour in our stags and hens, shout and piss in the streets, demand the cafés serve shakshuka for breakfast, and laugh at the stupid names that stupid people give their stupid tourist businesses.

We don't deserve nice things. What we could have had, just down the street and around the corner from My Fucking Restaurant, was grilled tuna steak with chopped garlic and parsley, a mixed salad, a jug of house red, and an espresso with brandy, at the Romesco. It was the cheapest restaurant in Barcelona, basically a counter, an open kitchen, and a rear dining room, with old-school waiters who gave not a fig and brought the food when it was ready. It was great. But you can't have that because the Romesco is long gone, and most of the other places like it, too.

At least the Romesco shop front is still there, with its offer of 'comidas caseras' (homemade meals), but there's an estate agent's sign hung outside, so it'll doubtless be a designer chewing-gum emporium by the time you read this.

I realise I'm ranting at the dying of the light. Doing that thing that old people do – complaining about the continuous and irreversible progression of existence. Wishing that the Romesco defied the laws of physics so that I could have just one more cheap dinner.

Wishing, in effect, that I wasn't so damn old and where did the time go?

It's not Barcelona's fault that everything's changed. In fact, you could say that it's partly mine.

I worked for a guidebook company, and wrote a successful book about Barcelona, that sold thousands upon thousands of copies. I must be culpable in some way, however much we – as travel writers – justified the popularising of places like Barcelona. A bit rich, me then complaining about how touristy it all is.

Then again, when I first started writing about Barcelona, unless you flew from London with British Airways or Iberia, you could only get here by train or bus, which took two days. It took a particular sort of person to want to come – the sort of person who fancied themselves as an independent traveller, bought a Rough Guide, and liked eating and drinking in the sort of places that you only got in Barcelona. Like the Romesco.

It wasn't me that made Barcelona easy and cheap to get to; it wasn't me that bought up all the apartments; it wasn't me that let the cruise ships, and the sweary stags and hens in; and it wasn't me that jacked up all the shop rents so that the only businesses that can afford to stay in the old town are those selling olive-oil soap and gourmet cupcakes.

I'm not sure I should have come. Maybe I should have just changed trains and moved on? I'm a bit too close to this city by the Med – a bit too over-familiar. It's hard to come and see it for what it is today.

Which is still, I promise, a fabulous city, despite the changes. I urge you to go if you haven't already. It won't be my Barcelona you'll be visiting, but that's the beauty of travel. Even to a thoroughly over-visited destination.

If you're adventurous, and prepared to get off the Ramblas, you'll find your own special corners and hide-away restaurants. Your own favourite bars. Your own secrets and discoveries.

And then one day, many years in the future, you too can moan about how it's all different now, what with the youngsters careering down the Ramblas on their hoverboards, and the robot artist in Praça Reial churning out AI sketches for the airship tourists.

CHAPTER 17

BARCELONA TO VALENCIA

After a couple of days off, I've been looking forward to getting back on a train.

There are still over a thousand kilometres to go to reach Algeciras. I could do it in one long day by taking the high-speed, Málaga-bound train to the junction at Antequera and changing there for the final run south.

But where would be the fun in that?

Instead, I'm going to catch Spain's greatest long-distance service, the Torre Oro. This leaves Barcelona Sants station early each morning – before eight am – and trundles its way south, crossing the country from the Mediterranean coast to the Atlantic. The 'Golden Tower' runs via the coast as far as Valencia, and then turns inland for Córdoba and Seville, finishing up in the southern city of Cádiz anything up to fifteen hours later.

I'm not going all the way, because even though Cádiz is relatively close to Algeciras, it's further west and there's no direct train service between the two. It would mean doubling back on myself by bus to get to Algeciras, and that's against the rules.

I'll need to change trains, and spend the night at Córdoba instead, for the complete run to Algeciras by rail. And I've got at least one other overnight stop in mind, too, in Valencia, which is going to push my journey to the far south to three days.

Slow travel, in anyone's book.

For the Torre Oro is a true hangover from the past. Despite the posh name, it's not a grand train: four carriages and a stand-up buffet, no Wi-Fi, and no phone-chargers at the seats, though there is a space for 'voluminous luggage.' It's laughably billed as an express service, although it leaves most stations a few minutes late and barely ambles along at times.

It's the last of the old, slow, long-distance trains that used to wind across the entire country, most of them replaced by the extensive high-speed network that has transformed travel in Spain over the last thirty years.

These days, you can zip from Barcelona to Madrid, or Madrid to Seville, in under three hours, at speeds of up to three hundred kilometres per hour. But I wouldn't get much of a book out of that. I'd barely be able to see what's flashing past the window.

Instead, I'm going to take this opportunity to meander through Spain on a kind of back-in-time service, because who knows how long the Torre Oro will continue to operate?

We start with a dull chug out through Barcelona's suburbs, and it's almost an hour before we hit the coast at Cambrils. The scenery picks up as the train cuts across the wetlands of the Ebro river delta, with its tilled fields and immaculate allotments. Every farmhouse has a protective ring of shady trees, and at least one soaring palm.

It already feels 'southern,' although we're not south by any means yet. Perhaps it's the sight of orange groves – always a delight to this northerner – and the way the light glints off the ponds and waterways.

I'm interrupted by some early train-manager announcements, always a source of entertainment.

For example, "Please turn down the volume on your phones, which are only to be used between carriages" (i.e., in the carriage entrance).

Has the Spanish train manager on the Spanish train service ever been to Spain? He should have a word with the man across from me watching TikTok videos with the sound up loud, and with every other person currently conducting shouted conversations from their seat.

Also, good luck with, "There is no smoking allowed anywhere on the train." That rule is already being tested to the limit, what with the gaspers out of the doors at every short stop, or the evidence in the train toilets.

Meanwhile, when stopping at stations, we are

advised to "exercise caution when crossing the tracks." Obvious, really, although the added rider – "one train may be hidden behind another train" – is much more specific, indicating some hard-earned experience at the expense of a terribly unfortunate passenger.

Halfway to Valencia now, and idly gazing out of the window, my notes go – oranges, vines, oranges, oranges, vines, oranges, ooh palm tree, vines, vines, oranges.

This is a lush agricultural area, although one that's under threat from an ongoing water shortage. There's been an official drought in parts of Spain since 2021, and the public-service posters at the bus stops in Barcelona make more sense now – "Water doesn't fall from the sky," they say, urging households to restrict their water use.

Even the catastrophic flooding that killed so many in southeastern Spain in 2024 didn't do much to alleviate the drought conditions. A single storm dumped an entire year's worth of rain in under a day, but flash flooding simply rolls over built-up urban and dried-out agricultural land alike, causing devastation.

Traditional crops can't cope with the rising temperatures from climate breakdown, or with the lack of, and then over-supply of, rain. In this new normal, even the famous Catalan vineyards of the Penedès region are looking to move further north and east to higher, more temperate ground.

And now that I've depressed you thoroughly, I draw your attention to the train's brief stop at a town named after the world's worst soft drink, Peníscola.

We eventually close in on Valencia, which has taken a lazy four hours. I can tell we're approaching a city because instead of oranges and vines my notes now go – cement factory, kebab preparation warehouse, salt-cod production unit, crematorium. And this wonderland of attractions is where I'm going to get off and spend the night, because I've promised myself a proper paella in its place of origin.

We pull into Valencia Nord, the original city station, a rather glorious Art Nouveau building, with an eagle-topped clocktower, a long sweep of decorative crenelations, and highly floral ceramics. The old bull ring is right outside, and the equally fancy town hall just a couple of hundred metres away.

This is a fitting station for the old-school Torre Oro train, with a genuine sense of arrival. High-speed trains all use the nearby Joaquín Sorolla station instead, which is fine if you like your stations grey and windowless – more like a DIY home stores depot than an inspiring transport hub.

I drop my bags at my hotel – also grey and windowless, as it happens – and head for the central market, one of the glories of foodie Spain. This is another beautiful Art Nouveau building – the style known here as 'modernista' – a soaring construction of cast iron and multi-coloured tiles, with a vast central cupola.

If you saw it for the first time and thought 'cathedral,' you wouldn't be far wrong. Spain does markets brilliantly, it has to be said, and Valencia's is one of the best, with long aisles of produce under light filtered through church-like stained glass.

I marvel, as always at the fruit and vegetables, so much larger, more vibrant and mis-shaped than anything sold back home. The artichokes look like they've been working out, and you could disable a robber with the asparagus spears. There are tomatoes as big as a baby's head, ten types of mushroom, a dozen varieties of rice, and huge sacks of dried and fresh beans, lentils and peas.

Skinned rabbits, like degloved arms, decorate the butchers' stalls. Snails come in five grades, from the tiny ones on your shed wall to I'm-not-eating-that – seriously, they're the size of Brian in *The Magic Roundabout*.

There are bright red Mediterranean shrimps, octopus from Galicia, twitching crayfish, lobsters and crabs with their claws tied, and some things and bits of things that don't look like seafood at all. Goose barnacles, for example, which resemble dead men's fingers, or pin-cushion sea urchins, sliced open and ready to eat, along with a glass of vermouth from a stand-up bar.

If you want to understand the story of paella, the market in Valencia is as good a place to start as any. Wherever you may have had it in the world, it's a dish whose distant origins are right here – the Moors planted the first rice paddies in Europe in the tenth century, in the wetlands to the south, around the Albufera lagoon.

The first thing to know is that paella is not a bright yellow chicken and shellfish dish, of the type you might be used to. It's a rice dish of the huerta – the cultivated fields of the Valencian wetlands.

The farmers and labourers ate what was to hand, cooking rice over orange-branch and pine-wood fires, and adding things such as rabbit, snails, eels, beans, tomatoes, artichokes, peppers and rosemary. Basically, nothing you couldn't grow or catch in a soggy ditch. That combination is a true Valencian paella, and all those ingredients are still front and centre at the market today.

What you cook it in is more familiar – the flat-bottomed steel pan, with a handle on either side, seen in every restaurant. Fun pub-quiz fact: it's the pan that is actually the paella (or sometimes paellera), with the dish eventually taking its name from the utensil.

Outside the market, under a bright yellow awning, you can buy anything you need, from a pan and a wooden paddle to an outdoor gas ring. A pan big enough for two will set you back around fifteen euros. One to feed the street – a metre or more wide – is still under a hundred, but I'd be carrying it around on my back like a turtle for the next couple of weeks, so I reluctantly let go of the idea.

And now I'm fully up to speed with what to expect, it's time to sample the real deal. I have a table booked at La Pepica, a famous haunt a few kilometres out of town, overlooking the beach. It's been recommended as a place to try authentic Valencian paella, and has been in business since 1898, so I'm going to take that as a good sign.

I get there at opening time, and there's already a queue, reservations notwithstanding. We all sidle slowly through the vast kitchen at the rear, where white-hatted chefs are wrestling with huge pans on a blackened range. One party at a time, we approach a maître d's desk, where the reason for the delay becomes clear. The tourists – for there are many in the queue – are being forewarned, and now it's my turn.

"Reservation for one?" she says.

I nod.

"The paella," I am informed, "is for a minimum of two people."

Luckily, I already know this – it's standard across Spain – but let's hear the spiel.

"You may order it for one person…"

"Oh, really?"

"But you will pay for two portions, do you understand?"

I do, madam. Worry ye not. I did not come all this way not to have a paella. Anyway, having checked the menu in advance, I am reassured that even a double portion costs about the same as a large glass of wine in a Parisian restaurant I could mention. Lead on.

The dining room is typical of these sorts of places – vast and tiled, like the banqueting suite on a second-rate cruise ship, with a gang of waiters exuding an air of supreme professional indifference. They are *very* good at what they do, just as long as you don't expect to be able to catch their eye or engage in menu chit-chat. There's also a wall of photographs of illustrious visitors, none of whom are recognisable to anyone from outside the Valencia region. In short, it's all as it should be, and I expect great things.

The menu doesn't disappoint. There are ten paellas listed and they would all put the wind up a chef in a British tapas bar. Or even Jamie Oliver, who almost caused a riot in Spain when he published a paella recipe with chorizo and frozen peas in it. There's no chance you're going to get that in La Pepica.

There's one with duck and mushrooms, another that's entirely black, made with squid ink, and – there it is – the traditional paella valenciana. This one comes with pieces of chicken on the bone, but also rabbit, large white and fresh green beans, and sprigs of rosemary tucked here, there and everywhere.

You can order a paella with prawns, crayfish or crab – there's a school of opinion that these fisher-style paellas are authentic in their own right – but I'm going old-school, farm labourer. Stick an eel in it and call me José, as the Valencian farmhand said to the milkmaid.

When it arrives, I do a double take, because it's all wrong for any paella I've ever had before, meaning it's exactly right. Rather than Simpsons yellow, the rice is a dark, rich brown – no turmeric in sight – and the entire dish has been cooked in a flat layer against the pan, not piled in a stodgy mound. The meat and green beans stand out on top, and everything has a caramelised, ever-so-slightly burned taste.

What do you want me to say? It's fantastic.

There's crispy rice sticking to the sides and bottom

of the pan, where the paella has caught on the burner. This is not a mistake, it's the good stuff, known as the 'socarrat,' and needs to be prised from the pan with the side of a spoon. Or you can get the waiter to come by with a scraper and do the job for you. But you don't want to leave it. The nutty flavoured scrapings are the soul of the paella. I devour the lot.

Two portions, my eye.

After that, all that remains is to squeeze in an egg-custard flan and head back to my windowless cell. I'll be picking up the Torre Oro again tomorrow, winding across country towards Córdoba on the penultimate leg of my great southern journey.

CHAPTER 18

VALENCIA TO RONDA

There's another long day ahead on the Torre Oro – it's seven hours from Valencia to Córdoba – but I'm getting used to the slow, stop-start nature of this journey.

The train is heading into uncharted territory as far as I'm concerned, given that almost all my time in Spain over the decades has been spent in the north. I'm looking forward to seeing another side of this vast country, as we head further into Castilla-La Mancha – the windmill-filled land of Don Quixote – and on to Andalusia.

And vast and unpopulated much of it is. With Valencia receding in the distance, there's very quickly nothing on the horizon, save a farmhouse every few miles and olive plantations as far as the eye can see.

English gentleman traveller, Richard Ford, passed

through these lands in the 1830s and later published his pioneering *Handbook for Travellers in Spain*. His observations on parts of the Spanish countryside could have been written today: "hedgeless, treeless tracts of cornfield, bounded only by the low horizon; uninhabited, uncultivated plains, abandoned to the wild flower and the bee, and which are rendered still more melancholy by ruined castle, or village."

As the day wears on, there will be plenty of stops at small stations in the middle of nowhere, but they are rarely idyllic, *Railway Children* stations – the sort that feature hanging baskets and kindly old gentlemen. There are a couple that still speak of former times, with their tiled station names and shaded platforms. But others – peeling, graffitied, concrete structures, with broken windows and cracked walls – look like crack-houses on the Lower East Side. Like all the crack-houses I've ever been to, anyway.

Two hours in, and on any other day I might have stopped in Albacete, enticingly billed as Spain's Cutlery Capital. A quick check shows its Cutlery Museum is sadly closed today and tomorrow, and though I'm always game for a mad diversion, even I'm not prepared to spend two nights in Albacete just to see some knives and forks.

An hour later, the landscape has changed again as the train snakes through embankments of red earth, past olive trees and almond orchards. There are expanses of old vines cut right down to the root, and impressive, rolling vineyards around the wine town of Valdepeñas.

Just as we cross the regional border into Andalusia, five hours out of Valencia, the route reveals one more surprise as the train follows the river through the mighty Despeñaperros gorge. This natural north–south pass through the rugged Sierra Morena has been used for thousands of years by migrating tribes, itinerant traders, opportunistic bandits, and invading armies alike, as a way to move between the plains of central Spain and Andalusia.

High-speed trains bypass this traditional route altogether, which alone makes taking the Torre Oro a no-brainer if you have the time.

Laid out in the 1860s, the rail track cuts straight through the gorge, with soaring, almost vertical, rock walls above. We rattle through a series of tunnels and cross latticed-steel bridges, with slower sections and sporadic halts as the train makes its careful way along the deep gorge. Hikers on a platform above wave to us, and then we're off again, eventually leaving the heights behind and chugging ever onwards.

It's been as dramatic as it was unexpected – a short interlude to brighten a long day's journey.

Córdoba, I'm sure, is delightful, despite its apparent lack of a cutlery museum. But it does boast the Mezquita, the former mosque, now cathedral, and one of Spain's most glorious historic monuments. You can't come all the way to Córdoba and not see that.

However, I arrive at close to seven pm, and am out

of here the next morning on the first available train. Algeciras is getting closer, I only have time for one more stop on the way, and Ronda has got the vote. Sorry, Córdoba and its – hello, what's this? – Museum of Alchemy. Never mind, next time.

After a change at the high-speed station of Antequera – an incongruous steel and glass interchange in the middle of huge olive plantations – I'm finally on the train that will take me right to the end of the line at Algeciras.

It's a slow jog, as we leave the vast plains of olives behind and climb, imperceptibly, into rockier heights. There are stone outcrops and yellow gorse by the side of the track, flocks of sheep and goats, and a goatherd glimpsed on the hillside in the distance. An occasional farm, an abandoned station platform or two, and then the train climbs further still, straining at times on the slower stretches.

According to my phone, the temperature has dropped. Not by much, two or three degrees, but enough to confirm we're at a higher altitude and approaching somewhere special – the town of Ronda, over seven hundred metres up in the Sierra de las Nieves. Set on a clifftop plateau, and split by a deep canyon, it's a remarkable place – and a marvel that you can reach it by train.

I am staying the night in the Hotel Extremely Loud and Incredibly Close, which ticks all the boxes: on a road junction with idling traffic and screeching motorbikes (check), above a late-night bar (check), and opposite a church with loud and regular bell-ringing (check). My room also features the special upgrade bonus of overlooking the flashing, fluorescent light of a pharmacy, which bathes the room in an alarming green glow every thirty seconds. Sleep, boomer pop-pickers, will not be so much a matter of "Hello darkness my old friend" as "Blinded by the light."

However, all is forgiven, because the woman who runs it is delightful, and scurries around calling me Mr Julian, and asking if there is anything else she can do. Yes, you can kill the motorcyclists, the pharmacist, and the bar owner, thank you. Oh, you mean more towels, sure that will be fine.

I say woman, singular, although I'm beginning to think there's more than one of them. Elaine always maintains, with no evidence – how was I supposed to know we had a new car? – that I'm not very observant. But I suspect there are two sisters running this gaff, because they keep appearing at random intervals in entirely different parts of the hotel.

They both call me Mr Julian, so that's no help. Unless one of them is out murdering noise polluters, and the other is fetching me towels, I've no idea what's going on. There's potentially even a *third* one – also on point with the Mr Julian business – or else the single woman owner is a shapeshifter, but either way, the service is impeccable. If disorientating.

The train ride in – a gradual ascent – only hinted at Ronda's grandeur. Even on a short walk from the hotel,

I soon see that it's an extraordinary place – or, at least, in an extraordinary location.

The town gardens cling to the edge of a sheer sandstone cliff, from where you look out over the broad and fertile Guadalevín river valley, hundreds of metres below. Balconies and promenades provide magnificent views, and it's easy to see why Ronda has been fought over many times for the strategic advantage it offers. One of the oldest places in Spain, settled by Celts, Romans and Visigoths, it was later a Moorish citadel for six hundred years, and then contested again during the Napoleonic Wars and the Spanish Civil War.

Ernest Hemingway first came here in the 1920s, and always spoke fondly of the town. There's a bust of him in the gardens (the sculptor clearly working from an image of Captain Birdseye), and another of Orson Welles, both aficionados of the bullfight, whose spiritual home Ronda claims to be.

Without the town's notable Romero family, who introduced the use of cape and sword, and other stylistic elements, modern bullfighting perhaps wouldn't have quite the same cultural heft. As it is, the town bullring, the oldest in Spain, gets pride of place right by the clifftop gardens, and there are statues of renowned bullfighters outside the ring – said cape billowing behind them, like they've just emitted the most tremendous of farts.

Over the road, meanwhile, is a restaurant named after Pedro Romero, the most famous Ronda bullfighter of all. Pedro, it is said, fought over five hundred bulls, and killed his last one at the grand old age of seventy-seven – which makes Pedro Romero Spain's greatest torturer and murderer of bulls. No offence.

Oh, sod it, offence.

If ever there was a 'sport' that was a shrine to threatened masculinity, bullfighting is it. Men, terrified that something has got a bigger horn than them. I'm very macho – here, let me just put on my pumps and sequinned waistcoat, and pirouette around an exhausted, spear-stuck bull with my big, manly sword.

I walk through the gardens and onto the Puente Nuevo, the famous symbol of Ronda, which crosses the gorge that divides the town in two. The 'New Bridge' is scarcely new, finished in 1793, but its construction seems jaw-dropping even today. Its towering arches plunge down into the 120-metre-deep canyon known as El Tajo – genuinely gasp-inducing when you lean over for a closer look. During the Civil War, several fascists were reputedly thrown from the bridge, a detail that makes its way into Hemingway's novel, *For Whom the Bell Tolls*.

You can get closer still by descending into the canyon itself, underneath the bridge, and I join a small queue to pay an entry fee.

I'm handed a narrow strip of white, almost lacy, elasticated material, around twenty centimetres long and two centimetres wide.

"You must wear this."

I look at it. That, madam, is a thong. I don't know

what sort of establishment you are running here, I've just come to see the canyon.

"It is for your hair," she says, "Look," and she unfurls it.

This explanation is not the clincher she seems to think it is. I now have what looks like a pair of white, frilly panties, and on the voluminous side. Still, when in Ronda, so I stand there at the kiosk with some pants on my head. Imagine grandma's knickers. Well, I mean don't, obviously, you'll have that image in your head all day.

"And now this," she announces, and it's only at this point that it makes any sense, because next she hands me a hardhat with a chinstrap. Pants under the hat seems to be the watchword at Ronda's gorge, and who am I to argue?

I'm waved through, down the path into the canyon, pants flapping around my ears, with the hat perched on top.

The path clings to the canyon walls and descends to an exposed viewing point directly below the bridge. It's quite something to stand here and look up at the sheer canyon walls and the brickwork that clings to them – to imagine an eighteenth-century architect examining that same chasm, and still thinking they'd be able to build a bridge across it, no problem.

It's possibly no surprise to learn that the current bridge was the second attempt. The first one, earlier in the eighteenth century, fell down, killing scores of people. So, no pressure on the new architect – I look him up later – José Martin de Aldehuela, but he did a grand job.

The older part of town is on the other side of the bridge, and I wander through, with the aid of a map from the tourist office. There's an older bridge to cross, the Puente Viejo, which is far less dramatic, and an even older one known as the Arabic Bridge, though it's probably built on Roman foundations. There are the remains of an Arabic bathhouse, more gardens and views and, right at the foot of town, an enormous, fortified, twin-towered gate.

I've got directions from here to another gorge, hidden away a few kilometres out of town, the Tajo del Abanico. It's the work of half an hour to be fully out in the countryside, on a minor road with olive groves and almond trees in all directions.

The road turns into a track and then a dusty path that picks its way through oak trees as it descends into the gorge, corrugated sandstone bluffs rising high to my left. There are blankets of five-petal flowers on either side of the path, which – thanks to my botanical knowledge, acquired after years of travel – I am able to identify as 'Purple Ones', and a smaller, tight-petalled variety that I believe are 'White Ones.'

Eventually, the path becomes a medieval stone track in a carefully laid herringbone pattern, an amazing sight out here in the middle of nowhere, although a reminder, I suppose, that people used to have to walk everywhere. And this indeed once formed part of an old medieval trading route between Ronda and the surrounding villages.

At the foot of the gorge, I can hear – but not see – water, which isn't entirely comforting. I follow the dry riverbed around a long bend, until I find myself under a vast, curving, overhanging canyon wall, where some adventurous types have hammered in bouldering handholds and pinions for ropes.

A little further on is a huge cave, which supposedly looks like a fan ('abanico' in Spanish, hence the gorge's name), although I don't see it myself. What I do see and hear is that the whole place is entirely silent, empty, and very definitely spooky. You can't tell me there aren't bats and worse inside that cave.

You also wouldn't want to be here in a flash flood. There's plenty of evidence in the canyon bottom – worn plastic, torn fabric, frayed rope, smashed branches – that earlier deluges have torn through.

I don't like to point the finger at Spain, but if this was anywhere else in Europe, there would be skull-and-crossbones signs, and words like 'Danger of Death' posted everywhere. It being a verifiably and obviously unsafe place to be clambering around. You wouldn't be allowed to do this in Helsinki, that's for sure.

Here, though, it's all fine. Sure, step right up to Doom Overhang and never mind the falling rocks.

This is the one place where the frilly pants and helmet combo might have come in useful, but I suppose you can't carry around said items on the off chance you'll need them. I've heard there are nightclubs where pants on your head and a hardhat are de rigueur, but otherwise it's just asking for trouble.

By the time I get back to the hotel in Ronda, footsore, tired out, twenty thousand steps under my belt, it's about all I can do to think about dinner. One of the Mr Julian women – possibly a fourth, by now, though I am somewhat dehydrated – recommends a place up the street, the Bodega San Francisco.

This turns out to be underneath an apartment block and opposite a car park, which – if you know anything about dining in Spain – almost guarantees it's going to be excellent.

The tourists are all sitting in the pretty squares with a view of the old bridge or the historic bull ring, but what they are not doing is having Cantabrian anchovy on toast, and grilled ribeye with Padrón peppers. That would be me.

The toast, drizzled with olive oil, is smeared with sweet jam, with the fat, salted anchovy layered on top. It sounds like one of the appalling dishes from Mike Leigh's film, *Life is Sweet*, where Timothy Spall's chef character is opening a restaurant serving liver in lager, quails in treacle, and pork cyst. But that surprising, counter-intuitive anchovy dish alone is worth the trip to Ronda.

Let the motorcyclists, the church bells, and the flashing pharmacy light do their worst. For tonight I dine, and tomorrow I reach the end of the line.

CHAPTER 19

RONDA TO ALGECIRAS AND TARIFA

The last leg, south from Ronda, feels special.

After thousands of kilometres on trains, I have only a hundred to go until I reach Europe's southernmost railway station. It's still not the culmination of the trip – not until I've gone as far west as I can – but this last, short, southern section marks the end of an epic, cross-continental ride.

What a journey it's been, from the fjords and lakes of northern Europe to the Pyrenean peaks and dry plains of Spain. I've seen every kind of scenery from the train window, but there's one more surprise to come, because the slow line from Ronda to Algeciras provides another unexpectedly glorious ride.

You get little impression of the height of Ronda on arrival from the north, because of the gentle climb up. But leaving is different – the train sweeps away from the station along the ridge, and then careers down the valley, with huge views away to the surrounding mountains.

There's a foot-off-the-brake feel as the train barrels downhill. I picture the driver, feet up on the dashboard, saying "Let's see what this baby can do." Either that, or Keanu Reeves is at the controls, trying to keep it above fifty.

Whoever's in charge does slow right down to take a big curve, otherwise the good folk of – examines map – Arriate would be waking up to the otherwise inexplicable news of a train in their municipal swimming pool.

After the station of Benaoján, it's a gorgeous ride down a narrow valley, following the Rio Guadiaro just above the swirling green water, with tree-covered hills to either side. There's almost a Lost World feel to the scenery – bulrushes in the water, stunted palms on the banks, and deep-red earth. Keanu goes back to ambling at mule-train pace, as the valley widens out and becomes more pastoral.

There's a pretty, mustard-yellow-and-white painted station at Cortes de la Frontera, and then another valley section to Gaucín, where we're close to the river again. The train cuts through short tunnels, one after another, to suddenly appear above a dramatic, carved gorge (where higher water, thousands of years ago, rounded out the rock). Galleried sections flash kaleidoscopic images of the sheer walls, with the river below appearing as a glimpse of jumbled rocks and splashes of water amid the trees.

We pass by Jimena de la Frontera, another so-called 'frontier' settlement, which is puzzling if you only look at a contemporary map. These days, the nearest frontera, the Portuguese border, is three hundred and fifty kilometres away, but they have long memories in these parts. All Andalusian towns with the suffix 'de la Frontera' – and there are many of them – date from the medieval period, when Christian forces were slowly taking the Iberian peninsula back from the Moors.

In the eighth century, Muslim forces had made it as far as the Pyrenees, as I saw earlier in Núria. By the thirteenth century, the frontier zone was in present-day Andalusia, and towns were named accordingly; and when the last surviving, Moorish kingdom of Granada finally fell, in 1492, the reconquest was complete. However, the Moorish names have endured – as in Andalusia itself, from 'al-Andalus,' the name given to the historic, Muslim-ruled territory.

Entertainment *and* history. This is all gold, I tell you.

The hundred kilometres from Ronda should have taken a couple of hours, but it's been closer to three, factoring in some random stops and delays. That's about thirty-five kilometres per hour, which – given the scenery – is not a complaint. Indeed, information signs and trackside building material suggest they are modernising the line, but speeding up this journey will hardly be an improvement.

Finally, we roll through the outskirts of Algeciras and come to rest in the station.

I've made it.

S for Shredded and for South – mainland Europe's southernmost railway station.

I'll admit, it doesn't look like much, inside or out. There's a vague Moorish thing going on, with its low, white, blocky design and arched entranceways, and I take a few pictures, but this is not the grand arrival or departure point I might have been hoping for. Still, I've travelled a long way for this, so I stick around for a few more minutes.

Playing around with the compass on my phone, I discover that the southernmost points *inside* the southernmost train station in Europe are as follows: platform four (extra points if you disembark the train on this platform), the station toilets and, finally, drum roll, the Hertz parking lot, which is still within the station confines. That's as far south as you can go in the southernmost train station in Europe.

I can do no more. The subject is exhausted. It's time to go and have a look at Algeciras itself.

It sits on the west side of a wide bay, with Gibraltar right opposite, and I'm predisposed to like it – partly because I've travelled a stupidly long way to get here, and partly because I like ports. This one has daily ferries to Tangier in Morocco, and to the Spanish-North African enclave of Ceuta, which are romantic destinations, at least on paper.

But, my word, Algeciras is hard to like.

The lower town, especially around the port and in the back streets behind the market, has an edgy feel. I pass loitering groups of men smoking outside cafés, kebab shops with a Leeds-night-out-at-three-in-the-morning feel, and cheap hotels with names like Hotel Kidney Exchange and the Pension Assault and Battery.

There's the occasional grander building from a nineteenth-century shipping heyday, and a central avenue running down to the port that's been given an urban makeover, with benches, flower beds and sculptures. But the harbour views are of cranes, container stacks and distant tankers, and it all seems a bit grim. You can get a kebab for under a fiver, and a tagine for a tenner in any number of small cafés, but unless you're catching the night ferry to Morocco, that's hardly a reason to come.

Pushing on, I eventually discover that Algeciras is a town of two halves. Climbing up from the port, I emerge in the upper town – literally, a breath of fresh air, high above the harbour, with unimpeded views across to the Rock of Gibraltar.

The shops have changed from selling vapes to displaying fancy pastries, and there's a handsome square, Plaza Alta, with Moorish tiling, orange trees and palms. It's ringed by rather more salubrious cafés than down below.

A long street leads past the remains of the old city walls and to the municipal gardens, where more cafés spill out over the pavement. These are packed, with a loud chatter that is the Spanish nation at play – little kids turning cartwheels while their parents have a cheeky wine, teens entwined on benches, strolling gents in blazers, and women in heels with fans.

It's better, but is it enough?

Would I have come here, if it wasn't for the southernmost train station in Europe? Well, no, obviously not, but I did rather paint myself into a corner with this book concept.

I wouldn't even come here to catch the Morocco ferry, seeing as Tarifa, half an hour down the road, has quicker services that dock more centrally in Tangier itself.

Now I am here, however, I have a choice to make about my onward travel.

My next – and final – target is the west of Portugal, which you can get to by train from Algeciras, but there's a catch.

If you check a rail map of Spain, you'll see that there's no link to the west from Algeciras. There are no railways, in fact, until you get to Cádiz or Seville, and even then, the line west from there, towards Portugal, terminates at Huelva, which is sixty kilometres from the border. I could retrace my steps north from Algeciras all the way to Ronda and Córdoba, and then take the train to Seville and Huelva, but I'd still be left with a bus ride to fill in the missing link.

If I'm deadly serious about completing the entire journey by rail, I'd have to take the high-speed train four hundred kilometres north of Córdoba to Madrid, and then change onto slower trains for the only east-west, Spain-Portugal crossing, via Badajoz.

This route would take several days from here – probably four – because it's notoriously slow and inconvenient, which is how Spain and Portugal must like it, because they're certainly in no hurry to fix the train connections between their adjacent countries.

If you want to know why, you only have to watch a Spanish TV news report about something in Portugal, or vice versa. Their languages are different, but not so different that they can't understand each other, yet they gaily subtitle every speaking Portuguese or Spanish person, just to be arsey.

I digress, but the gist of my dilemma is that I can travel all the way to the westernmost station in Europe by train from here, but I'd have to go absolutely miles out of my way, at great expense and inconvenience.

Or I could simply get the bus from Algeciras down the coast to Tarifa, and then another bus up the coast to Cádiz, where there's a train station with regular services to Seville. And, if you've been paying attention, you'll know that there's one final bus from the end of the Spanish line at Huelva to get me to the Portuguese border, and the rather more sensible Portuguese train network.

Stick with the plan? Or break the rules and take three buses?

Look, I might be daft, but I'm not that daft. Apologies to all who believed in me.

The bus it is, which turns out to be an enjoyable ride through low, green hills. We eventually crest the brow for a view of the distant sea and then descend into Tarifa. This is immediately more enticing than Algeciras, with a walled old town defended by a harbourside castle, and long, white-sand beaches stretching away to the north.

If Tarifa is known for anything, it's as a windsurf and kitesurf centre on the breeziest bit of the Costa da Luz. I spot sails in the air and on the beach almost the minute I arrive. The measure of the surf dudes who descend here can be taken from the graffiti down on the sea wall, which reads, 'A friend in need is a friend indeed, but a friend in weed is better.'

However, I'm interested in Tarifa's location for another reason, because – as far down Spain as you can possibly go – this is the southernmost town in continental Europe. This, for me, is a geographical BOGOF, or two-fer: the southernmost train station, followed by the southernmost town. How could I not come?

It's the closest European town to the North African coast, just fifteen kilometres away across the Strait of Gibraltar, at its narrowest point. Those hills I can see are Morocco, and the ferries are making a dash for Tangier; while the North African cities of Algiers and Tunis, a couple of thousand kilometres away to the east, actually lie further north than Tarifa.

This proximity, of course, put the town right in the firing line during the centuries of Muslim conquest and withdrawal, hence the impressive castle. Tarifa changed hands several times, and endured many sieges, the most famous associated with the defence of the town in the 1290s by its governor,

Alonso Pérez de Guzmán. It's a curious tale, to say the least.

The besieging Moors, in cahoots with a rebellious Castilian prince, captured Guzmán's son and paraded him in front of the castle, threatening to kill him unless the town surrendered.

Guzmán was having none of it. According to legend, not only did he tell the Moors to feck off, he threw down his own knife from the castle ramparts and told them to use it to kill his son. That'll show them, he thought. That's how hard *I am*.

Even worse, this noble, selfless sacrifice – "Dad, hang on, what are you doing? Why are you giving them your – uugh" – played out rather well for Guzmán. He got promoted, given lots of land, and is remembered – non ironically, it seems – as Guzmán el Bueno, Guzmán the Good. And not Guzmán el Bastardo Loco, for example.

From the castle ramparts, there's a good view across the harbour to a slender causeway leading to an offshore islet. This is my ultimate destination, for if there's a southernmost point inside Europe's southernmost railway station (Hertz parking lot, remember?), the same is true of continental Europe's southernmost town.

On the far side of that islet, around fifteen hundred metres away from me now, the Punta de Tarifa is the furthest south you can go in continental Europe. The southernmost point of the entire European landmass.

I stroll out along the causeway, looking away to my

right at the sweeping beach and the swooping, coloured sails of the kitesurfers. The blue waters sparkle – Atlantic one side of the Strait of Gibraltar, Mediterranean the other. It's a beautiful day, and a fitting setting for a walk to a continental extremity.

I felt the same sense of appreciation and achievement, decades earlier, when I made the similar walk out to mainland Europe's northernmost point, Nordkapp, in northern Norway. Beyond there, nothing but ice, Arctic islands, and the North Pole; here, next stop, Africa.

Where the causeway meets the islet, a ring of fortified walls stretches away to either side, blending into craggy rocks above crashing waves. This, too, has long been considered a defensive position, with troops from the Phoenicians onwards stationed here to protect the approach to the mainland.

I get closer. There's a high iron gate between dressed stone columns, and old garrison buildings visible beyond. Behind the gate is an island of around five hundred by five hundred metres, with a lighthouse at the very southern tip, where Europe ends.

If you've followed my travels over the years, you know what comes next. Sure as night follows day.

I think these trips up, set off, and see what happens. Things don't always go according to plan – and that's even when I have a plan. This trip to Tarifa was more a whim wrapped in a fancy, but it did all seem to be working out.

Until this point, when I discover that the gate to the island is padlocked shut.

It seems that the southernmost point in continental, mainland Europe is closed.

Of course it is.

Feel free to join me in laughter. I think mine is probably more hollow than yours.

Who knew that a geographical location could be closed? Every day's a school day.

That's it, then, for the extreme south. From now on, like the Village People, I shall make my plans, work and strive, start life anew, and Go West.

WEST
ALGECIRAS TO SINTRA AND PRAIA DAS MAÇAS

∼

Cádiz-Jerez de la Frontera-Seville-Huelva-Vila Real de
Santo António-Tavira-Sintra-Praia das Maçãs

CHAPTER 20

TARIFA TO CÁDIZ

It's ninety minutes by bus from Tarifa to Cádiz, where I'll pick up the train route again, and as bus rides go it's not bad at all. We steer a leisurely course through coastal lowlands, which fracture further into a tidal estuary of streams, marshes and lagoons the closer we get to the city.

This scrub-like expanse is the Bay of Cádiz Natural Park, once the heart of a major salt-production industry, with abandoned salt pans and tumbledown buildings still much in evidence. Where "water, sun, wind and man gallop at the same rhythm," according to the rather overblown website. There's not much galloping going on today, but there are circling storks settling in large nests on old stone towers.

It all makes for a highly scenic approach to Cádiz,

which then becomes ever more dramatic as we run along a narrow, four-kilometre causeway, with golden sands on the seaward side as far as the eye can see.

Cádiz itself – once an island – lies on a long spit of land, with the old town occupying a bulbous nub at the far end, ringed by huge defensive walls. The bus swoops through a battlemented gateway, swings around the port, and deposits me at the back of the impressive train station. Cádiz certainly knows how to make an entrance, and I immediately like the look of the place.

Even on the short walk into the centre, with the town hall tower and dome of the cathedral visible ahead, it's clear that this is a city with some history behind it. There's a long, unbroken record of settlement, dating back three thousand years to the arrival of the Phoenicians, making Cádiz one of the oldest cities in western Europe.

It was an important Roman naval and trading base, and then changed hands – as usual around here – between Moorish and Christian forces for centuries. Columbus sailed from Cádiz on two of his voyages; the city was fortified against constant British attacks, including by Sir Walter Raleigh; Napoleon's fleet set sail from here before the Battle of Trafalgar; and it later played a significant role in the reestablishment of the Spanish monarchy.

In short, Cádiz has rizz, an historical ton of it, and I decide to stick around for a while.

Unfortunately, so have a bunch of other people, currently pouring off the cruise ship that's parked in the harbour, at the foot of a long, wide, seafront plaza. I've only said 'parked' to see if my cruise-loving friend, Steve, has read this far, because that's bound to annoy him. But frankly, Steve has got a lot to answer for.

Despite its storied history, Cádiz used to be something of a tourist backwater – on the wrong, western, side of Andalusia for most visitors, and a long way from anywhere. But then cruise ships started docking – see, I do know – in the deep-water port adjacent to the old town, and things began to change.

As the only major cruise terminal between Lisbon and Gibraltar, it's a popular stopover, not least because visitors can walk right off the ship into town. More than three hundred ships a year call in – almost one a day – disgorging thousands of people at a time. The out-sized scale is blindingly obvious: there's a ship in today and it towers ten storeys high, well above the palm trees, blocking all views of the port behind it.

Accordingly, the locals have a point – just as they do in Barcelona and Valencia – when they complain about being inundated by day-trippers, losing their traditional shops, and being unable to afford the rent.

Steve has been to Cádiz at least twice on his round-the-Med jaunts, so you might say that this is all Steve's fault. Indeed, if you find yourself priced out of the local housing market, or stuck behind a crocodile of cruise-ship tourists in the old town, I shall be providing his address later – feel free to send your concerns to him directly.

The trick is not to go where the tour groups are

going, which seems to be straight to the cathedral. Instead, I walk further up the harbourside and follow the line of the city walls, which turns out to be an excellent idea – a nice, breezy circuit around town, with the aquamarine sea a constant presence to my right.

At times, I'm high up on the whitewashed ramparts, with ancient cannons on trundles pointing through gaps in the walls, out into the bay. By the seafront gardens, shaded by huge, multi-ribbed plane trees, shirtless men on the promenades are uniformly failing to catch fish.

A couple of castles defend the western reaches, one dangling on an islet reached by a slender causeway. There's a sandy town beach, La Caleta, and big views south to more beaches – the ones I passed on the bus on the way in. It's easy to see why the cruise tourists like the city so much.

You lose the views and the sense of space the minute you set foot inside the tight grid of old-town streets. They form high, narrow canyons, lined with bars and shops, opening out now and again to reveal tucked-away squares ringed by palm trees.

Wikipedia claims this is one of the most densely populated urban areas in Europe, and while I don't know about that – Naples, for one, seems far more intensely crowded – I do find it hard to get my bearings. I circle around on myself a couple of times, before realising it scarcely matters. If I walk in a straight line I'll hit the sea again eventually, since the old-town area is not much more than a kilometre across in any direction.

Somewhere in the distance, a block or two away, there's a rumble of noise that rises to a terrible racket the closer I get. Outside what appears to be a local government building, a fair-sized crowd of people has gathered, with a couple of police cars in attendance.

I shouldn't jump to conclusions. In Spain, two hundred people shouting their heads off, with cop cars stationed nearby, could all just be waiting for lunch. This lot, though, are holding banners and placards, and producing an absolute cacophony courtesy of air horns, cow bells, whistles, and chanting. It's obviously a very serious matter – the local restaurant must have changed its menu without notice, or something.

Half the people in the crowd are wearing blue smocks, and there are a few, rather bemused, dogs in the mix. I chuck some of the words on the banners into Google translate, and it turns out that these are protesting vets. Not ex-forces, but actual veterinarians.

It's either the Popular Veterinarian Front, or the People's Front of Veterinarians, it's not quite clear, but they are furious about something. (When I look it up later, I discover that the protests – not just in Cádiz – are about a new national law that limits veterinary use of antibiotics.) This manifests itself in traditional, demo-style chanting, mixed in with more of a hen-party vibe – mass selfies, Mexican waves, and photo-bombing the roving local TV reporter.

After about ten minutes of nonstop bedlam, the

lead rabble-rouser vet – not a phrase I ever thought I'd use – uses her megaphone to announce, "Right, now I want you all to make some real noise". And I'm just wondering what she thinks has been going on for the last ten minutes, when all sonic hell breaks loose, someone lets off an air horn next to my head, and I almost pass out. The police officers raise an eyebrow but otherwise stand firm as every noise abatement law – surely, even in Spain – is wilfully broken.

I leave them to it. Fair play, who knew vets had it in them? But I can't help feeling that if the Veterinary Popular Front of Cádiz want to effect real change, they need to take a leaf out of the French farmers' handbook. French farmers get shit done. The air horns, placards and chants are all fine, but there's nothing like dumping tractor loads of manure on local government buildings to make your point. And you can't tell me that vets don't know where to lay their hands on grade A animal poop?

There's still a queue outside the cathedral, and guides with little flags trying to corral cruise passengers who think this is Lisbon. I skip down a side street instead, through an arch cut into an ancient stone wall, looking for the remains of the Roman theatre.

As the author of a magisterial, handwritten, two-volume *History of the Roman Empire* ('A+, this is an excellent piece of work, Julian'), carefully illustrated in felt-tip pen, I take a keen interest in all things Roman.

Obviously, the research opportunities available to a ten-year-old in the 1970s were rather limited – I note the bibliography of my masterwork cites as a source, *We Go to Rome: A Look and Learn Comic* – but I like to think I've kept up with developments. Cádiz, the internet tells me, has a Roman theatre, and this A+ student would very much like to see it.

Built near the water in 70 BCE, to hold up to ten thousand spectators – making it both the oldest, and second largest, Roman theatre in Spain – you'd think it would be easy to spot. The big, semi-circular, stone thing with tiered seats; follow the snarls of the lions and the screams of the condemned.

However, it fell into disuse by the end of the third century CE, and was then plundered for stone, repurposed, and built over. Hidden under the surrounding neighbourhood, it only resurfaced in 1980 during building works, but it now has a visitor centre attached to a large section of the exposed seating.

I walk up the street and down the street. I catch glimpses of tiered seating through iron gates across dead-end alleys. I follow occasional signs that promise an entrance that never materialises. I tell you, *We Go to Rome: A Look and Learn Comic* was considerably more reliable than this.

Eventually, I realise that I have already walked past the entrance at least three times. The unobtrusive doorway is on the ground floor of an old townhouse, while the sign is of fashionably distressed metal, with lettering styled like that of a hipster bar. If the Teatro Romano de Cádiz would like a top tip, here it is – know your audience. For ancient Roman stuff, it's old gits like me. Not someone looking for a charred-chilli Aperol spritz in a backstreet speakeasy.

For all that, it's very well done inside. It's not the most dramatic of theatres by any means, given that it was buried and disguised for centuries, but there's no one else here and I have the exhibition and theatre to myself. Also, everything is translated into English, which is a great relief, because despite my long interest in the Romans, my Latin is not what you'd call *bonum*.

Long ago, at Oxford, I had to struggle through a term of Latin translation to be able to continue my studies, and it was completely baffling. Not because you needed to know the ancient language of Latin to study – checks notes – modern history. That was just Oxford being Oxford. Baffling because of my previous education at a state school, where Latin was not an option, but woodwork and metalwork were. Or *opus ligneum* and *opus metallicum*, as both Plinys, Younger and Elder, would have it.

Our tutor persevered with us for eight painful weeks. "And soon they climbed the table that overlooks the city," one of us would tentatively proclaim, faced with that week's 'gobbet' of translation from Virgil or one of the other Osmond brothers.

"That's certainly one interpretation," he would say, not unkindly, "but is it perhaps 'hill rather than 'table'? I rather think it is, don't you agree, gentlemen?" And then we would move on to the next impenetrable section of text, accompanied by the gentle whimpering of an Oxford history don who had never encountered anything like it in his life.

All this is by way of saying that, when confronted with a Latin inscription, I feel I should know what it says, but tend to get stuck after the numerals. And I'm not too hot on those, if I'm honest, especially once we get to the thousands. I'd have been all right in ancient Rome buying two, six or nineteen of anything, but don't send me out to negotiate a house sale.

Luckily, other than 'Theatrum,' which I think I can manage, there are no inscriptions to translate. Instead, I sit outside for a while in silent splendour, next to rows of seating that had Roman bums on them two thousand years ago.

Its inhabitants knew the city as Gades, and they were *gaditanos* – known throughout the empire as prominent traders of salt, spices, cereals, wine, and olive oil. Their waterside theatre matched their ambition: built by the Balbus family, friends of Julius Caesar, no less, it's a mighty 118 metres across, with a vaulted gallery underneath the seating that was wide enough for the city's upper classes to arrive on horseback.

Four-storey houses tower over half the theatre even today; the stage, and portico behind it, lie buried still. Other parts of the theatre complex were used as storerooms and stables in medieval times, or incorporated into the city's defensive walls.

Like anywhere historic in Europe, if you dig down far enough, you'll find remnants of other peoples' lives. Here, in the remains of the theatre by the sea, there are just echoes from the submerged stage. A final curtain call. Noises off.

I make my way back across town for lunch, with one eye on the city's speciality, deep-fried fish. Or 'varied fishes frying,' as I saw on one menu. Every tapas bar and restaurant do the honours – a platter filled with floured and fried sardines, anchovies, whitebait, squid, baby hake and sole, and shrimp fritters the size of a saucer.

The only consideration is where to have it, and I think I'm going to steer clear of the places around the cathedral, in favour of a pretty, traffic-free street I spotted earlier, Calle Virgen de la Palma. There were tables out in the street, and shade from awnings and palm trees. Perfect.

And it is, too, or at least as close as I'm going to get. I suspect divine intervention, because the church at the end of the street is dedicated to the eponymous Virgin, who saved Cádiz from disaster.

On 1 November, 1755, an enormous earthquake and subsequent tsunami destroyed Lisbon and caused devastation along the Portuguese and Spanish coasts. In Cádiz, the waters rose to two and a half metres high – a plaque on the street shows the line – but began to subside when the local churchmen paraded the crucifix and banner of the Virgen de la Palma. While other coastal towns were washed away, Cádiz survived, with limited casualties.

So that's a big thank-you to Our Lady, and to the *gaditanos* and their fondness for fried fish. After Tarifa, I needed a win, and I think we can all agree that a crispy shrimp omelette and an ice-cold glass of rosé in a charming street is not a shabby way to celebrate a fine city.

No one tell Steve where it is, though, all right? It's the tourist traps for him, until he mends his ways.

CHAPTER 21

CÁDIZ TO JEREZ DE LA FRONTERA

The train from Cádiz, north to Seville, first has to travel the long way around the bay, south along the causeway to the mainland and then up through the salt pans and marshlands.

If I'd stayed on the Torre Oro train all the way from Barcelona, this would have been my final approach to the end of the line in Cádiz – coasting in late in the evening, with grass-tufted dunes and long, sand beaches framing the view of the Atlantic beyond.

I've already travelled part of this route by bus, but I'm happy that I get to see it from the train, too. I don't mind this bit of backtracking if it means squaring the circle, filling in the gaps.

My destination today is the town of Jerez de la Frontera, a mere forty-five minutes away. There's that 'frontier' name again, and of all the places in Andalusia tagged 'de la Frontera,' it's Jerez that's the best-known.

That there's something notable about the town is obvious from my very arrival. After the disappointment of Algeciras, *this* is what a railway station should look like.

The main platform has acres of blue-and-white and polychrome tiling – heraldic shields, dragon tails, nymphs with harps, gods and cherubs, grapes and flowers. It continues in the waiting room and ticket office, which has an upper gallery with sculpted reliefs that run right around the hall. The exterior, meanwhile, trumps the lot, with its curlicued, wrought-iron window grilles and Juliet balconies, and no fewer than seventeen brick arches with more inlaid pictorial tiling.

This is Islamic-inspired, Mudejar styling at its finest, applied to the train station in a small provincial town. The company that built it in the 1850s has left their name in the tiling, and I think they should get a shout-out, so hats off, Constructores Fierro, S.A., that really is a beauty.

Incidentally, if you turn to your left on leaving the station, the blank, brown box with slit windows, and every ounce of despair etched into its construction, is the adjacent bus station. The bus station, I might add, has two clock faces showing different times, both wrong. The central clock tower at the train station is accurate to the second. Just saying.

And why does Jerez have a fantasy railway station that is far bigger than a town of its size warrants?

The clue is in the name, and in the short walk from station to town centre, where I pass winery after winery, for Jerez is sherry, and sherry is Jerez.

The Phoenicians called the town Xera, the Moors Sherish, and wine has been made here for three thousand years. Strong wine that would keep, and that could be exported over long distances – traded to England in medieval times, in return for wool. Wine that was brought back after the sack of Cádiz in Elizabethan times, mentioned in Shakespeare's plays, sent to the Americas, and served at presidential and royal tables. Wine that is Spain's greatest and longest enduring export; that requires an entire industry behind it, including a massive, beautifully designed train station.

My experience of sherry until now is probably similar to that of most British people. You have a bottle in for your granny at Christmas, or you're given a glass if you're invited to the vicar's house, or accidentally find yourself in a 1970s TV sitcom. That said, it's fashionable these days, I believe, in the sort of bars that only have a buzzer to identify them, where it's probably mixed with, I don't know, ginseng, or popcorn, or grass cuttings.

My only serious encounter with the drink came in my third year at college, when the long-suffering history tutor – the hero of the Latin anecdote – gave a few of us half a dozen bottles from the college cellar and asked us to organise a drinks reception for the new undergraduates.

I know, what did he think was going to happen?

Suffice it to say that, despite the evidence of six empty bottles, the freshers didn't get their drinks reception and the college never repeated the experiment. And I never drank sherry again, until now.

If ever there is a place to discover its true appeal, surely Jerez is it?

That's because sherry can only be produced in what's known as the 'Sherry Triangle,' which is like the Bermuda Triangle except with schooners and not ships.

Schooners, I said. Like the boat *and* the sherry receptacle. Do try and keep up.

This is the region north of Cádiz, bounded by the towns of Jerez, Sanlúcar de Barrameda to the northwest, and El Puerto de Santa María to the southwest. If it's not made from grapes grown in vineyards and matured in wineries within that region, it's not sherry. They have very strict rules about it, just like the French with champagne, and the British with pork pies.

If you're going to make sherry, you also have to do it in a bodega, which is what they call both the companies and the warehouses where the wines are stored and matured. There are about ninety of them in the Triangle – forty-odd in Jerez alone – and you'll doubtless know some of the bodega names and sherry brands from your nan's drinks cabinet: Gonzalez Byass, Osborne, Croft Original, Tio Pepe, Harvey's Bristol Cream.

Note, by the way, the preponderance of English names. The historic export market was such that British businessmen muscled in early. The nineteenth-century traveller in Spain, Richard Ford, had a particularly xenophobic view of things. The various sherries, he proclaimed, "owe their excellence to foreign, not to native skill [...]; nothing can be more rude, antique, and unscientific, than the wine-making in those localities where no stranger has ever settled."

Whatever their provenance, it's unusual to find so many companies in such a confined area – the small town of Jerez seemingly has a bodega on every corner, each offering tours and tastings. They all make sherry in largely the same way, from the same grapes, but some bodegas are very fancy indeed. The 'Tio Pepe Experience,' for example, at Gonzalez Byass, runs you around vine-shaded streets and gardens on a little train, and offers a stylish restaurant and boutique hotel on site.

I'd like to say that I chose my sherry tour after a rigorous selection process, but I'm here on a Monday, which is closing day for almost all of them. Thus, Gonzalez Byass is a non-starter, although if I'm honest I was only interested because of the little train. Instead, I book onto the eleven am tour of the Bodegas Diez-Merito, which I've never heard of, but is very easy to find, as it's on the road into town from the station.

It's a lovely eighteenth-century building in, what's now, a slightly odd location – a vaulted winery with gated gardens, slotted in between modern apartment buildings and shops. But the bodegas were here before

Jerez expanded and developed. They were all family affairs at one time, though most of the brands you've heard of are now part of multinational conglomerates. Diez-Merito, though, is still owned and run by a Jerez family, which bodes well.

There are only six of us on the tour, and we're led into an arcaded courtyard, with the vaulted cellars stretching off to either side.

It's immediately cooler in here, a steady temperature, and it needs to be if the wine is going to mature properly, as it can easily reach forty degrees Celsius outside in summer. Yellow, compacted, sandy earth underfoot – the same stuff that's used in bullrings – kicks up a slight dust. It's watered in summer to retain the humidity, and we leave footprints as we go. At night, they open the windows to allow in the cooling breeze.

Our guide, Maria, is on top of her brief, and for the next hour we learn in great detail about the sherry producing business, whether – frankly – we want to or not. Maria has facts, and we're going to hear them.

For example, there are 4,500 barrels in this cathedral-like bodega, each containing between 425 and 500 litres, but they don't measure it in litres. They use an old Spanish unit called an *arroba*, which is 16.67 litres, and they measure the amount of wine in each barrel by shoving a wooden stick inside and counting off the *arrobas*.

The black-painted barrels themselves are made of

American oak and last up to a hundred years. They are stacked three high in aisles under a vaulted ceiling, and the wine in them is mixed from top to bottom to achieve the correct blend for each type of sherry. The wood of the barrel is the magic ingredient, soaking up the wine for decade after decade, imparting depth and flavour. The barrels are so valuable to the process that they are repaired and re-filled, and then put back in exactly the same place.

Maria even has a barrel with a cutaway side that we can peer into. This is so she can demonstrate how the different wines mature – for there is no such thing, of course, as one single drink called 'sherry.'

Three grape varieties are employed – Palomino, Pedro Ximénez and Moscatel – and depending on what you do to the wine in the barrel, and how long you leave it in there, you end up with drinks of differing age, colour and sweetness.

A naturally occurring yeast layer – and time – produces drier, lighter Finos, Manzanillas, and Amontillados; grapes higher in alcohol kill the yeast layer and develop darker, sweeter wines, such as Olorosos; while naturally sweet grapes, like Pedro Ximénez, produce stronger, highly concentrated wines. The semi-sweet Creams – the ones traditionally popular in the UK – are a blend of Oloroso and Pedro Ximénez wines.

The fascination for me, in the end, is not in the barrage of facts, figures and processes, though Maria is doing her best. It's how low-tech it all is.

The Diez-Merito building dates back to 1760,

making it one of the oldest in town. The caverns filled with barrels haven't changed their appearance for centuries – and all those barrels are older than I am. A man with an actual wooden dipstick measures the amount in each one, also employing the most advanced piece of tech we see on the whole tour – a stepladder. Maria doesn't have a fancy video presentation or state-of-the-art visitor centre – she has a see-through barrel, and a thousand facts.

It's all rather glorious, and reassuring to know that when the end-times come, and the lights go out, we will still be able to have a glass of sherry of an evening, before closing the gates against the frenzied hordes.

"And now," says Maria, "for the tasting."

Hello. Everyone perks up a bit.

There are five sherries to try at a pop-up bar in a corner of one of the vaulted rooms, starting with the palest and driest, and ending with the sweetest. That's going to be Fino, Amontillado, Oloroso, Cream, and Pedro Ximénez, in that order.

In my defence (and I am aware that paragraphs beginning "In my defence" rarely end well), the tasting begins at a minute or two after twelve noon, which in Spain is a long way from breakfast and a similarly lengthy time before lunch. Maria is not a shy pour and she's at pains to say there's no hurry. It's cool in here, it's hot outside, and the bar is open.

By sherry number three, even the more reserved Brits on the tour are throwing their arms around each other and saying, "You're my best mate, you are." At which point, Maria completely ups the ante by introducing an extra free drink into the proceedings – a glass of their excellent brandy – before we get to the final two sherries.

I'm not sure that Maria has fully understood the British character. If she's expecting a studied inspection of each glass, a swirl and a sip, some sluicing through the teeth, a discussion about the wine's qualities, and then for us to pour the rest away, she is sorely mistaken.

For example, my personal tasting notes for the five wines go:

'Oof;'

'Jeesh;'

'Better;'

'Now you're talking;'

'Give me that bottle.'

The last one – the Pedro Ximénez – is basically liquid raisins, and I could no longer give two figs about how it's been produced. They could make it in a steel vat out of sugar and heroin, for all I care. This is not your granny's sherry. This is a hardcore portal to a different kind of existence.

By one pm, I have had five sherries and a brandy, and it's still at least half an hour before any restaurant will serve me lunch. I wave farewell to my new best mates – we're all going on a cruise together next year, Maria's bringing the Pedro Ximénez – and totter into town.

The obvious thing to do, while I wait for a restaurant to open, is go to the nearest bar, sit in the sun, and have a glass of rosé wine. I make this choice on the basis that rosé is relatively low in alcohol and will probably soak up, if not counteract, what I am now calling the sheroin. The science is still unproven, but it's worth a try.

That takes me to lunchtime, where I recall eating something, though I couldn't tell you what. I do remember employing the Spanish for 'Another rosé wine, please' a few more times, because rosé wine – as I am discovering – barely has any alcohol in it at all.

In fact, rosé wine must be completely non-alcoholic, because I now feel GREAT.

Afterwards, I stagger to the cathedral, looking for somewhere cool to lie down, and stump up a whacking eight euros to get in – with not a sniff of sherry included in the price. Damn straight, I wouldn't have paid that if I was sober. The Catedral de Nuestro Señor San Salvador is soaring and majestic, and completely empty, and I think it's clear where the diocesan authorities in Jerez are going wrong with their pricing and drinks policy.

I have two thoughts upon waking the next day.

Is that a chainsaw in my head? And, bugger me, sherry.

And then a further realisation. That actually *is* a chainsaw – wielded by a man in a cherry picker outside the hotel, who's taking lengths off a hundred-foot-high palm tree. From the top downwards, obviously, the man's a professional.

I watch with the detached demeanour of someone

who's vaguely interested in how it will all pan out, the tree shrinking a few feet at a time, until all that's left is a stump and a pile of expertly cut sections.

But mainly I'm wondering if he'll kindly take my head off after he's done, because, bugger me, sherry.

CHAPTER 22

SEVILLE

I pull into Seville later that day fully intending to spend just one night, and end up staying two, because it's just so damn attractive.

In truth, I didn't expect this. The last time I was in Seville, forty years ago as a backpacker, it had a bad reputation for drugs, petty crime, and the indiscriminate use of flamenco. We were warned to keep our wits about us, and not venture out into certain neighbourhoods, which looked no different from the run-down neighbourhoods we were out venturing in.

I don't remember Seville with any fondness, put it like that. But this is the way the train comes, so there's no avoiding it.

All I can say is that Seville – at least in the historic centre – has got its act together. The 1992 Expo held here had something to do with that, in the way that the

Olympics in the same year kickstarted Barcelona's revival. Budget airline flights, and high-speed trains from Madrid and Malaga, have done the rest. The city is packed with tourists, no question, but there's a charm to it, even right in the old centre.

Take the famous Seville oranges. There are thousands upon thousands of bitter orange trees in the city, lining every street and square, even within the cathedral grounds. The smell from the white blossom is intoxicating – like walking through an open-air Jo Malone – and fallen oranges lie everywhere, strays on every kerbside and corner. When it rains, even briefly – as it does while I'm here – you get a full-face, signature whiff of orange-infused Seville.

Even in its less welcoming days, the city always had something about it. It's the great city of the Spanish south, with its palaces, gardens, ducal mansions, museums and galleries. Roman, Moorish and Christian rulers all left their mark, while the city was the gateway to trade with the Spanish Americas. Its traditions are colourful and theatrical – bullfighting is revered, and it's the centre of the country's spectacular Semana Santa processions, when huge, wooden images are paraded through the streets by ancient religious brotherhoods.

A keen tourist could easily spend a week here. An ex-guidebook writer, say, who was too frightened to sightsee much the first time around, might well want to delve into the history, to check out the Zurbaráns, Murillos and El Grecos in the Fine Arts Museum, and peruse the treasures in the Alcázar, citadel of the Seville's rulers since Roman times.

Please, have you ever read one of my books? As I often say plaintively to Elaine, when she suggests we go to an art gallery – "But I haven't done anything wrong."

I am, however, minded to go to the cathedral on the trail of Christopher Columbus, who's indelibly associated with Seville and this part of southern Spain. I find him fascinating, or his voyages at least.

Obviously, he no more 'discovered America' than I did. Sailing the ocean blue in 1492, he first fetched up on the island of Guanahani in the Bahamas, in the Caribbean, whose inhabitants were probably surprised to find that they needed discovering. Columbus himself thought he'd reached Asia and the East Indies, which had long been his goal, so in short, he was in the wrong place to discover the thing he thought he'd discovered, and he didn't even discover the thing he did discover.

But like Captain James Cook, whose eighteenth-century voyages I also admire, Columbus did set sail on true voyages of discovery, in vessels that seem as if they were put together for a joke.

"You're going to sail *there*, in *that*? Sure, Chris, whatever you say."

I live near the Yorkshire coast, where all Cook's boats were built, and from the histories, drawings and accounts know well the hardships his sailors endured. Columbus, though, had it even tougher. His ships – some of which were built near Seville – were ridiculously small and ill-equipped in comparison. He was sailing off into the unknown a full three hundred years before Cook, and that makes him doubly brave and intrepid – if not the hero-discoverer that history once thought him.

The cathedral in Seville is Columbus' last resting place, and my first port of call. And everyone else's, it seems, because there's a giant queue to get in. It moves quickly, though, for if there's one thing that Seville's cathedral has, it's space.

Quite how much is a matter of some debate. The cathedral website – and most other sources – proclaims it the third largest cathedral in the world, after St Peter's in the Vatican, Rome, and St Paul's in London.

Guinness World Records, however, lists the Basilica of Our Lady of Peace in Côte d'Ivoire as the new champ, pushing Seville into fourth place. This didn't wash at all here, where cheeky Spanish maths nerds set about recalculating the internal spaces of each, based not on the square-metre footprint, but on a cubic measurement. Seville jumps from fourth to first if you do that, though less contentiously, Seville is indisputably the largest Gothic cathedral in the world.

Whichever way you slice it, it's magnificent in its scope and grandeur. Vast and echoing, almost with streets and squares instead of aisles and ambulatories. The very essence, you might think, of a mighty Christian cathedral in the most quintessential of Spanish cities.

Yet that's not what this is at all. As in much of

Andalusia, there's a different story to tell here. For this was the site of the grand mosque in Moorish Seville, which endured for almost seven hundred years. Even when Christian forces eventually took back the city, and built a new cathedral, they adapted the floorplan and many of the elements of the old mosque.

The famous Patio de los Naranjos, for example – a central courtyard filled with geometric ranks of the city's orange trees – was the original mosque entrance. Today, it's a teeming mix of tourists looking for the subterranean toilets, which have their own signature scent, and it's not oranges.

Meanwhile, the ornate cathedral belltower known as La Giralda – symbol of the city – was once the minaret, from where the faithful were called to prayer. It's a stunning structure, built in the twelfth century, and modelled on a minaret in Marrakesh. The intricate brickwork, scalloped arches, and filigree windows present a perfect expression of – what? Nothing Castilian Spanish, that's for sure. Religious adaptability, maybe, or just the simple recognition that some things are perfect as they are?

I join another queue to climb the inside of the tower, circling up and around thirty-four levels on ascending ramps with a herringbone brick floor. My old guidebook says these ramps were constructed to be wide enough for mounted guards to pass each other, which clearly can't be true, unless Castilian knights rode Shetland ponies.

A final flight of steps and there I am, a hundred

metres up, under the belfry added later by the Christians, which is topped by an enormous bronze weathervane, just to gild the lily. The views are spectacular, down to the neighbouring Alcázar palace, and across the rooftops, terraces, squares and gardens of the old town. The only discordant note is the repeated injunction not to throw anything from the top of the tower – a warning presumably made because some idiots do just that.

Big Chris C, meanwhile, lies in state down in the cavernous cathedral, in a tomb raised upon the shoulders of four giant kings wearing golden crowns and tabards. It's of a piece with the rest of the building – ornate, overblown – but has a sense of grandeur that's appropriate for someone whose voyages helped change the world.

Incidentally, Captain Cook wasn't so lucky. I've also been to his final resting place, in a remote bay on Hawaii's Big Island, where he was cut down by islanders as he came ashore. All Cook gets is a simple white monument and a plaque in the surf. His surviving bones were buried later at sea.

Columbus, though, got full honours from the minute he died in 1506, in Valladolid, in northwestern Spain. True, his remains were then carted around for centuries between there, a monastery in Seville, Santa Domingo in the Dominican Republic, and Havana, Cuba. His remains only came back to Seville, to be laid to rest in the cathedral, after Cuban independence in 1898, following the Spanish-American War.

Given that he'd been exhumed at least four times by then, there was long a debate about whether the remains in the tomb belonged to Columbus at all. DNA familial testing in 2024 finally revealed that the bones in the tomb in Seville cathedral were conclusively his – a final discovery, if you like, which seems apt.

The other place I'm interested in seeing lies over the river, which bounds the western side of the old town. It was the wide, navigable Rio Guadalquivir that made Seville the main centre for trade with the newly exploited Americas, despite the city being almost a hundred kilometres from the coast. When the river silted up in the seventeenth century, and trade moved south to Cádiz, Seville didn't recover for another two hundred years.

The riverside is prettified now, especially the stretch around the Torre del Oro, a gorgeous Moorish tower where the Spanish later stored gold (*oro*) from the Americas. The train I first caught in Barcelona borrowed its name.

The Giralda tower of the cathedral is behind me, and the monumental bullring further up the riverside, and I keep going on a shaded promenade up to the bridge that crosses over into the neighbourhood known as Triana. It's a pretty prospect, with cafés and pastel-painted houses lining the river, and I'm here to get a different perspective on the Columbus story.

I didn't come to Triana on my previous visit to Seville, it being one of those neighbourhoods I was warned about at the time.

It was the site of the old Americas docks, from where sailors and deckhands were plucked for trans-Atlantic voyages. Clay from the river supported a noxious brickmaking and ceramics industry from Roman times onwards, while bandits and cut-throats roamed the back alleys and courtyards.

Visiting it in the 1840s, Richard Ford reported Triana as "the home of bull-fighters, smugglers, and picturesque rogues." If I'd have wandered in back then, I'd have relinquished the contents of my backpack to some large, roguish gentlemen in the first five minutes, and ended up indentured to the surly overseer of a brick factory.

I'm not much better-informed today, because in lieu of any actual research I grabbed a book off my travel shelves at home, thinking, that will do for when I'm in Seville. I'm of the generation that thinks something in print is intrinsically more trustworthy than anything I might find online. However, I suspect that my 1998 copy of the Rough Guide might no longer be the most reliable source available.

Triana, I am told, is "scruffy, lively and not at all touristy."

Look, we all know how time works. That Triana is now demonstrably touristy – Airbnb key-boxes, pavement cafés, ceramics galleries – isn't exactly a surprise. This neighbourhood has clearly come up in the world. If I'm going to be pressganged into anything, it will be as the sales assistant in a designer lighting shop.

But as a public service let me walk you through the

two other adjectives, for those old enough to remember slavishly following a guidebook around an unknown city.

For "scruffy" read "Looks a bit dodgy from a safe distance." In my guidebook-writing days, I described many sketchy neighbourhoods in Barcelona as scruffy. If it was a verifiable hellhole, I might have gone as far as "edgy," meaning, "No way am I going there, you're on your own."

"Lively," meanwhile, is the travel writer's way of saying there were some other people on the street when they were there. See also animated, popular, and bustling. These are all nothing, guidebook words that don't tell you very much.

So, here's what Triana is like today.

There's a red-brick market by the bridge that isn't even mentioned in the 1998 guide, so I assume it's been built since then. It's a bit pristine, with shrink-wrapped display fruit and some fancy deli stalls, which makes it a great find if you come from provincial Britain, but it's not a patch on the neighbourhood markets of Barcelona or Valencia.

The surrounding buildings were once part of the San Jorge castle, whose whitewashed walls still dominate the riverside. For three hundred years, this was the headquarters and prison of the Spanish Inquisition, and if you scout around between the back of the market and riverside, you'll happen upon a covered alley called Callejon de la Inquisicion. I think you'll find no one expected that.

The ceramics museum is actually pretty interesting, housed on a site where there's been a pottery workshop since Islamic times. It was a grim, polluting trade – which is why it was kept on the far side of the river from all the fancy buildings – but the elaborate ceramic designs that came out of Triana travelled the world. There were twenty factories operating until well into the 1920s, while the Cerámica Santa Ana – whose site this was – continued until 2010.

I love their more prosaic, day-to-day work – things like street signs, shop advertisements, and even a Pirelli tyres promotion, all in yellow and blue tiles. "Eight delightful day excursions by motor coach," says one in English, "Departure from Madrid every Thursday." Meanwhile, in the gift shop, I wonder how much I want a salt and pepper shaker of two entwined figures, a decorated wall thermometer, or an admittedly cute lemon-glazed espresso cup. Not enough to part with any money, is the answer.

After that, it's a short walk through Triana to the Santa Ana parish church, whose baptismal font, consecrated in 1499, is known as the 'Font of the Gitanos,' after the Romany gypsies whose stronghold Triana once was. It's an impressive, two-in-one piece of kit, with a kidney-shaped, baby-sized marble receptacle sitting in the much wider, circular font. The guidebook goes big on this, as being, "according to tradition, where the gifts of flamenco singing and dancing are bestowed on new-born infants."

If this is indeed the case, then a quick go with a

hammer and chisel, or a power drill, should sort that out. There is, as my good friend John says of the many and varied things that annoy him about the world, "no need for any of that," and in the matter of flamenco, he's not wrong. Ear-splitting racket, worse than morris dancing; a right pain in the castanets. Or, in the interests of balance, UNESCO-protected art form; you decide.

I'm not in Triana for the flamenco, or anything else – you can probably tell, my heart's not in it. I'm here instead to track down another monument to the 'discoveries,' which has far less prominence than the Columbus tomb in the cathedral. It's down at the far end of the neighbourhood, in Plaza Virgen Milagrosa, which is a grand name for an unprepossessing triangle of traffic surrounded by apartment blocks.

In the middle of a tiny fenced-off garden, with just a couple of orange trees for decoration, is a statue of one Rodrigo de Triana, a fifteenth-century seaman who sailed on the ship, La Pinta, on Columbus' first voyage. I can barely squeeze through the parked cars to get close enough to see it, but there he is, holding onto a mast, arm outstretched, fingers extended.

Columbus and other mariners took men from the neighbourhood to sail the world – it's why Rodrigo is 'de Triana,' although he originally came from nearby Huelva. Many were experienced sailors, like Rodrigo. A few were prisoners and ne'er-do-wells, offered a way out if they'd sign on for what promised to be dangerous voyages of exploration. The prospect of coming back was slim.

We don't know very much about him, but Rodrigo took his chance, and on 12 October, 1492, there he was, a lookout at the mast, when he sighted land. Three months out of Spain, Columbus' ships had reached the Bahamas, and Rodrigo de Triana became the first European to set eyes on the Americas.

And now here he is, in a hemmed-in Seville square, peering out and mouthing the word that's inscribed on the base of the statue: Tierra. Land. Or, bathetically, given what he's actually looking at, parked cars and the Mercadona supermarket, but I don't suppose they could get all that to fit on the monument.

History honours Rodrigo, though at the time Columbus already had his eye to the main chance. He noted in his ship's journal that he'd already seen a light from the shore before Rodrigo's shout (yeah, right, Chris), and later claimed the honour for himself – which was convenient, because it meant Columbus also trousered the lifetime pension promised to the first person to sight land.

It was always thus. Columbus gets the grand tomb in the mighty cathedral, while Rodrigo has to make do with a rather mean tribute in a backstreet. Reason enough, anyway, for me to wander the scruffy, lively streets of Triana, which – at this end of the neighbourhood at least – are also not at all touristy. I knew that the 1998 guidebook would come up trumps.

I raise a glass later to Rodrigo de Triana in the

Bodeguita Romero, a renowned tapas joint close to the cathedral. There's already a queue when I arrive, but through some mysterious alchemy a cheery waiter immediately lets me have a table for two, instead of making me stand up at the bar.

It might not surprise you to learn that I have strong opinions on standing up at a bar to eat. I've been walking around all day. I want dinner at my own table.

I also have views on tapas – what in Yorkshire we might call a 'picky tea.' It shouldn't be up to me to curate my own dinner. Call me old-fashioned, but surely it's the chef's job to combine ingredients into a pleasing whole? How would they like it if, next time they read a book, it started off like a thriller, then had a few pictures of a monkey, then some random lines of sixteenth-century poetry, and finished with a scratch-and-sniff page from a perfume catalogue?

I explain my misgivings to the waiter – not in quite those words – who does the ordering for me, so I end up with slices of seared tuna; a scramble of eggs, baby broad beans and shavings of ham; fried potatoes, and a crispy shrimp pancake. Not all on the one plate, that would cause conniptions in the kitchen, but still, more like a proper dinner. And eaten from a seat, at a table.

Which, as I'm ordering a third glass of a rather nice, crisp, white wine, and considering dessert, I see is causing a different kind of consternation in the queue at the door. The couple at the front have been waiting for a table for the entire hour and a quarter I have currently been in situ, and glares are being exchanged.

There are literally a hundred other tapas bars in the immediate vicinity, though none as good as this. The Romero has a reputation for a reason. Accordingly, I salute the grim determination of the man, who is buggered if he's giving up now, heavily invested as he is. It's the classic sunk-cost fallacy. His partner, on the other hand – his soon to be ex-girlfriend, I suspect – is shooting murderous glances in my direction.

What would Rodrigo do, I wonder?

I'll tell you, he'd stay the course. Rodrigo didn't get to spy new and mysterious lands by slacking off from the mast and going for a nap. No, the chief mate would have told him, "Suck it up, buttercup" – I'm extemporising now – and probably granted him another glass of grog to keep him going.

Grog it is. And dessert. For Rodrigo, and for the new world!

CHAPTER 23

SEVILLE TO HUELVA

There's an almost perverse attraction to this slow, meandering journey of mine by train. Towns and cities of note come and go, but in between – well, those are the quiet places, the forgotten parts, the tracks that remain defiantly unbeaten.

Spain, vast as it is, has a lot of those places, and the railway threads them all together, until suddenly it doesn't – until the tracks just stop. Like at Huelva, end of the line in the Spanish southwest, marooned on a river delta, a hundred kilometres from Seville.

The journey is typical, and one I've become accustomed to. Out of Seville's Santa Justa station, past tower blocks, allotments, and industrial estates before rolling through orange and olive groves, with covered tunnels of strawberries and ranks of neatly trimmed vines to all sides. A green blanket of crops extends to the horizon, while abandoned stations at barely noticeable towns – Aznalcazar, Aljarafe – bear the 'Al' prefix that gives away their Moorish past.

At Escacena, we pass an old chickpea processing factory; storks rise languidly from nests atop every nearby pylon. Castle walls loom over the tracks at Niebla, encircling the small town – another story of an important past in somewhere that's now a backwater.

You wouldn't make this journey by rail unless you had to – the express bus is a lot quicker. Or, I suppose, unless the quiet places and forgotten parts speak to you, like they speak to me.

An hour and a half from Seville, we reach the end of the line at Huelva. The border with Portugal is just sixty kilometres away, marked by the wide River Guadiana. My next leg west will have to be by bus.

You'd think they could have continued the railway to Ayamonte at least, the last Spanish town, and in fact for a while they did. A minor line operated for fifty years until 1987, although it never continued over the river to Portugal. When it closed, through lack of use and investment, Huelva was left high and dry – a reasonably large town of 150,000, in the deep southwest, with a slow line to Seville.

That's going to change, now a new high-speed line has been approved, straightening out the circuitous amble that I've just taken. With thirty new bridges and viaducts, and a two-kilometre tunnel, trains will be able to travel at over three hundred kilometres an hour between Seville and Huelva, slashing the journey time to half an hour.

Good for Huelva, obviously. I'm more ambivalent. I prefer to see storks, strawberries and cement factories from the slow train, but I realise that I get no vote in the deliberations of the Spanish Ministry of Transport and Sustainable Mobility.

At first glance, there's no discernible reason why I'd spend any longer than necessary in Huelva itself, beyond jumping on a bus for the border.

It lies a few kilometres inland from the Gulf of Cádiz, between the estuaries of the Tinto and Odiel rivers, and is known, above all, for its mining industry. The Rio Tinto is *tinto* (coloured) for a reason – an unnatural red-orange hue in its higher reaches because it's highly acidic and toxic, saturated with critical levels of iron, copper, manganese, silver, and gold.

Ore of all kinds has been extracted and refined here for five thousand years. The Roman Empire relied on copper from Huelva, while the multinational Rio Tinto mining group started out here in 1873, taking its name from the river. Metals are still shipped from the port today, and the lower estuary remains heavily industrialised, with loading piers sticking out at intervals along its length.

Meanwhile, the town's most notable sight is the long, wooden, nineteenth-century cargo pier that extends for over a kilometre into the Rio Odiel. I'm not sure I'd recommend coming all the way to Huelva to see it, unless you're really into ore-mining history, but I've had to get off the train anyway, so why not?

It's simply huge, built by the Rio Tinto company to ship out the ore, having transported it fifty-odd kilometres down from the mines on their own cargo railway, which connected directly with the pier. The three decks curve a long way out into the river, so that goods trains could run right to the ore ships and back, and the pier stayed in use until 1975.

While it's not exactly a tourist attraction, the latticed structure does look like someone lost the plans for the return half of a rollercoaster. I walk all the way to the end, climbing up and down between the levels, which is quite an experience, especially when the wind picks up and spray hits me in the face.

At least the water at this end of the river isn't hideously toxic. By the time the Rio Tinto reaches the confluence with the Odiel at Huelva, it's mixing with more benign Atlantic tidal waters. That's the hope, anyway. If this chapter ends abruptly, in the middle of a sentence, and all you can hear is the gentle beep-beep of the intensive care unit, I may just have swallowed more heavy metal than is good for a person.

The thing that is an undoubted tourist attraction hereabouts – and the thing that persuades me to stay the night – lies just out of town.

No, it's not the riverside stadium home of Real Club Recreativo de Huelva, the oldest football club in Spain, founded in 1899. That team is hopeless, bobbing around in the lower leagues of Spanish football, though

I sense a certain affinity with my own historic, hopeless team, Huddersfield Town, when I discover that Recreativo, too, wear blue-and-white striped shirts. The Spanish version will have to do without my support; I can't have my weekends ruined any more than they already tend to be.

Instead, I jump in a taxi for the ten-kilometre ride down to the confluence of the two rivers and across the bridge to La Rábida. A short walk up a steep hill stands the Franciscan monastery of Santa María, notable as a retreat for Christopher Columbus during his long years trying to persuade one European monarch or another to finance his voyages.

Columbus had been turned down several times by the Portuguese crown before he turned to the 'Catholic Monarchs,' Ferdinand and Isabella, and even they took some convincing. In the meantime, Columbus roamed from court to monastery while he waited for a chance to present his case again. At Rábida in 1490, he found some support from scientifically minded friars, and when he finally got the funding he needed, Columbus assembled his fleet and acquired sailors at a small riverside port a little way up the Rio Tinto from here.

The monastery is filled with paintings, documents and models related to Columbus and his voyages. Most of the original building was knocked down in the 1755 earthquake that ravaged this area, but there's one surviving part that Columbus would have recognised – a graceful, double-decker cloister with Moorish-style arches and stonework. Otherwise, the leaflet I'm given falls back on the coy use of 'might have' and 'probably,' but there's still enough in these quiet, cool rooms to be able to picture Columbus shuffling around in borrowed robes, patiently making his arguments.

I'm more interested in the voyages themselves than the financial and political machinations that enabled them. The Rábida waterside is my next stop, where the three ships of Columbus' first expedition have been reconstructed, moored on the wharf behind a visitor centre.

These are the Santa María, La Pinta, and La Niña, which set sail from Palos de la Frontera, just upriver, on 3 August, 1492. They passed this point of the river, with the monastery above, and then turned for the estuary and the Atlantic beyond. First port of call, a week later, was the Canary Islands; fully provisioned, the ships set off again in the first week of September and sailed into history. Columbus was on the largest ship, the Santa María; our friend, Rodrigo de Triana, on La Pinta.

Those are the bare facts, which become almost immaterial the minute I walk out onto the wharf. There they are in a line – one, two, three – with steps up to each, so you can clamber around them. And I naturally assume that these ships are scale models, because they are ludicrously small.

"I'll have three like that," Columbus presumably said, "just, you know, full size. On account of how I'm going to the East Indies and all. Not just a lads' cruise up and down the river, Ferdy and Izzy will never go for that."

But no. This is what Columbus had to work with. These are the actual sizes, as far as anyone can determine, given that the exact measurements aren't known. But based on the records of similar vessels, and crew and cargo manifests, the ships here at Rábida represent as close a picture as possible to those that sailed the Atlantic six hundred years ago.

Frankly, it's terrifying. They're like miniature *Pirates of the Caribbean* theme-park rides. There's even a Jack Sparrow lookalike halfway up the rigging. What they don't resemble is anything you'd want to sail in across the stormy Atlantic. Your regular multi-millionaire's day cruiser is bigger than any of these ships.

The Santa María is the largest, maybe nineteen metres long and not even six wide, yet it carried forty-one men, including Columbus. Nine of them were called Juan, and there were six Pedros and five Rodrigos, which must have been a complete pain when it came to organising the watch rotas.

The deck curves and slopes, so that water would run off. I can't imagine what that would be like to walk on in squally conditions, let alone a full-blown gale. The cooking was done on open fires in the galley, with provisions stored in barrels – salt-cod, dried beans, chickpeas, lentils, rice, oil, vinegar. Only the captain had his own study and cot, high on the upper deck.

There's a school party touring the ships while I'm

there, and with a classful on board, there is no room – let alone personal space – for anyone.

And this, remember, is the flagship. La Pinta and La Niña are even smaller – refitted merchant ships called caravels, built for sailing the calmer Mediterranean, with a design that offered little respite from the elements. They look barely survivable, La Niña in particular. There were twenty-six men on La Pinta, maybe a couple fewer on La Niña – a total crew across the three ships of around ninety. It seems impossible that anyone would come back from such a voyage.

In fact, only around fifty did, including Columbus and Rodrigo, but the story has a twist. Despite the relative merits of the ships, it was the biggest and best, the Santa María, that was lost, when it ran aground on Christmas Day, 1492, off the coast of Hispaniola (the island split today between Haiti and the Dominican Republic).

Scenting gold and riches, Columbus left thirty-nine men here, who built a fort from the ship's timbers that they called La Navidad – the first European settlement to be established in the New World.

Columbus, and the remaining crew on La Pinta and La Niña, returned to Spain, sailing back up this very river in March 1493. And when Columbus returned to La Navidad a year later, on his second voyage, he found the settlement destroyed and his former crew all dead, many at the hands of the island's indigenous Taíno people.

If you know anything about colonialism, or even

just have a heart, you'll have been wondering about them. Being 'discovered' by Europeans never ends well, and I fear for the presentation of the facts when I see how the wharf area is laid out. There's an ersatz village of the 'Indians,' which goes full *Night at the Museum* with its dioramas of naked natives in thatched huts. I walk through a market area displaying plastic fruit, and get a poorly made coffee from a café hut run by a disinterested teenager. It's not great, to be honest.

But the accompanying information boards spell it out, unambiguously, in measured tones. After Columbus came back, and others followed, the Taíno were "enslaved, maltreated, and dispossessed." They were worked brutally in the mines, fields, and newly built towns of Spanish America. Up to ninety percent of them died in just a few, short years, from disease, starvation and forced labour.

That's also the story that has to be told whenever we – all right, I – marvel at the extraordinary voyages made in these ships.

In the end, I'm glad I came. Here, to this historic riverside, and to Huelva, which is a nothing sort of town that, without the Columbus connection, you'd struggle to make a case for.

But as Columbus left Huelva behind, so do I. After almost two weeks in Spain, travelling from the Pyrenees to the Atlantic coast, it's time to head west into my final country of the trip.

Next stop, Portugal.

CHAPTER 24

HUELVA TO TAVIRA

There's no choice but to take the bus west from Huelva, but it does at least have the decency to terminate at the old railway station in Ayamonte, the Spanish border town.

There hasn't been a train service for forty years, but Ayamonte station – now the bus terminal – still retains vestiges of its former glory in its arched, tiled façade. There's absolutely nothing else here, though, and the one-star Google reviews are merciless ("now completely abandoned… no life… a horror"). I'm not sure what kind of person reviews an abandoned railway station, but I thank them for their service.

Portugal lies across the Guadiana river, and there never was a rail connection onward, in any case. Ayamonte had to wait until 1991 for a bridge to cross the river, and that's the way the road traffic – and the express bus – goes today, speeding across marshy waters five kilometres north of town.

Instead, I'm going to go the traditional way – the way I came when I first made this international border crossing in the 1980s. Across the river, on a boat that's barely worthy of the name.

The flat shuttle, sitting low in the water, is just wide enough to drive half a dozen cars on. It's the sort of craft you'd expect to see nudging its way up the Amazon, or propelled by Humphrey Bogart, waist-deep in the Guadiana. Such is its lack of facilities and obvious unsuitability, if Columbus had seen something like this, he'd have signed it up for his Atlantic crossing, no question.

At least three men are stationed on the dockside asking for tickets which, of course, they can't sell me. Apparently, I have to run back across the road to a shuttered office, which in my experience – with the ferry due to depart imminently – will almost certainly be closed.

However, another man, hunched over a desk, rubbing sleep from his eyes, coughs up the relevant bit of paper. It costs two euros fifty cents, which is a true bargain for dedicated international-border-crossing transport.

I love all this. Proper travelling. No messing about with a system that has worked perfectly well for decades. There's a river, there's a boat, and that's all you need to know.

There is also a timetable, which – again, love this

– is complicated by the fact that Spanish time is an hour ahead of Portuguese time. It isn't *that* hard to work out, but it does rather throw a spanner in the works when it comes to figuring out lunch, because in Portugal that might start at noon and in Spain you'd be lucky if the chef's left home for work by one-thirty.

All aboard, and the boat chugs across the Guadiana, which is muddy, wide, and windy at this point, close to the river's mouth at the Atlantic. The castle of Castro Marim is visible on the shore opposite, and then we steer a course for the Portuguese town of Vila Real de Santo António, docking there after an uneventful ten minutes, or not even that.

And that's it – Portugal.

Vila Real de Santo António is an intriguing town, and – having passed through several times before – I'll come onto that. First, though, some housekeeping.

For a start, I'm going to call it Vila Real from now on, because my typing fingers can't be bothered with the full name. No one in Portugal would do this, because there's a town in the north called Vila Real, and they all seem easily confused by that. You do see VRSA written instead sometimes, but that just looks like a communicable disease.

Second, I'm going for lunch before heading on. I've had a restaurant recommended to me, somewhere along the dockside, but it takes some finding. You'll understand what I mean, if I tell you that the directions go – follow the abandoned train tracks, past the rusting containers and trailer park, and watch out for the feral cats.

The Tasquinha – a blue-and-white dockside shack – turns out to be as good a welcome to the country as you'll find, a world away from the fancier cafés in town. You'll need the courage of your convictions because there's no menu, just a case full of the daily catch and some gesticulating when it's your turn to go and peruse.

I point at a sea bream, which turns up on the table fifteen minutes later, char-grilled and sprinkled with chopped garlic and parsley, accompanied by a plate of boiled potatoes, a hefty side salad, and hunks of crusty, coarse bread. There's chilled wine of dubious provenance in a stoppered bottle, and everything arrives without me having to say much except *Obrigado*.

Looking around, I'd say I'm the only English person here. There are a few Spanish day-trippers, who are all looking quizzically at their watches, wondering if this is breakfast, but otherwise the Tasquinha is going about its daily business as a rough-and-ready fish shack. No frills, just like the ferry. Why change it?

When I first came to Vila Real, trains used to dock right on the quayside, next to the ferry terminal. Obviously, that was far too convenient and couldn't be allowed to continue. The station is now right on the other side of town, which means a longish walk through the centre – and a glimpse of what makes Vila Real interesting, other than its end-of-the-line appeal.

Until the eighteenth century there was little here, at the mouth of the Gaudiana river, save for a fishing village. Castro Marim, a little way upriver, was the main town, defended by the castle I saw from the boat on my way over.

Then, on the morning of 1 November, 1755, a huge earthquake struck the Iberian peninsula. Its epicentre was two hundred kilometres out in the Atlantic Ocean, but the shock – and the accompanying tsunamis – reached as far as North Africa, northern Europe, and western Ireland.

Lisbon was devastated, and almost completely destroyed – up to forty thousand people died in what's known as the Great Lisbon Earthquake – but the Algarve and Andalusian coasts were battered, too. Castles, houses, wharves, towns, and entire fishing villages were inundated, or simply swept away, including the former settlement here at the river's mouth.

Under the direction of the Portuguese king, Dom José I, and his chief minister, the Marquês de Pombal, recovery was swift. Lisbon owes its ordered, grid-like downtown to the post-quake reconstruction, incorporating wide avenues, large squares, and wooden-framed buildings designed to withstand future shocks.

When Dom José later ordered the construction of a new town at the very eastern edge of the Algarve, it was this – so-called – Pombaline design that prevailed. The site of the old village of Santo António became a Vila Real, or 'Royal Town,' with a uniform grid of streets marching away from the river. The whole town was erected in under two years, which explains its harmonious look and feel today.

I take a walk along the landscaped riverfront, where the buildings are blindingly white, with matching iron balconies and pitched, tiled roofs. In the grid itself, the streets are handsome and wide, paved with the small cobbles typical of Portugal, laid out in geometric designs. There's an enormous main square with benches and lemon trees that wouldn't look out of place in the capital itself, and a fancy, townhouse hotel down one side that occupies several of the eighteenth-century houses.

It's all very charming – quintessentially Portuguese, yet a long way from the more traditional, medieval layout you usually find in such towns. Most visitors are over for the day from Spain, hence the cafés advertising 'Portuguese tapas,' which isn't a thing, but they've worked out that it's the only way to get a Spanish tourist to eat a salt-cod fishcake or a pickled lupin bean.

In many ways, Portugal – with all its idiosyncrasies – was my original travel crush. Fresh from quitting an unsuitable job, and with nothing else planned, I came here for the first time in 1985, and spent two months travelling the length of the country, from north to south.

I immediately loved everything about it – the time-warp towns with their encircling castle walls, the mountains and gorges of the north, the olive and cork plantations of the south, the golden beaches and rust-red earth, the custard tarts, the vintage cinemas that showed films in their original language, the half-bottles of wine, the unheralded Roman remains, the triple-carb meals, the street elevators and port-wine lodges, the language that sounded almost eastern European, the great outdoor markets that seemed almost medieval.

Above all, I loved the trains.

In the north, especially, there were narrow-gauge lines with wooden carriages that rocked and rolled down river valleys and canyons, delivering people and cargo to remote villages and hamlets. It was like travelling in the 1930s, or in deepest Africa or South America, on rail lines with truly evocative names – the Corgo, the Tâmega, the Tua. It was exhilarating for a young man from Huddersfield to be somewhere so utterly foreign, where no one spoke English, and someone had just put a chicken on my lap.

Those old lines are long gone – replaced by better roads and faster buses – but there's still plenty to love about rail travel in Portugal.

Trains hug the banks of the great rivers – the Minho and the Douro – and cross the stunning Dom Luís I bridge in Porto to arrive at the magnificently tiled São Bento station. At tiny Pinhão, at another beautifully tiled station at the far end of the Douro line, you emerge on the riverside to see vineyards and river cruisers. Lisbon has its own majestic, historic, central station, Rossío, while from another – the riverside Cais do Sodré – trains run right along the sparkling Estoril coast to the seaside at Cascais.

My favourite route, however – and one of my favourite rail lines in the whole of Europe – starts here at Vila Real station, the eastern terminus of the 140-kilometre-long Algarve line to Lagos, via Faro.

When I first encountered it, the carriages were six-seaters that opened directly onto the platform, and the tickets were made of cardboard and clipped by a ticket inspector in a peaked cap. The rolling stock has changed since then – of course I'm going to say, not for the better – but the experience is much the same, on a slow route through the backwaters of the Algarve. There are thirty stations in all, some of them miles from the town they ostensibly serve. Good luck finding a beach if you get off at 'Albufeira,' for example, where the station is six kilometres from the resort.

In fact, the train doesn't hug the coast much at all, with the track lying a few kilometres inland. There are distant sea views at times, and halfway – at Faro, where you have to change – the train runs in alongside the sandbanks of the estuary waters. But mostly, the Algarve line is an amble through a rural Portugal that maintains a separate existence from the coastal resorts it's known for.

Allotments, orange groves, olive trees, and polytunnels filled with strawberries. Tilled fields around country houses. Abandoned buildings covered in graffiti. Marshy channels and a chain of sandbar islands. Tethered donkeys. An occasional castle, or a hillside bank of modern apartments. Distant Atlantic waters to one side; green, villa-clad hills to the other.

It's an absolute joy, from end to end – two and a half hours if you travel the whole length of the line. The longest stretch between stations is just ten minutes, and as little as three or four at times. The doors open and close, and on and off get tourists, schoolkids, commuters, market-goers, shoppers, hikers, and the occasional travel writer, lapping it all up, as I have done maybe thirty times before over the decades.

After weeks of travel, I'm finally closing in on the end. Just three hundred and fifty kilometres to go now, until I reach Sintra and the westernmost point of my journey. These last few sections haven't exactly dragged, but from Algeciras onwards it's been a stop-start kind of journey – bus, bus, train, train, train, bus, ferry.

I'm tired. I could get it all over within a day or two, catching the fast train from Faro to Lisbon and then heading out the short distance to Sintra. That has a certain appeal. It's time to wrap this up. I've been away so long, Elaine will probably have knitted and stitched a new husband by now.

But the slow train works its usual magic and I resolve to make one more overnight stop on the way, at Tavira, half an hour down the line from Vila Real. Because if the Algarve rail line is my favourite journey in Portugal, then this is my favourite town on the Algarve.

This whole eastern side of the Algarve is a different beast to the west, where the famous resorts are located – Albufeira, Armacão de Pera, Praia da Rocha, and others, with their golden sands and weathered, ochre-coloured rock formations.

Instead, Tavira is tucked a few kilometres inland from the coast, straddling both sides of a wide river. It's not a resort or even a port, as such, though it was once an important centre for tuna fishing. It does have beaches, though not in the town – for those, you have to travel out to the long, undeveloped, sandbank islands, known as the *ilhas*, at the river's mouth, which shelter this part of the coast from the Atlantic's wilder exclamations.

For these reasons, Tavira took longer to be discovered – "scarcely affected by the tide of tourism," says my original Rough Guide from the 1980s. If you turned up with a backpack in those days, you'd be met at the bus or train station by little old ladies offering airless rooms in old-town houses, which cost five hundred escudos, or a couple of quid. For another pound or two, you could eat fresh tuna steaks and drink rough, cold, red wine at fishermen's cafés along the harbour. Ice-cold Sagres beers were as cheap as bottled water.

In the daytime, you walked out, with a throbbing hangover, through the salt pans to the ferry pier, a couple of kilometres from town. Here, you jumped on a rickety, diesel-spewing boat, in the company of like-minded Germans, Swedes, Australians, and anyone else who had an in-the-know guidebook.

Five minutes across the estuary was the sandbar island, where vast, exposed beaches stretched as far as the eye could see. The more intrepid backpackers, bags clinking with bottles and supplies, would slope off into the distance to camp out among the dunes for days on end.

Tavira is not really like that now. I know, because I've been back many times since. Also, and let's be clear – thank God I don't have to do that anymore.

Tourism here is far more upscale these days. The old riverside market now sells crafts and souvenirs, and not fish, and while some traditional restaurants remain, you don't have to search hard to find sushi and cocktail bars, Indian restaurants, and pizzerias.

There's also an ersatz Irish pub on the riverside, beyond the bridge, which even though Elaine's not here, I can't go into. She has some sort of early-warning device sewn into my backpack, I think, which alerts her – and any other genuine Irish person in the vicinity – to the unauthorised drinking of foreign Guinness.

Happily, the town is still quite the charmer, with its shady riverside gardens, a minor castle, and a low, ancient, stone bridge that's often claimed to be Roman but isn't. It's easy to spend a lazy day here, and that's what I intend to do, girding myself for the final push to Sintra.

There are still pockets of the past, in the tiled houses along the backstreets, and in restaurants like the Zeca da Bica, which I track down eventually. It's been here since the 1960s, and I have vague recollections of it from the eighties – simple wooden tables, tiled walls, and a menu of good Portuguese dishes.

I can recommend the pork with clams, a traditional dish which, although it sounds an odd combo, is delicious; Zeca da Bica's version is enough to feed a small family or a large writer. I finish the meal with another classic, Baba de Camelo, a whipped mousse made with eggs and condensed milk, whose most alluring aspect is its name – 'Camel Drool.' Like almost every Portuguese dessert, it is insanely sweet and uses a ton of eggs. I have a Portuguese recipe book at home, for example, where the first recipe out of the block starts, "Take sixty eggs…"

After emerging from my lunchtime coma, I discover that my boutique hotel for the night – get me! – is inoffensive in every way except one. In the old days, in the little old lady's house, there would be a mildewed shower down the hall, from which would issue a trickle of lukewarm water. All fine, what did I expect for a couple of quid?

Here, my small but perfectly nice en-suite bathroom is right next to the bed, behind wall-to-ceiling glass. Everything is entirely visible, and while I realise I'm travelling on my own, I don't want to sit on the toilet right next to my bed. Or indeed, lie in bed with a view of the throne.

But wait, what's this? There's a pull-down roller blind so you can screen the bathroom off if you like, but for some unaccountable reason it is operated from the bedroom side of the glass, and not the bathroom side. This means limbo-dancing under each time I enter and exit what is already a small room.

The shower, meanwhile, is a rain shower, which as we all know, is the worst kind of shower. It issues roughly the volume of water used by a small nation state, and points it straight down. Never mind washing my hair whether wanted or not, it could hose down a baby elephant. As the glass shower screen only extends laterally for about twenty centimetres, the bathroom floor is soon under water, while the floor-to-ceiling glass of the bathroom is now thoroughly steamed up.

This all rather negates the whole see-through experience that the hotel was keen for me to enjoy. But the bathroom is 'designer' and 'boutique,' let's never forget that, and the perfect example of what Elaine likes to think of as the Hospitality Patriarchy in action.

I check in with her, just to make sure, but it's exactly as I thought – "designed by a man who has never met a woman." See also: nowhere to hang or put anything, not enough toilet rolls, mirrors set at the wrong height, lighting that doesn't light anything useful, and sockets in all the wrong places.

I am sluiced, rinsed, steamed, and cleaned, though, you have to give it that.

I've got time to relive a bit more of my past before today's train, and when I discover that there's now a direct ferry from the town centre to the island beaches, that seems like it was meant to be.

I also discover, from the weather forecast on my phone, that there is currently a Severe Coastal Event

Warning, with an asterisk that says, "meaning a significant threat to life or property."

I look up at the sky. Mostly sunny, mostly blue.

I look down at the water. Mostly muddy.

I look at my phone. "Waves may reach a maximum height of eleven metres."

It may be coincidental, but the caramel-coloured water in the river is also running backwards at a lick. Either the tide is going out – fast – or there's an imminent tsunami. I've seen this sort of thing on the Discovery Channel, just before the articulated trucks and houseboats end up in the trees.

The boat captain seems entirely unconcerned. He's got more important things to worry about, namely shouting at the man on the quayside who's trying unsuccessfully to remove a swirling mess of driftwood and old plastic bags from the propellers.

After a bit more shouting I'm given to understand that we're off, eleven-metre-high waves be damned. We chug down the river away from town, past low mudbanks and salt pans. The old tuna canneries on the opposite bank have been converted to another luxury hotel, but there's nothing boutique about this boat trip. It's noisy and windy, and fabulously retro, even down to the price – a ridiculous two euros fifty return.

The weather holds and the beach is just as wonderful as remembered – a long stretch of golden, Atlantic-facing sand that curves towards Faro, forty kilometres away. It's littered with clam shells and driftwood, and pounded by surf.

A couple of beach cafés are stirring, the staff cleaning the seats and tables, and sweeping the sand away. Signs invite me to "Vibe. Relax. Love. Smile," but I think I'm good. Instead, I could walk for solitary miles along the sands if I wanted, and maybe another day I will. There are some places I know I'll never visit again; I've passed through a few already on this trip. But Tavira? I'm sure I'll be back.

For now, it's enough to grab a coffee – trying hard not to vibe too much – and sit around waiting for the return ferry to depart, bamboo-clogged propellor and mystery tsunami permitting.

CHAPTER 25

TAVIRA TO SINTRA

If you heard me talking in a restaurant or hotel reception, you'd say I can speak Portuguese. I've spent so long here over the years – even living for a while in a small, riverside town in central Portugal – that I've mastered the basics of getting around, and feeding and accommodating myself. I've even been told I sound vaguely Portuguese, at least for a sentence or two.

It's a more complicated language to learn than, say, Italian, and the pronunciation differs from the more familiar Spanish. But as long as simple conversations about meal choices, or directions to a train station, are conducted in the present tense, I can get by.

As is often the case with learning languages, I can understand more than I can speak, but nodding comprehension is rarely my friend. It will all go swimmingly – Does the room have a shower? Is breakfast included? – until the receptionist goes off-piste and mentions the roadworks in the street outside, and how the council never even consulted the local businesses, and honestly, what do we even pay our taxes for anyway? And all the while, I'm nodding and going, "Yes, is difficult in modern times. Where is bus station, please?"

Consequently, when there is something I really need to get right – buying a long-distance train ticket with a tight connection, for example – I'd rather do that in English if I can.

Thirty years ago, that wasn't always an option, especially in smaller towns. But here I am today in Faro, main town of the Algarve, the most heavily touristed region in Portugal, approaching the ticket counter at the train station.

Faro station is littered with signs about things in English. The assistant behind the glass is in his early forties, I'd say, of an age to have learned at school. He definitely speaks English; it's probably why he's on the counter.

Still, I play it safe. I'm not one of those travellers who simply assumes that everyone speaks English. It's polite at least to make an effort at the start.

"Excuse me, do you speak English?" I say, in my best Portuguese.

"No, but you obviously speak Portuguese," he replies.

Oh, well played, sir, very well played indeed.

"A little," I say, which is what I always say, hoping someone will take pity on me.

"Good," he continues – in Portuguese, his own language, how very dare he. "How can I help you?"

The reason I didn't want to do this in Portuguese soon becomes clear. Buying a ticket to Sintra involves changing trains in Lisbon, which is not as straightforward as it sounds.

There are, at a conservative estimate, about a thousand suburban train stations in Lisbon – I haven't counted them all, it may be more – and you can change trains at any number of them. They all have mysterious names, none of them with 'Lisbon' in the title – or 'Lisboa,' as we Portuguese speakers say.

Not only that, a journey on the connecting Lisbon suburban line out to Sintra requires a chargeable pass called a Navegante card.

"Do you have a Navegante card?"

I don't know the Portuguese for, "Why on earth would I?" Hypothetical conditional tense, very tricky.

Without a Navegante card, he can sell me a ticket as far as the gloriously named Sete Rios – Seven Rivers – which is not the idyll you might imagine, but an unlovely downtown Lisbon neighbourhood near the zoo. To take a connecting train from there to Sintra, I'll need to get off at Sete Rios, go to the ticket counter, and conduct another trying conversation like this – all in seven minutes, because that's how long before the connecting train leaves.

"Or," he says, tantalisingly.

I'm listening.

"I can sell you a Navegante card, and give you a ticket that will get you all the way to Sintra."

Why a man in Faro has got a bunch of under-the-counter Lisbon travel cards, we don't get into. It's not even a scam. He charges me the princely sum of fifty cents for the card, does some nifty e-charging and printing, hands over a fistful of tickets and a yellow Navegante card, and I'm all set.

"Enjoy your journey," he now says, in English, as I leave, which I take to be Portuguese ticket-office-clerk humour.

There are no announcements, and no platform departure board, but there is only one train, so I assume it's the right one. It looks shabby from the outside, and could do with a good wash-down, including the windows. But first class is roomy and comfortable, and has cost me just eight euros more than standard, and not the mortgage-and-firstborn-child-sacrifice premium you have to pay in the UK. I sit on board, ascertain that it's heading towards Lisbon, and wait.

And wait.

A man holding a plastic bag and a spanner walks past at one point, looking puzzled, never a hopeful sign.

The train finally departs twenty-three minutes late, so that's the seven-minute window I had for the connection at Sete Rios already blown out of the water. And the driver, clearly not in any hurry, has managed to stretch the delay to thirty-two minutes by the time we reach the first station.

Despite all the evidence to the contrary thus far, this route from the Algarve to Lisbon has undergone a dramatic transformation since the first few times I travelled it.

Trains used to take up to five hours to rattle across the vast, southern plains of the Alentejo region, and they didn't even reach Lisbon directly. When they got to the wide River Tagus, you hopped out at Barreiro and jumped on a ferry. This took you across the river, arriving right on the downtown waterfront on the edge of a huge eighteenth-century square featuring a regal mounted statue of the builder-king Dom José. Now, *that* was an exciting way to reach Lisbon.

Today, the trip can be done in three to four hours, crossing the river instead by rail bridge, and ending up at one of the city's large, peripheral hub stations, Oriente or Santa Apolonia. But while they've speeded up the line, particularly at either end, there's nothing much to be done about the long slog through the Alentejo, which has its own kind of attraction. I settle down in the buffet car – a glorious Seventies throwback, with contoured, white, leatherette seats and bar stools by the windows – and watch the countryside roll by.

This is the sparsely populated, agricultural heart of Portugal. The breadbasket of the nation since Roman times – endless plains punctuated by holm oak trees, olives, cork plantations, pines, citrus groves, and grain fields. There's an occasional village of whitewashed houses with red, tiled roofs, a church tower, and the obligatory castle ruin, but no reason to stop.

It's the other side of Portugal, the side that people leave for better lives, that few visit, that rarely features in travel itineraries. Vast estates here were run along feudal lines for centuries; when revolution came in 1974, the Alentejo was at the forefront of change.

The train makes a brief halt at the small town of Grândola, a name etched into every Portuguese heart. The song, 'Grândola, Vila Morena,' was played over the radio to signal the start of the army-led coup that became the Carnation Revolution, its lyrics pregnant with revolutionary intent: "Grândola, Dark Village/Land of fraternity/The people are the ones who rule."

Shortly afterwards, we cross into the estuarine lands of the Rio Sado and then circle the Setúbal peninsula, making the final approach to the Tagus river, so broad at this point that it's more like an inland sea. Lisbon lies across the river. We're almost there.

Of all European capital cities, Lisbon is one of the hardest to reach by train. Admittedly, it's out on a limb, but it is next to Spain and not that far from France. It's not like it's Kazakhstan or anything. For 130 years, you could travel from London via Paris on the Sud Express, or later on the Trenhotel sleeper train between Madrid and Lisbon. Covid put paid to them both and, frankly, getting to Lisbon on the train from almost anywhere outside the country is a chore these days. You have to change twice, even coming from Madrid, the neighbouring capital city.

But if you're already here, then this final approach – from the south – has to be one of the most dramatic ways into any city in Europe.

I'm waiting for it because I know it's coming, but the first glimpse – out of the righthand side of the carriage – is always arresting. Just before the water, the giant, white statue of Christo Rei – Christ the King – looms ahead. An eighty-metre pedestal topped by a thirty-metre figure, arms stretched out in a wide embrace. It's better than the one in Rio de Janeiro if you're Portuguese, worse if you're Brazilian, and quite the sight for the rest of us.

The train then dives into a short underground section, and all seems lost, before we suddenly emerge on the long, latticework Ponte 25 de Abril, the iconic suspension bridge that crosses to Lisbon proper.

It used to be known as the Salazar bridge, built in the 1960s and named after the dictator who ran the state for thirty-six years. It later got a name change for the day of the 1974 revolution, and train tracks were added in 1999, and here we are, trundling across – wait for it! – the forty-eighth longest, and most celebratory revolutionary suspension bridge in the world.

We're crossing west of the city centre, seventy metres above the water. The cranes and barges of the Alcântara docks are below – some of those old warehouses have been inexcusably turned into yoga-jazz clubs, natural-wine bars, and health studios. The huge building away to the left, set back from the river, is the stunning, sixteenth-century monastery at Belém; over to the right are the famed seven hills of the city itself, topped by the castle of St George.

Like I said, dramatic.

Also, we're not going there. This isn't a guidebook. If you want Lisbon, may I refer you to a Rough Guide I wrote earlier.

Sete Rios station is a swirling mass of suburban lines, where I discover that my seven-minute window to change trains has all been a mighty misunderstanding. Or another Portuguese train clerk joke. Not that there wasn't a connecting train. There was – and I missed it by at least half an hour. But as there's apparently a service every half an hour anyway to Sintra, no harm done.

The route, through apartment-heavy Lisbon suburbs, gives no hint of what's to come. The stations are grey and utilitarian, the sidings heavily graffitied. If this is the final stretch of the rail journey proper, it's disappointing.

I haven't made this trip in years. Decades, probably. But on this occasion I do know that, contrary to popular belief, it's the destination that counts, not the journey.

For Sintra is a fairytale, a temperate Portuguese hill-resort set amongst steep crags and deep valleys – a retreat for those escaping the heat, the flies and the noise of Lisbon. The Moors built the castle, Portuguese royals summered here for over five hundred years, and every Tom, Dick, or Lord Byron swanned in on the Grand Tour and swooned at the surroundings. It's the very definition of picturesque, as the Romantics dubbed such places – reminiscent of a beautiful, painted scene.

Sintra railway station ups its game accordingly. It might be at one end of what's now a workaday commuter line into Lisbon, but the building harks back to the glory days of the late-nineteenth century.

I'd forgotten how fabulous it is – a gingerbread confection outside, with its white walls and red-brick detailing, plus an eye-boggling array of interior tiling. What the Portuguese call *azulejos* – painted ceramic tiles – cover the entrance hall in a swirl of bucolic scenes of hanging fruit and vines in gilded frames. Stand at one of the cut-out windows to buy a ticket, and you're flanked by cherubs with curly hair and fat fingers, tut-tutting at your poor Portuguese.

I know chapter one was a long time ago, but if you recall, I'm still holding out hope for Praia das Maças as Europe's westernmost station. That's still a tram ride away, but even if I ended the journey here – at, indisputably if confusingly, mainland Europe's westernmost *mainline* train station – Sintra would not disappoint. It's ornate and impressive, and an entirely apt place to finish a rail odyssey.

In fact, there's a competing school of thought that says the longest train journey in the world begins at Sintra station and ends in Singapore, those being the two places furthest apart on the planet that are directly linked by rail. That's nineteen thousand kilometres across thirteen countries, including Russia, Mongolia, China, Laos, Thailand, and Malaysia.

It's a nice thought experiment, but it doesn't stand up to scrutiny, not least because no one is travelling through Russia any time soon. Add in the inconvenient fact that you'd have to change stations, not just trains, in Paris, Moscow and Vientiane, and the unbroken 'direct' train journey across half the world is suddenly lost in time, like tears in rain.

Mind you, I would very much applaud the person who attempts a conversation – in Portuguese – at Sintra train station that starts with the phrase, "A one-way ticket to Singapore, please."

Outside the station, the modern world intrudes somewhat, in the form of a waiting line of tour buses, tuk-tuks and mini-mokes. My battered, old, 1980s Rough Guide says, "remarkably few people stay in Sintra," but that is absolutely not the case anymore.

I walk the ten minutes into town on a well-signposted pedestrian route, following crocodiles of sauntering tourists who fan out into a cobbled square dominated by a glaring, white palace with distinctive conical chimneys. Narrow side alleys shoot uphill, lined with souvenir shops and restaurants, thronged with almost impassable crowds.

Picturesque, yes. Relaxing, not exactly.

Yet, while it's far from the genteel retreat of bygone days, there is something about Sintra that still tugs at the senses. The colour of the buildings, for a start:

avocado green, sky blue, burnt orange, and flamingo pink. Most of the grand villas clinging to the hillsides sport perky turrets. Even the town post office has a turret, as well as the burger bar opposite the train station.

Every building has tiles on it somewhere; every street is paved with geometric cobbles. I lift my head to see the crenelated castle on the heights above, and the shockingly pink Peña palace beyond. Sintra still has fairytale vibes.

But does it have what I'm really looking for? Time to go and see.

The tram terminus lies across town, back up past the train station and into the more modern part of Sintra. I walk past the art gallery – not going in, haven't done anything wrong – and look for the sign.

Here I am, finally. At the tram terminus for the service to Praia das Maças, ending at the westernmost stop in continental Europe.

There's no tram at the terminus.

There is, however, a note pinned to the departure board.

A note is never a good sign.

CHAPTER 26

PRAIA DAS MAÇAS

"We regret to inform you that, for technical reasons, the Sintra Tramway – the thing you have travelled eleven thousand kilometres to see, across all four corners of the continent – is currently suspended."

That was the gist of it. 'Technical reasons' unspecified. Dated three weeks earlier. No other information available.

Now, I know what you're thinking. After the whole, 'southernmost point of Europe is closed' debacle at Tarifa, you'd imagine that I might have checked if the trams were running. I may be packing a forty-year-old copy of the Rough Guide, of questionable help, but I do also have a phone and an iPad.

The thing is, I did check. Not a single website suggested that anything might be amiss. I saw timetables and photos, and was encouraged to believe that the

Sintra Tramway was in tip-top condition and raring to receive passengers. Not suspended for technical reasons, which in Portugal could equally be the tracks washed away in a storm or the driver having a cheeky lie-in.

This situation would defeat a lesser travel writer. A Bill Bryson, say, or a Paul Theroux. They would be crying right about now, I can tell you. Colin Thubron doesn't stop moaning if his slippers aren't warmed. Michael Palin would be calling for a helicopter. Don't get me started on Bruce 'Where's My Taxi' Chatwin, or Elizabeth 'Eat, Pray, Complain' Gilbert.

Not me. I haven't travelled thousands of kilometres to a selection of entirely pointless destinations just to be scuppered at the last. I'm going to the westernmost station in continental Europe if it kills me. Or makes me very tired, at least, Praia das Maças being twelve kilometres away, according to the map.

However, a quick search brings up the possibility of a bus from Sintra, the number 1254, so I can at least go and have a look at this now mythical destination.

And then here's what happens. Here's when the manifesting works, when the universe listens, when the stars align, when the unicorns dance in harmony, when all the other things I don't believe in, for once actually just happen. In the way they are supposed to.

The 1254 bus doesn't only go to Praia das Maças, it follows the exact same route as the missing-in-action tram. By which I mean the road shadows the very track, sticking right alongside it, down the valley on loops and switchbacks, past agreeable villas and cultivated fields, through the charming village of Colares and its vineyards.

We lose the track briefly, on the outskirts of Colares, but pick it up again at the bus stop in the middle of the village. Then we stick with the tramline again for the final run through a row of residential villas – their driveways crossing the track – to the small resort of Praia das Maçãs itself.

I get off at the bus stop, and walk a little way down to the buffers and the end of the line. The track is laid out next to the road, open to the elements, with an old, closed, blue-and-white ticket office of the Companhia Sintra Atlantico, and a wedge of sandy beach beyond.

The electric tramway, the Eléctrico de Sintra, saw its first journey in 1904, connecting mountain to sea. Day-trippers came down from Sintra in their top hats and bonnets, with parasols for shade – a line of vintage photos on the terminus wall show the tram through the ages. The square, marble cobbles under the tracks are laid out in such a way that they resemble proper train tracks – black for the horizontal sleepers on a surrounding sea of white.

Can we call this open-air halt a station?

Frankly, if you make it this far yourself, you are entitled to argue the toss, but as I'm the only one here, I'm calling it.

Praia das Maçãs is the westernmost railway station in continental, mainland Europe.

I walk along a bit of the track, and take photos of

the end of the line, and that's it – that's good enough for me.

Things usually work out, if you roll with the setbacks. And if they don't work out in exactly the way you'd hoped, then they are often close enough.

I got here in the end.

Thirty-two separate rail journeys, alighting on the way at forty-three different railway stations. Seven bus rides. Two sleeper trains. Two overnight ferry crossings. Around eleven thousand kilometres, and seven weeks' travel, give or take.

I take a walk down to the beach, where a bubbling river cuts its way through dunes to the sea. I stroll over and stick a piece of sea-drift bamboo in the sand, and watch the surf pound it for a while.

Praia das Maças is apparently named after the apples – *maças* – that used to wash downstream onto the beach in the autumn from the surrounding orchards. There's no such sight today, just rather a lot of plastic glinting in the sun. Praia da Plástica doesn't have quite the same romantic ring to it.

Sitting on the dunes, I muse on one last journey – one more thing I can do, one more adventure, for the sake of completeness.

I can go to the actual westernmost point of mainland Europe, Cabo da Roca – provided it's not closed, of course, always a possibility.

The good old Sintra bus company – my new travel heroes – have a direct service from town to the cape, and so I set out on one last morning, with the sky a non-approved Sintra colour of sickly elephant.

The bus doesn't take cards, and I only have a twenty euro note, and I'm just about to inwardly curse and try and get some change from the café over the road when the bus driver waves me on board.

"Don't worry about it," he says, and at that point I realise two things. That the universe really is listening, how could I doubt it? And, possibly more accurately, that the bus driver sees what I don't – what I can't, what we all can't as we age. I'm still a twenty-something backpacker in my mind. He doubtless sees an elderly person looking a bit confused.

The bus careers high over the hills between town and coast, through valleys so green and moss-grown you just know that rain is more than an unpleasant surprise in these parts. The cape itself stands out in the distance, a small concentration of buildings – tourist office, restaurant and bar, lighthouse and adjacent cottages – next to a large car park and bus turnaround.

It's a wild spot, on hundred-metre-high cliffs, sporting a landmark granite cross on top of a roughly built obelisk. The inscription leaves no room for doubt – "The westernmost point of continental Europe" – and they even throw in a phrase from a sixteenth-century verse by national poet, Luís de Camões: "Here, where the land ends and the ocean begins." Wikipedia, I note, also goes for "westernmost point of the Eurasian landmass," i.e., Europe and Asia combined.

It's a pretty big deal, then, Cabo da Roca, which

means the only other monument on the site makes me laugh – a simple block of stone dedicated to the seventy-fifth anniversary of the founding of the Sintra Rotary Club. Good on them, I suppose, for shoehorning their way onto the westernmost point of the Eurasian supercontinent.

I follow the fence along the cliff edge to a viewing point, where you can't miss the hazard warning signs. Even so, Darwinian natural selection is at work in the shape of several young men making their way across a narrow ledge to a further promontory. They are jumping from rock to rock as the ocean seethes a hundred metres below them. One stands there in silhouette, leaning out, hand on rock – I think of him as Endangered Specimen One – while Specimen Two films him for their @DumbAss TikTok channel.

I can't watch, and look out to sea instead, into the grey Atlantic. Due west of here are the Azores, and then – eventually – some town or other on the Virginia/Delaware coast of America.

That's quite a thought. As is the unbidden idea that the USA, too, must have a north, east, south and westernmost railway station. I can see Elaine rolling her eyes from here.

Enough, no more.

It's time to turn for home – not north or east or south or west, but back to the small corner of England that holds my heart. One where rolls of fabric are doubtless now stacked in my lounge like oversized papyrus scrolls, while the house throbs to the furious sound of duelling sewing machines.

The truth is that, to travel as I do – to go far out, to all the points of the compass and back – you only need one thing. Not a backpack, not an up-to-date guidebook, not even luck, or the smiling embrace of the universe.

All you need is the unquestioning love and support of a person who knows you have to do these things. Knows that it's in your nature. That you can't help it. Who helps you pack and waves you off, knowing that you'll be back some time soon, with a fistful of improbable tales and some wholly inadequate gifts.

You'll be back because your heart guides you back, every time.

Auden was right. "My North, my South, my East and West," it turns out, are all right at home, where Elaine is waiting.

Until the next time I say, "Darling, I've been looking at the internet…"

AUTHOR'S NOTE

This book had rather a lengthy gestation period. I first came up with the idea a few years ago, during the pandemic era, which put paid to it for a while. And then I got side-tracked writing other books. (SciFi, since you ask, available from all good booksellers under my pen name, Rex Burke.)

Then, finally, a couple of years ago, I sat down with a map and a bottle of wine, as mentioned, and really planned the whole trip out.

It was going to be a lot of travelling, but I'm used to that. And a lot of time spent on trains, but I'm used to that, too. What's more, I like it. Travel, trains – that's my thing these days.

The initial plan was to do the entire trip in one go, because it seemed like an exciting adventure to set off from home and go to all four corners of Europe by train. However, there was a problem with that.

The north and east had to come first – the whole

Never Eat Shredded Wheat business rather insisted on it – but there was no way I was going to go to Sweden, Norway, and Finland in winter. It would be all right inside the trains, but it's the Nordic wintry outside that bothers me – the cold, the snow, and the never getting light in daytime.

What I preferred to do was go to Spain and Portugal in early spring, when it's far more pleasant than being in the UK, and then do the northern leg in summer.

So, that's the first piece of the veil lifted from the book. I've presented it as one continuous journey, because it makes more sense of the concept. Otherwise, it was going to be Shredded Wheat Never Eat, which would have confused a new generation of schoolchildren.

As the book records, I set off from Newcastle to Amsterdam on the ferry, went to Osnabrück, but then worked my way south from Paris. At some point on this first trip I caught a horrible chest infection. There was stuff coming out of me that could have been collected and used a biochemical weapon. I soldiered on down through Spain, and even got as far as Algeciras (Shredded, if you're keeping up) but I felt worse and worse. And in the end, I had to do something I've never done before, in forty years of travel-writing, and abandon my trip.

I came home and recuperated, but life got in the way, as it has a habit of doing. I didn't pick up the rest of the southern and western Europe route until spring

AUTHOR'S NOTE

the next year, which I then did follow – after a short break – with the north and east.

I don't think you'll spot the seams. I did travel every centimetre of the routes described, and recorded the things that happened to me along the way. Indeed, I had to do some sections twice, because I'd been so ill the first time my notes just went – bleugh, ow, nurse, kill me now.

Some of the route timelines have either been slightly stretched or contracted, because you didn't need to hear about every hotel I stayed in, and every meal I ate. Only the ones that would make you laugh.

Other omissions were made on a case-by-case basis. For example, I didn't tell you about getting ill. Obviously, it would have been highly amusing for you to read about the terrible incident on the overnight train in France. But it wouldn't have done my reputation any good at all. Let's just say that, if you're not familiar with the term, I beg you not to Google the word shart.

As you've read in the book, I did have some help along the way, and I couldn't have kept going without the support and encouragement of my good friends, Steve and John. One day, we're all going to go on a sherry-and-flamenco cruise together, though I've promised not to write about it.

On the rails, I was indebted to many of the people I met who looked after me, told me facts, let me eavesdrop on them, and generally became part of the book. I've changed all their names, but if Lucas and Oskar, or Nils, recognise themselves, I hope they know how grateful I am to them for their kindness and knowledge. In the text, I honoured the very real Barbro Hunter – she of the endless gifts from the Swedish Tourist Board – who was my first angel in the travel-writing business. If I didn't thank her properly at the time (I probably didn't, being a twenty-three-year-old arse, as discussed) then allow this book to stand as my eternal gratitude.

I also found support in the excellent Facebook group, 'Interrailing for the older crowd,' whose international members are always on hand to put travellers on the right track – in my case, how to pronounce Uimaharju. Many thanks to Kimmo Kosonen for that, and for all his other useful insights into his native Finland.

I want to say thank you to the people who helped shape this book after all the travelling and research was done. My beta readers are a wonderful bunch of people, and helped spot the many typos, errors, and mistakes that are the lot of a first draft. I owe a huge debt to Chris Moore, Jill Pollock-Gore, Linda Foster, Lisa Rose Wright, Michael O'Sullivan, Simon Michael Prior, and Val Poore. Special thanks too to Cheryl Fujii who cast her terrifyingly keen eye over the final manuscript. Thanks to her, I now almost know how to use a semi-colon. It's not; like this.

It's here I'd also usually thank Elaine for all her love and support, but I did point out to her that she got a dedication at the front of the book, and a heartfelt tribute at the end. When I said this to her, she was wielding two giant needles, prior to attacking some blameless piece of fabric. The words, "Look, buster," may have been uttered.

So, on reflection – and as she truly knows, and I truly mean – I will repeat that I couldn't do any of this without her, and nor would I want to. She's the wind beneath my wings. In fact, she could probably knock up a serviceable pair of wings given reasonable notice.

Jules Brown, September 2025

TRAVEL NOTES

People often ask me *how* I do these trips, by which they mean the actual travelling – sorting out the routes, tickets, reservations, and all the other practical details.

Although it may seem as if I'm making it all up as I go along, there is quite a lot of planning that goes into a trip like the one in this book.

I love all that stuff – and it comes as second nature to me by now – and I thought I would set down a few helpful tips and hints for anyone who would like to embark on a European rail trip.

Not this exact trip, obviously. You'd have to be mad. Although I think you'd like Narvik and Praia das Maças, and the ride to Algeciras at least. Just don't get off at Uimaharju.

I start, as I often do, with an Interrail pass (Eurail if you're from outside Europe, it's the same thing). For those that don't know, you pay for a certain number of 'travel days' (three, five, three weeks, two months, etc), and then travel for free on the railway networks of Europe, with certain restrictions and caveats.

There are pass discounts if you're under twenty-six or over sixty, and sales a couple of times a year when you can save up to twenty percent off the price of a pass. It used to be a literal paper pass – and still can be, if you prefer – but I use the phone app, and it's always worked well for me.

The official Interrail website is the place to start, and there is plenty of supportive advice on the Facebook group pages for 'Interrail & Eurail Travellers,' and – my go-to – 'Interrailing for the older crowd.'

The Interrail website has tons of detailed European itineraries, if you'd like some help deciding where to go. It's aimed at young backpackers, but don't let that put you off because the suggested routes are well thought out. If you prefer a book and a more mature vibe then *Europe by Rail* (Nicky Gardner and Susanne Kries) is an unrivalled guide, with some wonderfully detailed itineraries alongside cultural and historical content.

I used Interrail for my trip north and east, and it covered all the train rides I made in Germany, Denmark, Sweden (including the Inlandsbanan), Norway, and Finland. You do have pay supplements for seat reservations where required, and I also paid extra for the overnight sleeper train to Helsinki, and for the Helsinki-to-Stockholm ferry, though the Interrail pass gives you a hefty discount on both.

Travelling by train in Europe in summer on popular routes, or any sleeper train, means planning well in advance, because seats and cabins sell out. I booked all my seat reservations at least a couple of months prior to travel – most booking windows open two to three months before departure dates, but some up to six months before. This is especially true of Eurostar, if you plan to get from the UK to the continent by train – you'll want to book that as early as possible and work from there.

The best single place for advice about train travel is the website of The Man in Seat 61. This covers every conceivable train route worldwide, with information on how to buy tickets and where to check timetables, as well as tips on the most scenic routes or handy hotels near railway stations, for example. It's invaluable.

What you learn from this, and I now know from long experience, is that while the Interrail pass is fabulous, it isn't always the best solution, or even the best source of information.

For example, the Interrail app and website has a useful journey planner (basically, all the European timetables), but it's not as reliable or as up to date as the websites for each individual country and train operator. I use the Interrail planner to sketch out my route, but then I usually double-check everything – and buy seat reservations – with the train companies direct.

This sounds complicated, but it isn't really. The Facebook groups above have pinned help-posts to talk you through each country, while The Man in Seat 61 provides step-by-step booking information (with links) for any journey you are likely to want to make.

In practice, it means that I also travel with a lot of other train apps on my phone – DB Navigator (for Germany and Europe-wide timetables and reservations), ÖBB Scotty (Austria), Trenitalia (Italy), Renfe (Spain), SNCF (France), VR Matkalla (Finland), CP (Portugal), etc. And you can also buy European rail tickets and seat reservations on the Trainline and Rail Europe apps and websites. I use all these regularly.

For my trips to the south and west I didn't use an Interrail pass, because in France and Spain, in particular, you often have to pay much higher supplements for seat reservations on the faster trains. And buying individual tickets on the slower trains I was mostly taking tends to work out cheaper than getting a pass. The Train Jaune mountain ride, for example, cost me just five euros, the ticket bought by happy accident during one of SNCF's annual promotions.

I still bought train tickets and seat reservations in advance for some journeys – using the websites and apps – but often I just turned up on the day and bought a ticket. This is especially do-able in Portugal, where train travel is still very cheap compared to most other countries.

If you buy a ticket at a station, it is of course a paper one. Most of the tickets and seat reservations I had on the whole trip were digital – emailed to me or stored within one of the apps. You can either complain about this, and mutter about how things aren't what they used to be, or embrace the ease that digital travel offers. I used to do the former; now I do the latter. But I do still print out tickets and reservations for the important journeys before leaving home, just in case.

For accommodation, I almost exclusively use Booking.com, because of the option of free cancellation if my plans change. If you can be bothered (I generally can't), you can do your research there and then book the hotels direct. But as I use the website so much and am now a Genius Level 3 (I know!), I often get better deals than by going directly to the hotel.

You may have read articles about Booking [dot] com scams ('Which' posted one recently), but I've never had any issues. I don't store my credit card details on there, and I don't click on suspicious links. If I get a message within the app that doesn't look right, I contact the hotel directly to check. I also don't book anything with a rating of less than 8.0, or with fewer than thirty recent reviews. That weeds out most of the shockers.

Finally, I did a lot of research about restaurants on TripAdvisor and followed all sorts of advice from the internet that sometimes turned out surprisingly well. I plan to get around to writing up individual recommendations, but in the meantime if you'd like specific hotel or restaurant recommendations for any parts of the trip in this book, please do get in touch –

julestoldme@gmail.com – and I'll happily share the details of the places I stayed and ate.

So that's how I did it. Now it's over to you. And if you plan your own mad, grand adventure, let me know! I'd love to hear about it, on the strict understanding that none of it is my fault.

LIKE THIS BOOK?

If you enjoyed the book, please take a moment to leave me a review on Amazon, Goodreads, BookBub, or anywhere else you like.

A word or two is absolutely fine (though please, go to town if you like!), and even just a rating makes the book that much more visible to other readers.

Thank you – I appreciate all your support.

ABOUT THE AUTHOR

Jules Brown took his first solo trip around Europe when he was seventeen, and has been travelling and writing professionally since he published his first travel guide – to Scandinavia – in 1988.

Since then he has eaten a puffin in Iceland, got stuck up a mountain in the Lake District, crash-landed in Iran, fallen off a husky sled in Canada and was stranded on a Mediterranean island. Not all of those things were his fault.

He wrote Rough Guide travel books for over thirty years, but now that he no longer has to copy down bus timetables for a living he doesn't know what to do with himself. So he comes up with ridiculous ideas for trips and then writes about them.

He still doesn't know what he wants to do when he grows up.

FIND OUT MORE

Sign up on the website for Jules' newsletter and receive a free travel memoir, *The Travel Writer Chronicles* – julestoldme.com

www.ingramcontent.com/pod-product-compliance
Lightning Source LLC
Chambersburg PA
CBHW020352080526
44584CB00014B/994